Crystal Power
Crystal Healing

Crystal Power
Crystal Healing

The *Complete* Handbook

Michael Gienger
Translated by Astrid Mick

CASSELL
ILLUSTRATED

Publisher's note

The information in this volume has been compiled according to the best of our knowledge and belief, and the healing properties of the crystal have been tested many times over. Bearing in mind that different people react in different ways, neither the publishers nor the author can give a guarantee for the effectiveness or safety of use in individual cases. In the case of serious health problems, please consult your doctor or naturopath.

This book is dedicated to my 'crystal healing friends' of the early days and the members of the first crystal healing research group in Stuttgart: Marcella Balzer, Wolfgang Bregger, Sibylle Daeschler-Geyer, Anja Gienger, Walter von Holst, Eveline Kopp, Marion Molitor, Lisa Muntwiler, Barbara Newerla, Joachim Rieger, Heide Ruf, Dr Gerald Rollett, Ulrike Scheffler, Beate Simon, Silvia Weller. This book would not exist without their contributions.

First published in the UK 1998 by Blandford
Reprinted 1999, 2000 (twice), 2001, 2002, 2003, 2004

Cassell Illustrated
2-4 Heron Quays
London, E14 4JP

A Member of the Octopus Publishing Group

Distributed in the United States by Sterling Publishing Co., Inc., 387 Park Avenue South, New York, NY 10016-8810

A Cataloguing-in-Publication Data entry for this title is available from the British Library

ISBN 0-7137-2677-6

Translated from the German by Astrid Mick
Editing of the translated text by Anne Trevillion
Original graphics and artwork by Fred Hageneder/Dragon Designs
Original colour photography by Ines Blersch
Typeset by Ben Cracknell Studios

Printed and bound in China through Colorcraft Ltd., Hong Kong

Contents

Part 2: The art of healing with crystals

Part 3: Healing crystals

3.1 The healing properties of precious stones 204

Fig. 1 (opposite) Advancing toe of lava at the front of a stream of pahoehoe lava, Hawaii, December 1992.

Appendices

Foreword

Among my earliest memories are those of stones, inseparably linked in my mind with running water, and mountain streams in particular. I loved to divert the flow of water with the aid of dams built with large and small pebbles, and delighted in dividing one stream into many small ones, connecting these up again, erecting dams and waterfalls, or creating a quiet basin of water in the middle of a fast-flowing stream. My favourite materials in all these endeavours were stones and rocks. Where others used twigs, sticks, wood or soil to reinforce their elaborate structures, these were only substitutes for me – the challenge was to solve the problem using only rocks and stones! With all these activities, which resulted in many a soaking wet pair of trousers for me and

The author at the age of six, collecting stones.

trials of patience and tolerance for my parents, grew a great love of the world of rocks and stones. First I was attracted by the spotted, striped, banded or peculiarly veined pebbles and stones in streams, but later my interest extended to all other stones and rocks that were in any way characterized by their shape or colour, or by any other special feature. Fortunately, my parents actively supported my growing collecting mania (by carrying my numerous finds home for me!).

Then, in the summer of 1972, I tripped over a very special stone on a field of scree in southern Tyrol, Austria. This particular stone was peculiarly angular and had an even, reddish-brown surface with a slight film of mica, and looked – well, different. It was too regular in shape to be an ordinary stone, at least as far as I was aware at the time. Just a broken piece of something, I thought, and threw it away again. A few minutes later, however, I came across it again and decided to take it with me. I never looked at it again during the rest of the holiday, but it was among the other stuff I had collected when I showed it all to my friend Thomas back home. 'Where on earth did you find this garnet?' he asked, and among all the colourful bits of stone, he fished out this unusual piece.

'Garnet?' I asked. 'How do you know that's what it is?' He pulled out a slim, hardback entitled *My Little Book of Minerals*, and one of the pictures looked just like my find. So, this peculiar stone was a mineral, a garnet, definitely something very special!

Of course, I just had to own a copy of *My Little Book of Minerals*, and with it I began to discover a completely new world – the world of minerals. I learned that all rocks and stones consist of at least one but usually several minerals, which generally remain small and unobtrusive, rarely becoming beautiful or large with a conspicuous shape and colour like the piece of garnet I had found. I also found out that minerals actually grow, beginning with a small 'seed' and, over the course of many years, become larger and larger, while adhering to a wonderful 'construction plan' that ensures exact and regular shapes. These shapes, my little book informed me, are called crystals, of which there are only seven groups in the whole world. So as a child of eight I was already familiar with crystal systems, minerals, Mohs' hardness and systems of minerals. All this awoke the collector's passion in me and I began to collect minerals.

No longer did I want 'ordinary stones' – they had to be minerals! Collecting became more targeted, my collection grew larger with every year, and I joined evening classes and went on outings to quarries. Anything I was unable to collect for myself was supplied at Christmases and birthdays by my parents and relatives. What a shame it was that there were not far more occasions throughout the year for present-giving! My mineral collection became huge and soon I had taken over the boiler room in the cellar of our house with 'Cosmos' kits and my first 'mineralogical' laboratory, where I loved to identify, test and conserve my collection. It was, therefore, not surprising that chemistry, the school subject most closely related to mineralogy, became my favourite subject and a firm foundation for a good grade average. When I left school, I began studying chemistry at university.

There, however, I came down to earth with a sinking feeling of disappointment. Chemistry, as practised there, led me into a dry, cold, sterile world that did not seem to have anything in common with the beauty of pebbles from streams or the fascination of minerals. Viewing the entire world as accidentally interacting matter seemed to rob our existence of all its magic and I was left with the strong conviction that this could not be all there was to our existence. I packed up my university studies. During the next few years, I tried hard to find answers to the deeper questions: are we humans merely the end product of a chain of random mutations, or are we really beings with a spiritual source? Is this Earth, with all its beauty and cruelty, merely a planet lost in space, or perhaps after all a world that makes sense and has a purpose? My inner world became a battleground between materialism and a more spiritual view. These inner conflicts resulted in an extremely chaotic phase of my life, replete with a series of accidents and illnesses.

All this resulted in my meeting with rocks and stones again – but in a very different way. In 1985 – my year of accidents and illnesses – someone first suggested to me that I use a mineral for healing purposes. At the time I was suffering from regularly recurring, severe sinusitis infections against which both antibiotics and homeopathic remedies remained ineffective. I was very sceptical when an acquaintance mentioned that emerald was very helpful for infections. The view that stones and minerals were attractive and fascinating but otherwise consisted of dead matter still was still dominant in my mind. Nevertheless, I decided to try it out. 'It can't do any harm' was my main thought at this point. I managed to borrow an emerald, stuck it to my forehead with a piece of sticking plaster and – it worked! Literally 'overnight' the persistent phase of illness just cleared up!

Initially, I tried to explain it away as a mere coincidence. I turned again to the study of stones and rocks, this time fully intending to dedicate myself to the study of the healing properties of minerals and precious stones. I collected all the literature I could on the subject, although there was not very much around at the time. Only a very few pioneers had so far become involved with the healing powers of stones – a situation that has not changed very much to the present day. Although the number of books available on the subject makes it appear otherwise, this turns out to be an illusion. Closer investigation reveals that, for the most part, these publications have been compiled mainly through the 'editing' route, that is, by collecting together secondary source information that, with very few exceptions, merely quotes and copies material from the pioneers of the last few decades.

While studying the literature on healing stones, I noticed two things in particular: first, that there were great contradictions with respect to the healing properties described and the use of the relevant stones, and second, a noticeable consensus when it came to explaining the effects of minerals and precious stones in terms of their colours. Both these points created a conflict in my 'scientific soul'. These contradictions in the descriptions of healing properties, I reasoned, either meant the whole thing was humbug, or else subjective experiences were being generalized into objective truths. Next, there seemed to be a dire lack of knowledge about minerals, as a mineral certainly consists of a great deal more than merely its colour! The circumstances of its origin, the structure and the mineral constituents of a given stone are of such great importance for the growth and later appearance of a mineral that all almost certainly must play a part in the acquisition of its specific healing properties!

For the moment, I could see no way of solving these contradictions, so I decided to study other natural healing remedies and methods and experiment with minerals 'on the side'. Again, it was a number of 'coincidences' that brought me into contact with *shiatsu*, the Japanese form of acupressure, as well as Chinese medicine and various traditional healing methods. I learned about the complete opposite to orthodox medicine at the School of Natural Healing, an experience which, with hindsight, I would certainly not have wished to miss. It was while I was studying there, in 1988, that I was encouraged by lecturer and outstanding homeopath, Wolfgang Bregger, to pass on the experiences I had with stones. I was amazed by the response I received. The demand for information on this subject area was so overwhelming that a seminar developed out of it and, even more important, a research group was set up which, from 1989 to 1993, continuously investigated and recorded the healing properties of minerals and precious stones.

From then on, I dedicated myself entirely to the world of stones. The research group tested stones according to the established principle behind testing new medicines and drugs: over a period of four to six weeks all the members of the group would wear the same stone. All psychological, spiritual or physical phenomena that were observed were recorded and were reported on at regular meetings. The results were amazing! With every stone tested, it became increasingly clear that a common thread seemed to run through the experiences of all those taking part. Mutual features and characteristics were so clearly demonstrated that coincidence could effectively be ruled out. By involving a large number of people of different types, from students to pensioners, and of all age groups as well as representatives of different fields of employment, the 'real' effects of the mineral or precious stone were easy to distinguish from other influences. In this way, the research group developed comprehensive, detailed descriptions that had not been made available in existing literature.

The results of these experiences were initially offered to doctors and non-medical practitioners for trials in their own practices. After we had received more and more positive responses, they were also offered in the form of seminars, training units and lectures to the wider public. My own task during the course of research and teaching activity consisted of analysing the parallels between the real mineralogical facts associated with the stones and their healing properties. Based on the protusion of experimental material gathered by the research group, I was finally able to carry out this analysis. The initially fairly vague supposition I had had when I first studied the existing healing crystals literature was now proved to be correct.

The healing properties of minerals and all other types of stone can be traced back to the manner of their origin, their inner structure, their mineral elements and their colours. These four principles can be described separately and, in the case of each individual stone, can be combined to form an individual portrait of its healing characteristics.

In this way, we were able to create a foundation for the art of healing with crystals, a method in which the principles refer to the nature and characteristics of the stones themselves. Until then, the use of crystals had usually been only as a supplementary method to other medical systems. As therefore crystals were only employed in healing in the context of some other system, their use was also usually restricted to a particular aspect of their healing power. Now it has become possible to understand the effects of crystals in a truly comprehensive way and to apply them to the whole person, to their psychological state, their spirit, mind and body.

In the meantime, early conclusions have had time to mature and are now bearing fruit at a rapid pace, so there is a clear need for our activities to be published in the form of a book. Many questions remain unanswered, however, as this rediscovered knowledge of the art of healing with stones is such a young discipline. The nagging feeling I always had that I would never be able to obtain a complete picture of the subject left me dissatisfied for a long time: I wanted this work to be better still, even more comprehensive, even more detailed... For this reason, I would also like to thank my publisher, Andreas Lentz, who last year finally 'held a pistol to my head' and quite pleasantly, but also very firmly, convinced me to take up my pen, or rather the keyboard, and complete the task.

In order to understand completely the effects of healing stones, we will need to become familiar with the world and nature of rocks, stones and crystals as well as that of humans. Only then will we be able to understand how and in what form communication between the two can be possible. As rocks and stones are by far the older partner in this, our earthly existence, I would like to introduce them first.

PART 1

The world of rocks and stone

The origins of minerals

The Earth's boiling interior

In the beginning there was magma. Not at the beginning of all things but at the beginning of the world of rocks and stones that we are interested in here. The Earth evolved out of a cloud of gases into a dense fog of dust and then, through contraction, became denser and shrank into an intensely hot ball. This fiery spherical body consisted entirely of hot molten matter, a viscous glowing mass. Very little has changed to this day. The Earth has now acquired a firm crust through cooling down but this crust is still comparatively thin. If you imagine the Earth to be an apple, then the Earth's firm

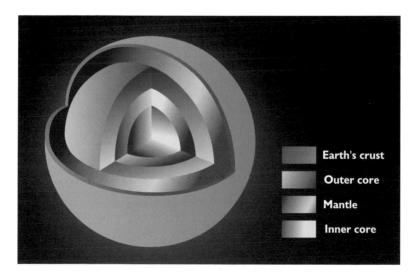

Earth's crust

Outer core

Mantle

Inner core

Fig. 3   *The internal structure of the the Earth: the core, which consists mostly of iron, with smaller amounts of nickel and other metals, has a solid inner core and a liquid outer core; the mantle is made of rock and magma; the crust (c. 0.1% of the diameter) is made up of solid types of rock.*

Fig. 2   *(opposite) A nocturnal eruption of the volcano Krakatoa, Indonesia, 1993.*

outer crust is about as thick as the skin around it. That is not exactly thick! The rest is still glowing hot and liquid and in constant movement. This 'rest' is called magma.

Although the thought of there being molten rock below the crust may be alarming, in fact there are several kilometres of rock between your feet and the magma and the rock has outstanding insulating properties. As long as your house does not happen to be situated in the centre of an earthquake zone, on a tectonic fault (a deep crack that reaches right down to the magma), or in the middle of the crater of a periodically erupting volcano, you will notice very little of the activities of the magma. Very occasionally an earth tremor may remind us that the ground beneath our feet is not quite as stable as it seems.

Indeed, the magma in the interior of the Earth is in constant flux. As the viscous, molten rock is considerably hotter near the centre of the Earth, and is therefore lighter than rock nearer the surface, hot magma is constantly rising upwards towards the Earth's crust. There, it cools down a little, becomes denser and heavier again, and gradually sinks back down towards the centre of the Earth. These constant movements, known as convection, cause the crust of the Earth, which 'swims' on the top, to move as well. This is how cracks are formed where plates drift apart (as, for example, in the Atlantic Ocean, where Europe and the Americas are being pushed apart), or how mountains form where plates are pushed into each other (still happening now, for example in the Himalayas).

Wherever these cracks open up all the way down to the magma, magma will rise up, driven by the pressure within the Earth's core. A volcanic eruption occurs when the magma is under such pressure that it bursts though the Earth's crust. In most cases, however, magma will never reach the surface; instead it gradually cools on the way up and solidifies. Whether at the surface or below it, the cooling of magma results in the formation of igneous minerals and rocks.

The formation of igneous rocks and materials

The formation of minerals from magma can be likened to the emergence of sugar crystals in jam that is oversaturated with sugar. Many of us may have observed this fascinating phenomenon when a home-made jam – particularly a jelly-like one like blackberry or quince – suddenly produced distinct crystals on its surface or on the sides of the jar. When this happened the crystals did not materialize immediately the jam was made, but, after it had been kept in a jam store for a while, they suddenly seemed to appear. And they carried on growing. What had happened to produce them out of a gooey, seimi-liquid substance?

While the jam was boiling, the added sugar was easily dissolved in it. It is a rule that hot liquids are able to dissolve larger quantities of solids than cold liquids. When the jam cooled down it turned into a 'supersaturated solution', which means that there was more sugar present in the jam than the now cooled liquid could hold. The sugar slowly began to precipitate out of the jam. Single, tiny grains of sugar formed, acting as nuclei for the growth of further new particles of sugar. This is how sugar crystals gradually grew in the home-made jam.

Minerals and rocks

The crystallization of minerals from magma occurs in exactly the same way. Magma is a mass of molten rock. Because of its high temperatures (several thousand degrees Celsius), all matter contained in it is in a liquid state. Once the magma begins to cool down, it is unable to retain all the different substances in solution and some of the matter begins to precipitate out: here, too, the process begins with small 'seeds' that gradually grow into larger crystals. The process continues until, at the end of the cooling phase, all liquid matter has become solid. If the 'end product' consists of homogeneous matter, we speak of a mineral, but if it consists of a mixture of substances, that is of several minerals, it is called rock. The size of the crystals will depend on how quickly the magma cools down, or the length of time that the magma is has had available for the mineral's growth. As the analogy with the home-made jam has shown, the crystallization process requires time. This is why the crystals of minerals that are created during a volcanic eruption are considerably smaller than those formed deep in the Earth. This makes sense: magma that has been released as 'lava' from the interior of the Earth onto the surface will have cooled down in a matter of hours or days, while millions of years may have passed during a cooling process taking place in the depths of the Earth.

Igneous rocks

In mineralogy the rocks and minerals that have formed directly from magma are called igneous or magmatic rocks and minerals. These magmatic minerals are characterized by the fact that they were formed through the cooling and solidification processes described above. Depending on where they were formed, whether at the surface or deep in the Earth, igneous rocks are divided into rocks or minerals of volcanic origin (vulcanites and volcanic minerals) and rocks of plutonic origin (plutonites, otherwise known as 'intrusive' rocks). The term 'plutonic' is derived from Pluto, the name of the Lord of the Underworld in Roman mythology, and is used for those rocks that have formed deep within the Earth. Minerals that formed in plutonites are subdivided into a further three categories, called liquid-magmatic, pneumatolytic and hydrothermal. They will be described in more detail in what follows.

Vulcanites

Vulcanites generally form fine-grained rocks containing minerals that produce only minute crystals. Well known among these are the lightweight 'lava rocks', such as pumice, which owe their structure to gases contained in the lava, or the more solid basalt, a very hard

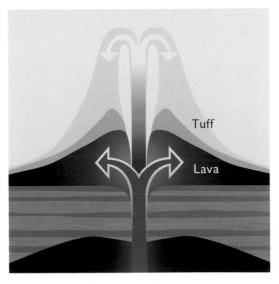

Tuff

Lava

Fig. 4 (left) The formation of vulcanites.

Fig. 5 (right) The formation of igneous and gangue rocks.

rock without gas bubbles. Vulcanites applied in healing with crystals are porphyrites and rhyolite, with the latter being traded as leopard skin jasper or orbicular jasper. Fire opal is also formed during the course of volcanic activity.

In some cases, when lava cools extremely quickly, for example by streaming into cold water, it may even be that no crystals are formed at all. Instead, the entire lava mass is practically 'frozen' through the temperature shock experienced, and the molten mass solidifies into a glass-like mass. This is how obsidian originates. Obsidian, being a mixture of many substances, is not strictly speaking counted among minerals, but is classified among the rocks; it is also called rock glass or volcanic glass. Owing to its varied composition, the appearance of obsidian can vary greatly, from the simple black obsidian to mahogany, rainbow, silver and snowflake obsidian, to name just the most important.

Plutonites

Among the plutonites, not all of the minerals form at the same time. The first minerals start forming freely in viscous magma where, depending on their density, they are able to sink down or rise up. This is how magma differentiates, or divides up, and how certain minerals accumulate at certain depths and become concentrated

Fig. 6 *Gangue rock containing quartz and calcite crystals.*

there. This initial step in mineral formation is called 'liquid-magmatic formation', which simply means 'the formation of minerals from liquid magma'. This process occurs at temperatures between 1100 degrees and 700 degrees Celsius and under enormous pressures (several hundred atmospheres). Examples of healing crystals formed in this way are aventurine, epidote, olivine, peridot, rose quartz and hyacinth zircon.

Sometimes, gases or vapours from the magma penetrate neighbouring rock. This may also lead to mineral formation through substances dissolving out of the rock and forming compounds with the gases from the magma. Mineralogists call this process of formation 'pneumatolytic formation' (derived from the Greek words *pneuma*, 'vapour', and *lyein*, 'to dissolve'). Of these pneumatolytic minerals, the following are applied in healing with crystals: apatite, lepidolite, topaz and tourmaline.

During the ensuing cooling phase, once the 'critical temperature' of water at 375 degrees Celsius and below is reached, aqueous solutions result. At temperatures above the critical temperature, water is only present as a vapour, whatever the prevailing pressure. Below 375 degrees Celsius water can become liquid if the pressure is great enough. Further minerals are then formed out of the substances dissolved in the water. Their formation is called 'hydrothermal', derived from the Greek *hydro*, 'water', and *therme*, 'hot spring'. Well-known healing crystals that have been formed hydrothermally are, among others, amazonite, aragonite, fluorite, kunzite and moonstone.

Because water is far more free-flowing than the viscous magma, it is able to penetrate more easily and quickly into cracks and fissures in the surrounding rocks. Here, the minerals are precipitated as druse on

22

the walls of cavities or clefts, forming so-called gangue rocks. The mineral solutions in these types of environment will only cool off very slowly owing to the insulating qualities of the surrounding rock (in Alpine clefts the temperature only falls by about 1 degree Celsius in 40 000 years). This means the minerals created here are able to form large, beautiful crystals. Another important factor is that they have plenty of space to grow undisturbed. Some of the most beautiful and popular healing crystals, for example agate, amethyst, rock crystal, chalcedony, smoky quartz and many more, are formed in these fissures and clefts.

The principle of igneous rock formation

A liquid substance becomes solid. This is the simplest way of describing the first and oldest formation principle of minerals. It is important – in order to understand the resulting effects of minerals on humans – to have a closer look at what the process really involves.

The first stage is represented by a free or non-ordered state. Free means mobile and non-ordered as all the substances contained are mingled and mixed together unbound in compounds. Magma, therefore, is like a thick soup containing many mineral-forming elements (chemical elements), but no mineral has yet been formed at this stage. Magma is the 'potential' out of which many minerals and rocks can be formed. According to the elements it contains, magma helps determine what particular minerals will eventually form, and which ones will not. Magma is not identical everywhere, which is why certain minerals are found only in certain parts of the world.

Apart from the magma itself, further factors will determine the formation of minerals: pressure and heat, as well as the speed of cooling. The same source substances may lead to very different final forms, depending on whether the magma reaches the surface in the form of lava and cools down very quickly , whether many 'closely packed' crystals are formed in liquid-magmatic formation, or whether the mineral has enough time in a cavity or cleft to develop, grow and form beautiful, large crystals.

In brief: The igneous formation principle demonstrates a crystallization process based on the cooling and solidification of liquid magma. The mineral-forming elements contained in magma represent the potential and predisposition for formation, as they already determine what can be formed. The crystallization process itself, however, is determined by the factors of pressure, heat, space and time, all of which decide in which manner the existing potential will be realized. As this is the oldest method of formation of rock (although, of course, it has continued through geological time and is still going on today) we will call the minerals so formed 'primary' minerals.

We should take note of this principle as it will continue to be of great importance for healing with crystals. Let us first turn to the second formation process which occurs in quite a different manner from the first.

The formation of sedimentary rocks and minerals

From the depths of magmatic formations, our path will now take us up to the surface of the Earth: here it will become clear that even stones and rocks do not remain the same forever. The teeth of Time are gnawing away at even the hardest rock; in fact it is the sun and rain, heat and cold, frost and wind that are doing the 'gnawing' and gradually wearing the rock away. This action of wind and weather that leaves nothing untouched is called weathering or erosion. It leads to the second way that rock is formed.

Weathering on a grand scale

Mountains are worn away by weathering. Rocks are split off by the action of frost and turn into the rubble that is found on mountain slopes in the form of extensive gravel (scree) slopes. This gravel will not remain lying there forever, but will gradually gravitate towards the valley bottom – gravel avalanches are greatly feared in such regions – where it is transported away by streams and rivers. The flowing water serves to transform the angular pieces of rock of all sizes into round pebbles, by rolling them about against each other, knocking off their corners, grinding them down, and polishing them. During the process, myriad small fragments are created; this is sand, right down to the finest, dust-like, floating particles that we find in mud. A small amount of some mineral-forming elements is completely dissolved in the water, particularly chalk, for example, or rock salt.

Fig. 7 Sedimentary rock.

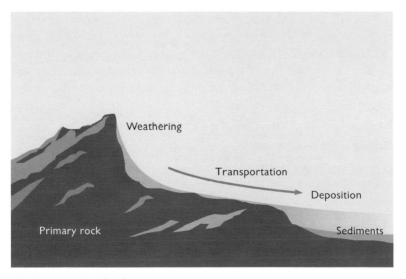

Fig. 8 Formation of sediments.

Fig. 9 *Limestone sinter deposits.*

Sedimentation

Water can only transport matter as long as it is flowing. Wherever a river slows down, in lakes, river deltas or where it reaches the sea, it will deposit anything it has carried along. Vast quantities of deposits can be built up in this way, out of which new rocks are formed. This kind of deposition is called sedimentation and the rocks formed in the process are called sedimentary rocks. Among these kinds of rocks we find such healing stones as anglesite, anhydrite, calcite, dolomite, oolite, selenite (gypsum) and pyrite, in particular the globular pyrite known as 'boji stones'.

Small-scale weathering

Wherever rocks are close to the surface of the Earth, surface water, whether rainwater or other water, will penetrate them. This surface water carries oxygen, carbon dioxide or acids with it. It penetrates cracks and crevices and begin to dissolve the rock and release mineral-forming elements. This, too, is a weathering process, although on a much smaller scale. It is going on beneath our feet worldwide and completely independently of whether the rock is exposed to the air ('unlocked') or whether there is a layer of humus on top.

Fig. 10 *Cracks filled with chrysocolla.*

The zones between the surface and the water table

The mineral-forming elements that are released form compounds with other substances contained in the water and are then either deposited on the spot as new minerals or are transported away to be precipitated and deposited in deeper locations. This 'miniature sedimentation' causes the formation of many new minerals, particularly in rocks rich in ore. These processes occur in the zone between the surface of the Earth and the water table.

The region above the water table is called the 'weathering or oxidation zone', as oxygen from the air is still active at this depth. Chemically, oxidation means a release of electrons. By releasing electrons, metal atoms transform into charged particles (ions) and only in the form of ions are they able to form new compounds or can they can be dissolved in liquids. Typical minerals in the oxidation zone are, for example, azurite, malachite, chrysocolla, dioptase, turquoise and variscite.

The region next to the water table is called the 'cementation zone', as dissolved substances are precipitated out here (this process is also called cementation). In this zone, reduction processes occur during which, for example, metal ions turn back into neutral metal atoms. Chemically, 'reduction' means 'collecting electrons', so it is the opposite process to oxidation. Neutral metal atoms do not remain in solution, so this is where we find typical minerals of the cementation zone like copper or silver. Other minerals from this region are copper-chalcedony and covellite.

The principle of sedimentary formation

'Weathering and deposition' are the main elements of this principle. The environment plays a decisive part not only in shaping rock but also in reforming it, both through the power of the wind and weather and through the work of weak acid solutions. Sedimentary formation starts with an already existing rock that is gradually dissolved, whether completely or partially, through the effect of outside forces. The rock iself represents only one element in what goes into possible later new formation. Logically, only the mineral-forming elements already present in the rock can be involved in the process of dissolving and new formation, but watery solutions in the form of acids make up another equally important component. It is the combination of these two influences that determines the formation of new minerals. We shall call such minerals 'secondary' minerals.

In brief: The sedimentary formation principle represents a process in which the solid structures of certain rocks are dissolved through environmental influences. The mineral-forming elements released out of the rock, together with other substances brought there through environmental activity, create new minerals.

So much for this part; all good things usually come in threes – thus after the first two processes we have a third: the metamorphic formation process.

The formation of metamorphic rocks and minerals

Leaving the surface of the Earth behind, we will now go right back down again into the depths, not quite as far as the magma but almost as deep, in the lower part of the crust. The rocks in these deep regions also enjoy little peace as the hot magma is always present and they are subject to the immense pressure that exists in the interior of the Earth. Here again, there are various different factors at work, contributing to a state of affairs in which nothing remains exactly as it was before.

The nature of the Earth's crust

In order to understand what follows, we must first get rid of the superficial notion that the Earth's crust is evenly thick and firm all the way round. This is by no means the case. In reality, the crust consists of discrete 'shields' or 'plates' that float on top of the magma, in a similar manner to ice on the surface of water. The individual plates vary in thickness: the oceanic plates are only about 5–10 kilometres (3–6 miles) thick, the continental plates, on the other hand, are more like 20–60 kilometres (13–38 miles) thick. As with icebergs, it is only the smaller portion that is visible at the top; the greatest part is below the surface. For this reason, the continental plates also rise up farther than the oceanic ones; this is why we have the distinct separation of oceans and dry land on our planet.

The formation of mountains

Owing to the convection currents of the magma in the interior of the Earth (explained above), the various plates of the Earth's crust remain in constant motion. During this process they are pushed together and on top of each other in certain parts of the world. This creates zones where they cross each other and become buckled or folded up, forming mountains. A glance at the world map will show these 'squashed' zones on the Earth as long chains and ranges of mountains. The largest, at present, are the Himalayas, then the Rocky Mountains and the Andes. These regions are also the places where the Earth's crust is at its thickest. According to the 'iceberg principle', only about 10 per cent of the total mass is pushed upwards; the rest is pressed down into the depths.

Metamorphosis

These processes do not, of course, occur without leaving a trace on the rocks involved. A glance at our mountains will give you an inkling of the enormous power of the forces in the interior of the Earth that have accomplished these folding processes. Rocks that are involved in such a process under extreme pressures begin to restructure themselves. Crystals that were originally randomly interlocked with each other in all directions begin to order themselves, under the action of the great pressure. As far as possible, they will organize themselves so they end up facing crossways to the direction of pressure. In some minerals, certain substances are quite literally 'squeezed out' of them; these accumulate and then form new, more resistant minerals. In some cases, neighbouring layers of rock are pressed together in such a way that they exchange elements with the moving rock and form new minerals in a kind of boundary layer. Any change in structure that will save space and provide more resistance to the pressure being exerted will inevitably take place: this is how a completely new rock is created.

The process is further promoted by heat acting upon the rock involved. The temperature of the rock in the interior of the Earth will begin to rise, particularly in layers of rock that are being pressed downwards by the formation of mountains. Temperatures even higher than those during the liquid magmatic phase of formation of igneous rock may occur as the pressures acting upon the rock prevent it from becoming molten. The transformation of existing rock under extreme pressure and heat, without it becoming molten,

Fig. 11
Regional metamorphosis during the formation of mountains.

Fig. 12 *Metamorphosis: rock (tiger iron) transformed and folded by pressure and heat.*

is called metamorphosis, meaning it changes its shape and appearance. The newly formed rocks are called metamorphic rocks and the minerals formed inside them are called metamorphic minerals.

Transformation of large areas

In addition to the example given above of the formation of mountains, metamorphosis also occurs if rocks become ever more compressed and hence heavier through overlaying with new layers, and thus end up sinking into the depths of the Earth. In both cases we speak of regional metamorphosis, as large areas are subjected to these transformations. Crystalline slate is typical of rocks formed in this way. Minerals formed in metamorphic rocks include disthene (kyanite), garnet, jade, nephrite, serpentine, thulite, tiger iron and zoisite. Another well-known example of a metamorphic rock is marble (transformed limestone), in which deposits of lapis lazuli or emeralds can sometimes be found.

Small-scale metamorphosis

Small-scale metamorphosis also occurs in the vicinity of rising magma. Owing to the enormously high temperatures, the rock

31

around a volcanic chimney, for example, is subject to contact metamorphosis. This process can form ruby and sapphire, for example.

The addition of new elements

Wherever an additional exchange of elements in surrounding rocks takes place, for example through pneumatolytic vapours dissolving certain elements out of the rock and replacing them with others, this process is called 'metasomatism' (addition of new elements by migration in the rock). Examples of minerals formed in this way are charoite and rhodonite, as well as falcon's eye and tiger's eye.

The principle of metamorphic formation

Metamorphosis is the key word for the transformation of existing rock under the influence of heat and pressure in the interior of the Earth. The important point here is that the rock is not melted down again, but still undergoes alterations in its structure and mineral content. It takes on a completely different shape and appearance, but the transformation occurs essentially from the inside out. Metamorphosis subjects the rock to severe testing. Only what is impermeable to pressure and heat will be retained, everything else is transformed until a new, stable state is obtained.

In brief: The third formation principle represents a transformation process in which everything that cannot withstand the heat and pressure is changed into a new form from the inside out. In this way, new minerals are formed through metamorphosis and exchange of elements. We shall call these 'tertiary' minerals.

The cycle of rock formation

It now becomes clear that even rocks, together with their minerals, are by no means as eternal and unchangeable as they often appear to human observation. It is really only the enormous time scale in which these geological and mineralogical transformations take place, compared with the relatively short span of our earthly existence, that gives rise to this false notion. How could we, who in our short lives barely experience the span of three generations, be able to grasp time spans of millions of years? Maybe an analogy will make the dimensions of these processes more obvious.

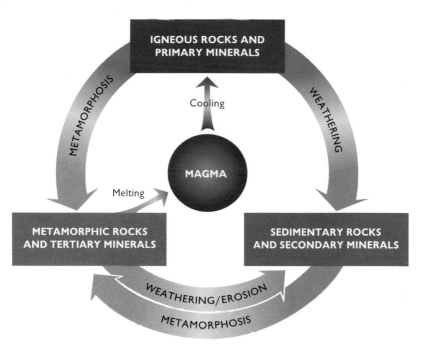

Fig. 13   *Cycle of rock formation.*

If our allotted span of, say, 70 years were to represent symbolically one minute, an Alpine rock crystal, for example, would be almost a year old and the dinosaurs would have become extinct about two years ago, diamonds could boast 30 years or more, the oldest rocks would be regular Methuselahs of over 90 years and the Earth itself could boast as much as 150 years. Again, compare these figures with the minute of our lifespan!

When the processes are viewed as a model with these dimensions, it is clear that even rocks and minerals are in a constant process of transformation. Here, too, there is creation, change and dissolution. From the magma arise igneous rocks with their primary minerals; through weathering these are transformed into sedimentary rocks and secondary minerals. Both formations may pass through a process of metamorphosis to become metamorphic rocks or tertiary minerals, which may then be transformed back into sedimentary rock or secondary minerals through weathering.

Finally, the heat of metamorphosis may become so great that the rock is melted down again. Thus the circle is closed if rock returns again to the state of magma.

The relationship between mineral origin and crystal healing

Very soon after the first results and experiences with the healing powers of minerals and precious stones had been established, I found myself asking the question as to how the ground beneath our feet might influence our human condition. Naturally, the rocks we walk about on daily contain a number of minerals and are present in such quantities that a possible influence could not be ruled out if a certain power were inherent in these minerals.

I dug out my old notebooks and diaries and gathered together geological maps of all my previous places of residence, remembering that I had moved house a total of six times between 1984 and 1987. I could be a useful research specimen myself for observing possible changes due to being subjected to different underground rocks. I was very surprised when I realized that of the total of seven different locations of residence, the first five had always been on the same type of rock strata. Could this be a coincidence? Or had I, intuitively perhaps, without consciously realizing it, chosen the same types of homes on the same types of soil and rock? Even when I moved to Nürtingen, a slightly larger town than the others where I had lived, I had chosen one of only two streets in which the same rock was present underground.

I should like to give the sceptics among my readers the benefit of the same doubts and considerations I had at the time and which occupied me a great deal. When I use the term 'rock', I do not mean a basic, overall type that is present in great quantities (large mass), but a very specific strata: lias alpha, a very narrow band of black Jurassic that was only a few metres thick in several places where I lived. Furthermore, another glance at the geological map also yielded the information that the clinic in which I was born also lies on the same layer.

That moment, after a total of 23 years, when I 'left' the familiar rock strata in order to take up residence on a different strata, also brought a visible turning point in my life. It was the moment in which the conflict between materialism and a more spiritual view of our existence was decided in favour of the spirit, the moment in which encounters with important teachers began and the moment when I decided to dedicate myself to natural healing methods and to start studying at the School of Natural Healing. After that, my life changed so radically that it could hardly be mere coincidence.

Following on this realization came a very intense period during which I spent a great deal of time outdoors, sitting, eating and sleeping on the most varied kinds of rock strata, trying to work out their influences and properties. Here again, I had the problem of trying to separate the actual influence of the respective rock from other environmental factors, and to try and find out whether it was the ground or the weather, or even accompanying people, who were responsible for creating a particular mood or atmosphere. In the end, I went on long walks in order to experience the influence of different rocks under similar conditions. During this period I was involved with seminars, in which I used not only to pass on my own experiences but also to check over them with other participants. These seminars all took place in the form of excursions during which we trained ourselves to the point where we were able to sense or perceive an exact transition from one rock strata to another in unknown terrain without first looking at a geological map (dowsing principle).

In spite of the fact that we had many enthusiastic participating seminar members and friends, it was still to take seven years until the connections between the manner of origin of rocks and minerals and their influences on human beings became clear and capable of being formulated. Several paths of research led us into cul-de-sacs; however, the repeatable experiences that were finally described in 1994 will be introduced here.

The healing properties of igneous rocks and primary minerals

If we think back again to the principles of origin of these rocks and minerals, we will realize that our human lives are bound up with very similar processes.

The first formation principle demonstrates a crystallization process based on the cooling and solidification of liquid magma. The mineral-forming elements contained in magma represent the potential and predisposition for formation, as they already determine what can be formed. The crystallization process itself, however, is determined by the factors of pressure, heat, space and time, all of which decide in which manner the existing potential will be realized.

From the first moments of our existence, beside eating and sleeping, we are mainly occupied with learning. If you look at the huge learning accomplishments of a small child in its first years of life, they are without a doubt amazing: grasping, sitting, standing upright, walking, talking, recognizing other people, objects, situations and understanding them. These are all such complex matters and are learned in such a short space of time that certain tendencies have to have been there right from the start.

These natural abilities are what distinguishes us from other creatures. We can, for example, talk but not fly like a bird and will not live to be as old as a tree. These factors are simply part of our natural, inborn tendencies. These tendencies, whether they are part of a spiritual inheritance or genetic, are as determining for us as is magma for igneous rocks. They represent the potential for what or who we can become.

There is, however, a second factor: what good are natural tendencies if we do not have the space, time, the energy and the possibilities to unfold them and develop them further? Only if the inherent potential meets optimal conditions will it have the opportunity to unfold fully. As an analogy, what good is an inborn tendency to be a concert pianist for who is never able to take piano lessons, or why does not every student of the piano become a concert pianist?

▶ Minerals and rocks may not change our inherent tendencies, but they may help us to develop our inner potential and to unfold it. Igneous rocks and primary minerals in particular, because of the similar manner of origin involved, will encourage learning processes. Every magmatic mineral represents certain spiritual values and will support and encourage their development. In connection with this, the mineral will also encourage a certain kind of spiritual experience and corresponding thought and behaviour patterns, and may help with healing if these values, experiences, thought and behaviour patterns in any given case are conducive to overall good health.

In all of life's challenges, perhaps where we have just embarked on a new beginning in our life that is confronting us with many new ideas, or where we are faced with a host of learning experiences, the primary minerals are the first choice of healing stones. They will encourage the necessary growth processes and help with diseases that will typically arise in these situations.

The healing properties of sedimentary rocks and secondary minerals

Sedimentary rocks and secondary minerals draw our attention to another aspect of our existence – the influences of the environment. Thanks to psychology, the fact that our environment – beginning with the home, kindergarten, school, training, profession, partner, children, friends and relatives and society, or even the total environment – has a massive effect on us is no longer a new idea.

It is, therefore, no surprise that sedimentary rocks and secondary minerals that originated through the influences of the environment will exactly reflect this aspect.

The second formation principle represents a process in which the solid structures of certain rocks are dissolved through environmental influences. The mineral-forming elements released out of the rock, together with other substances brought there through environmental activity, create new minerals.

The same processes occur in our lives: we are moulded and shaped by the experiences of our past. Childhood experiences in particular play a determining role in all this. Here we make decisions based on pleasurable or painful experiences – what is 'good' and what is 'bad' for us. We also develop survival strategies ('How do I get Mum and Dad to do what I want?') and during these years we are provided with 'explanations' for the way we find the world. As children, we are unable to check whether it is true that 'alcohol is evil' or whether 'beer is liquid bread'. We will tend to take on the opinions of those people whom we trust most.

In this way, first in childhood but also in later years, certain correspondences are created ('halt at red lights') and tenets of belief ('men only want one thing') that decisively shape our lives, behaviour and our feelings, as well as our imagination, ideals, goals and world views.

As long as this kind of shaping encourages our development, there is nothing to be said against it. Very often, however, it happens that rigid patterns that we have absorbed suddenly become useless at a later time or under changed circumstances. For example, when we were children, if we learned the survival strategy 'Keep your mouth shut and you won't get hit in the teeth!' which might have been quite appropriate at a given time, we should not be surprised if, later on in our working lives, we get lumbered with the worst jobs because we are known for never protesting. Or if the strategy 'Cry loudly and I will get whatever I want!' worked with our parents, we should also not be surprised if nobody likes us much later on because we never stop moaning.

Sedimentary rocks and secondary minerals make it easier for us to recognize this shaping based on learned correspondences, beliefs and painful experiences, to become fully aware of them, and then to dissolve them. Sedimentary rocks and secondary minerals will help with new orientations, looking at new experiences from a different angle and with developing more suitable strategies tailored to present situations. In this way, our inner needs can more easily be brought in harmony with demands from our environment. Stress and tensions are dissolved and harmony restored, which will bring about healing of all diseases that result from conflicts with our environment.

There are many situations in which we are involved in conflict with our environment or with other people. Whether or not these conflicts are imminent or belong to the past, sedimentary rocks and secondary minerals will be our first choice for healing purposes. The healing all diseases that have arisen through conflict or the avoidance of conflict is helped by them.

The healing properties of metamorphic rocks and tertiary minerals

Just as their strength and durability were constantly being tested during their formation, metamorphic rocks and tertiary minerals appear to test aspects of our lives in terms of their durability. Everything that is not of permanent value for us will begin to change and take on new shapes and forms. Many episodes in our lives will come to an end naturally, without there seeming to be any noticeable necessity for it. In theory we could have held onto many things for longer – a job, a home, a group or a partnership – but somehow a point came when it was all over, finished with and ended. If we withdraw at that moment, make the break and begin something new, then as a rule the change will take place painlessly and without difficulties.

Too often, however, we do not let go of the old but hold on to it because we are used to it, or because we do not (yet) know what the new thing is that is approaching us. We carry on as usual, only suddenly there is an unpleasant sense of 'something not being right'. The sensation grows stronger and gradually materializes into a feeling that we have to change ourselves and our lives. We may have forgotten the point at which it should have been obvious, or we do not notice when it should have happened. It may be that the feeling of wanting this new thing has no particular direction, and pressures and heat arise in us that begin to question everything fundamentally.

The metamorphic formation principle represents a transformation process in which everything that cannot withstand the heat and pressure is changed into a new form from the inside out. In this way, new minerals are formed through metamorphosis and exchange of elements.

The heat and pressure inside us may lead through a phase of dissatisfaction in which we are very self-critical. Everything is questioned as to whether it makes sense and is of value for our lives. We begin a radical clean-up. Lazy compromises, outworn habits, nostalgic relics from the past as well as meaningless rules and regulations are thrown out and replaced by genuine settlements, necessary activities, contemporarily useful attitudes and sensible agreements. In this way we transform our lives into completely new forms.

▶ Metamorphic rocks and tertiary minerals stimulate this inner transformation process. They encourage critical self-reflection and help us to realize and understand those things in our lives that are not durable and what needs ending because it makes us feel dissatisfied. These minerals and rocks bring radical changes that lead to a more fulfilled, purposeful life. They will, therefore, help with all manner of diseases that are rooted in the fear of letting go, in necessary changes that have not been carried out, or in a lifestyle that no longer makes any sense. By stimulating an inner transformation they help us to overcome attachments, habits and compromises.

In all life situations in which we feel strong inner dissatisfaction, where we have a feeling that we should change something but do not know what, or if we are confronted with a change but are afraid because we do not know what will happen afterwards – in all these cases, metamorphic rocks or tertiary minerals are the first choice of healing crystals. The healing of all diseases that have come about through such inner conflicts is stimulated and accelerated by these materials.

The application of the formation principle to healing

The three types of origin of minerals and rocks is very clearly mirrored in typical life situations. The principle provides us with simple opportunities to find solutions for our problems or difficulties with the help of the right minerals or rocks. The curing of all the diseases that have arisen out of these situations is also enhanced. To identify correctly the minerals needed it is important to make an exact and careful analysis of the situation. For this purpose, first make a sketch of the circumstances, that is, pick out the key issues and important features. Then, in your mind, run through all three possibilities: 'What should be present so that the primary/secondary/tertiary type of mineral may apply?' Once you have run through all three possibilities in your thoughts, it will become clearer which applies than if you just observe the given situation.

Once you have made a choice, matters become quite simple. Choose a location where the relevant rock is present in the ground and remain there for at least one day, and preferably at least three days at this location or in this area.

Typical rocks of igneous origin would be plutonites: granite, syenite, diorite and gabbro, for vulcanites: rhyolite, trachyte, basalt, phonolite and volcanic tuff (tufa) or 'lava stone'.

Typical sedimentary rocks (which give us secondary minerals) include: sandstone, breccia, conglomerates, clay-based rocks, as well as limestones, dolomites and gypsum rocks.

Typical metamorphic rocks (which give us tertiary minerals) include: gneiss, mica, phyllite, amphibolite, serpentine, hornfels and marble.

Geological or petrographic maps that will help you find the right strata can be obtained from Ordnance Survey offices, surveyors or the geological survey of the area.

Spend lots of time outside and moving about at these locations. You need not do anything else. The effects of the rocks are so strong that you will definitely experience changes very quickly. The third day is always the most interesting, on which the influence of the new type of ground becomes most clearly noticeable. It is also the so-called 'critical day', which is something all mountain guides and skiing instructors will be able to tell you about, as this is when the new 'feeling for life' begins, the urge to rebel against the old. People often lack concentration and become very careless and negligent at this time. The attention (unconsciously) turns inward and people tend to pay little attention to external demands and dangers. On the third day, you should definitely make time for yourself – even if you are already back at home!

The second possibility consists of choosing minerals of the correct formation from the table in the Chapter 2.2, *The analytical art of healing with crystals*. You may even discover minerals that you already know and with which you already have a connection. If not, choose the suitable mineral according to the profile given in Part 3 of this book. Carry this mineral on you constantly. As the effect, in this case, will not be as strong as it would be if you were staying somewhere with the mineral in the ground beneath you, the influence will take longer to make itself felt. Here, pay attention on the third and seventh days.

During our research, these two days turned out to be ones with a special quality. It appears that renewal processes have an underlying rhythm of threes and sevens. Think, for example, of the fact that all the cells in our body are completely renewed over a span of seven years. And it may also be no coincidence that a cycle of exactly seven days was chosen for a weekly rhythm.

Let us now turn to a completely different aspect of our lives. Just as the manner of origin of minerals throws light on (and in) our present life situation, there is also a secondary principle in the kingdom of minerals that will illuminate our lifestyle. This principle is revealed to us in crystals.

Crystals

The discovery of crystals

Throughout the ages people have noticed that minerals and precious stones display extremely conspicuous and fascinatingly regular shapes and forms in their naturally grown state. For a long time, these strange, precise shapes and forms were seen as evidence for the intervention of the gods during the formation of these

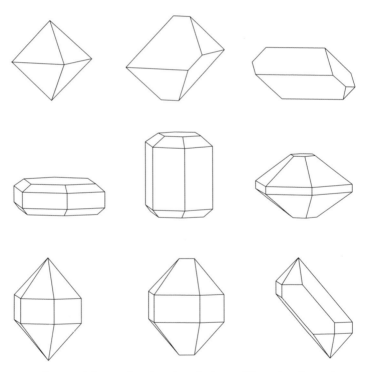

Fig. 14   *The crystal shapes of a mineral can look very different but the angles between the individual facets remain the same.*

stones. Who else would be in a position to create something as wonderful as this? Only a little more than 300 years ago, in 1669, the Danish naturalist, Nils Stensen, known as Nicolas Steno, published some initial research concerning the mathematical regularity of crystals. Stenson had discovered that the angles between the surfaces of a particular mineral, independently of their size, appearance or location, are always the same. From these observations he formed the 'law of constant interfacial angles'.

From this time on, it became clear that it was not random influences from the place of origin that gave a mineral its shape, but there it was some inherent property that would always cause the mineral to take on certain shapes. It was then discovered that a particular, typical shape could often be a more reliable feature of a certain mineral than, for example, its rather variable colour. This presented the science of crystals with the presently accepted definition:

A crystal is a solid body with a geometrically regular shape.

The name 'crystal' had originally been given to rock crystal which the Greeks had christened *krystallos*, 'ice', as they believed rock crystal was deep-frozen water that could never melt again! This belief was still prevalent at the time of Nils Stensen. Four years later, in 1673, the British scientist Robert Boyle first cast doubts on the belief. Nevertheless, scientists began to search enthusiastically for the laws governing the phenomenon of the 'crystal'. It was to take another 100 years until a French schoolmaster, Rene-Just Haüy, published his theory on the structure of crystals in 1784. A 'coincidence' had come to his aid: while handling a calcite crystal belonging to a friend, he dropped it and it split into several parts. Although this was very annoying, it allowed him to make an important discovery: the fragments of the shattered crystal all displayed a very similar appearance. Haüy concluded that crystals already have certain geometric shapes right down to their smallest 'elementary cells', that is, in the domain of atoms and molecules (the smallest building blocks of matter).

The crystal lattice

This realization had brought him very close to the truth. The atoms and molecules are not themselves geometrically shaped as Haüy

Fig. 15 *According to Haüy's theories, both the cube and the rhombo-dodecahedron (a twelve-sided object with diamond-shaped sides) can be formed out of smaller cubic elements.*

assumed. However, they are organized spatially in exact, geometrical patterns, the so-called 'crystal lattices'. This perfect order is explained by the fact that individual atoms and molecules (usually of varying sizes) of the mineral are packed together as closely as possible during their growth. This is partly because they are drawn together by strong electromagnetic forces, partly because pressure around them allows no space to be wasted. (Think back to the often extremely harsh conditions under which a mineral is formed!) A strictly ordered system will always offer a better use of space than a random muddle.

One small example may illuminate the nature of a crystal lattice: imagine you had to divide up an empty, white surface like that outlined below into lots of equal-sized fields without leaving any gaps. (The edges need not be taken into account.) What geometric shapes would be appropriate?

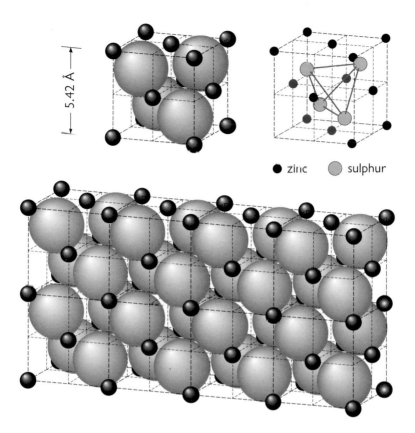

Fig. 16 *Above left: the crystal structure of schalenblende; it is not the atoms themselves that are angled but their distribution in the crystal results in a severely geometrical lattice. Above right: the atoms have not been shown here in their correct relative size to each other but merely as 'points of mass' in order to depict the lattice. Bottom: A larger section of the crystal lattice; the lattice should be imagined to extend further into all three spatial dimensions.*

If you try this out for a while, you will discover that only the following seven geometric shapes can be used for the purpose: the square, hexagon, triangle, rectangle, rhombus, parallelogram and trapezium (see Figure 17).

Only with these shapes will you be able to fill out the surface without leaving any gaps. In the case of pentagons, heptagons, octagons, dodecahedrons, or even circles, there will always be gaps between the fields, meaning wasted space that cannot exist in a

Fig. 17

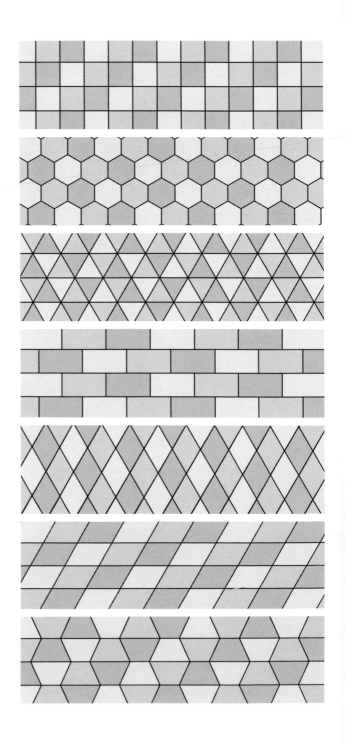

completely filled out crystal! For this simple reason, only crystal lattices exist that have squares, hexagons, triangles, rectangles, rhombuses, parallelograms and trapeziums as their basic structure. There are no other types!

These basic structures ensure that crystals only ever display particularly defined shapes. This means that the basic structure of the square, for example, will typically lead to shapes like the cube, octahedron and rhombic dodecahedron, while a basic hexagonal structure leads to hexagonal pillars, and so on. All crystals, not only those of minerals, but also crystals in the organic realm, as for example the sugar crystals mentioned earlier, are governed by these laws. Crystals can, therefore, be grouped according to their inner structure into seven distinct systems, the seven crystal systems.

The crystal systems

The **cubic crystal system** includes all crystals with a square inner structure. The word 'cubic' is derived from Latin *cubus*, hence our word cube. Cubic minerals often actually form cubes as crystals (for example diamond, fluorite, pyrite), octahedrons (diamond, fluorite, magnetite), rhombic dodecahedrons (garnet, lapis lazuli), tetrahedrons (pyrite, zinc blende (sphalerite)), pentagon–dodecahedron (pyrite) and others ...

Fig. 18   Crystal shapes based on the cube.

The **hexagonal crystal system** includes all crystals with a hexagonal inner structure. The word 'hexagonal' is derived from the Greek for 'six-sided body'. Hexagonal minerals in the form of crystals will, as a rule, also form hexagonal pillars, for example apatite, aquamarine, beryl, morganite and emerald.

Fig. 19   Hexagonal crystal shapes.

The **trigonal crystal system** includes all crystals with a triangular inner structure. The word 'trigonal' is derived from the Greek *trigon*, 'triangle'. Trigonal minerals have crystals in the form of trigonal pillars (tourmaline) or hexagonal pillars, although the latter are not quite as regular as those formed in the hexagonal crystal system (for example amethyst, rock crystal, citrine, smoky quartz, ruby, sapphire, tourmaline), and also in rhombohedral forms (calcite, dolomite, magnesite, rhodochrosite). The inner trigonal structure is particularly beautiful and clearly visible in tourmaline slices that display triangular or trident-like colour zones.

Fig. 20   Trigonal crystal shapes.

The **tetragonal crystal system** includes all crystals with a rectangular inner structure. The word 'tetragonal' is derived from the Greek *tetragon*, 'rectangle'. Tetragonal minerals generally form crystals with rectangular pillars, sometimes with flat boundaries and sometimes with pyramidal points. Examples include apophyllite, rutile and zircon (hyacinth).

Fig. 21   Tetragonal crystal shapes.

The **orthorhombic crystal system** includes all crystals with a rhombic inner structure. The word 'rhombic' is derived from the Greek *rhombus*. Rhombic minerals form either rhombic crystals, for example aragonite, peridote (olivine) or topaz, but sometimes also hexagonal ones, as three rhombuses fitted together form a hexagon. This type of growth is quite aptly termed 'pseudohexagonal'; an example is aragonite.

Fig. 22   *Rhombic crystal shapes.*

The **monoclinic crystal system** includes all crystals that have an inner structure in the shape of a parallelogram. The word 'monoclinic' means approximately 'with an inclined angle' (Greek *mono*, 'one', and *klinein*, 'to incline, bend'). Monoclinic crystals also display this 'crooked' angle. It is most obvious in gypsum that often has 'crooked' crystals with clearly visible parallelogram shapes (in this crystal form called selenite). Other monoclinic minerals include azurite, epidote, jade, kunzite, lepidolite, malachite, moonstone and nephrite.

Fig. 23   *Monoclinic crystal shapes.*

The **triclinic crystal system** includes all crystals with an inner structure in the form of a trapezium. The term 'triclinic' means the equivalent of 'with three inclined angles' (Greek *tri*, 'three', and *klinein*, 'to incline, bend'). There is nothing quite like 'crooked' or 'bent' triclinic crystals that have no right angles at all. The inner structure of this crystalline system is most clearly displayed in amazonite crystals, which form the shape of two trapeziums joined together. Further triclinic minerals are disthene (kyanite), labradorite, rhodonite, sunstone and turquoise.

Fig. 24   *Triclinic crystal shapes.*

There seem to be no rules without exceptions! The same goes for crystal structures. Sometimes, conditions are so extraordinary that a mineral has no possibility of forming a crystalline structure. These minerals are called **amorphous** (Greek *amorph*, 'without shape') and they do not possess any kind of inner structure. The reasons for this lack of structure are to be found in their too rapid creation, for example as in moldavite and obsidian, where there is no time for crystals to be formed, or because too many different substances are mingled together, as for example in amber and opal.

Fig. 25   *The appearance of amorphous minerals.*

Discovering the connections between crystalline structures and lifestyles

For me, crystals and their regular shapes were always the most interesting phenomena in the entire realm of minerals as it had been the strange, regular crystal facets of my piece of garnet that had started me off on my discovery of minerals. This structure and order fascinated me and, even as a ten-year old, I was tossing around terms like 'lattice structure', 'crystal system', 'axis of symmetry' and so on. I would not maintain that I properly understood everything then, in as much as many modern books on mineralogy still suffer from the same defects that Franz von Kobell complained about in his *History of Mineralogy* in 1864:

> Furthermore, at all times, it has been demonstrated that, although individual researchers have an unselfconsciously sharp eye for detail and a gift for explaining matters in simple terms, others place obstacles in the way of progress by demonstrating an even greater talent for passing on simple things in the most complicated manner and for seeing difficulties of all kinds where there are none!

So, whether I did or did not understand things then, at least the crystal systems were so familiar to me that I was rather surprised to find, during the early days of my studies on healing with crystals, that hardly any researchers or authors had taken much notice of them, let alone the possibility that they might incorporate these ideas into considerations of the healing properties of minerals and precious stones. There are only seven crystal systems in the whole world (not counting the amorphous exception). Surely there must be some kind of cosmic significance in this? Fortunately, a remaining residue of scientific suspicion prevented me from immediately setting up a table to incorporate the crystal systems in a row with the seven planets of the classical world, the seven chakras, seven notes, and so on. Instead, I began observing which humans felt drawn towards certain minerals and what effects these minerals had on them.

One of the most impressive experiences I had was during a visit I paid to the home of an acquaintance who was known throughout his circle of friends for his exactness, correctness and thoroughness, and also for his extraordinary stamina, discipline, ability to learn, his immense knowledge and untiring 'know-it-all' attitude. In his living room, I unexpectedly came upon a shelful of minerals – at the time, I did not even know that he collected minerals. This shelf accommodated fluorite exclusively. At this point I must correct my earlier statement: he did not collect minerals – he collected fluorites. Only fluorites! Now, fluorites belong among the cubic crystals ... Later, during the meal, when I noticed that I had never observed anyone sprinkling more salt (also cubic!) on his food than he did, a suspicion began to form in my mind ...

Could it be that there was a connection between the crystal structures of minerals and the lifestyle of humans? – that this inner structure of a mineral is mirrored in the way they conduct their lives?

Just as I began to come to grips with this idea, a bookseller in Stuttgart offered me regular advisory sessions on the use of precious stones. I saw this proposition as a challenge, first to check out the conclusions I had come to and to see whether they were applicable practically, and second, to collect further experiences through contact with other people. This was the beginning of a very fruitful phase in my work with minerals and precious stones. Looking back, I am now very grateful that there was comparatively little information available during this period (1988–1989). Because of this, there were very few opinions around and we were forced to research into the properties of relevant stones in these sessions by means of intense discussion.

During the course of these sessions, I was able to observe very clearly the real connection between crystal structures and lifestyles. Minerals with particular crystal systems were always chosen by certain people with particular traits. With time, I became increasingly conscious of the connections, until eventually I was often able to guess in advance the crystal system that someone would intuitively gravitate towards by watching them from their first entrance into a room, their manner of walking, talking and moving. Gradually, these observations led me to the conclusion that, even among the great variety of human lifestyles, there really were eight basic structures that corresponded to the seven crystal systems and the eighth amorphic state. The causes for this lie in the observed reality of each individual.

Human reality

Each one of us lives in his or her own reality. It is determined by our experiences and knowledge, by our opinions and observations and by the value systems we apply. This reality, which is defined by ourselves, will create mutual bonds with other humans or form boundaries between us and others. If you have shared experiences with someone, you will have the same reality. What do old friends do, for example? – They talk about 'the old days', that is, mutual experiences.

If you find someone who shares the same knowledge as you, you also share the same reality. Two experts in the same field will soon begin to exchange technical knowledge even if they have only just met five minutes earlier. An outsider (an interesting word!) who does not have this same knowledge will probably not understand very much about these conversations as he or she cannot share the same reality.

The same opinions or ways of looking at something create a reality, and this is how people who have the same political, world or religious views will quickly gravitate towards each other. The converse is also true, as there is hardly anything that will create deeper divisions between people. Thus, the example of religious wars shows that different realities can even lead to people into situations where they will kill each other, without gaining any significant advantage by doing so.

We are aware of this problem in everyday life: interview the witnesses of a traffic accident and you will be surprised how many different realities you come up with! Even shared experiences may lead to very different realities. A shared lesson at school will represent a very different reality to the star pupil than to the persistent problem pupil!

Or how about the very different realities of optimists and pessimists? For the former a glass is half full, while for the other it is half empty.

This means reality is something completely subjective, yet the individual experiences it as absolute and valid. It is very important to understand this and to give it due attention. Particularly in the field of natural healing, it is extremely important to get to know the other person's reality. We will not be able to help anyone if we attack their reality, deny it or devalue it. Only if we accept another reality as given will we be able to help someone to change, if that person is having problems or difficulties and wishes to overcome them.

Crystals can be employed in this field in order to bring about changes or encourage them. A very interesting phenomenon is displayed when one is observing human realities. If we ignore all common factors that have arisen through shared experiences, knowledge, opinions, observations and values, there are still certain basic structures. Even then, humans can be distinguished by their nature and divided into different 'types'.

These 'basic structures of human reality' have been observed at all times and many systems have been created to explain the structures: the temperaments, Jung's archetypes, the principles of astrology, the picture cards of the tarot, and many others. All of these descriptions are valid within their own framework and when applied in the relevant system can work very well.

The difficulty always arises when one attempts to transfer a particular definition to another system. Here conflicts will arise between the different realities of the systems themselves. An example for this is the typical problem encountered by ethnologists arriving in a different cultural circle, where they investigate and then describe what they have found but are only very rarely able to discard the 'spectacles' of their own culture and lay aside the ways of observing they have brought along with them. This is where the necessary appreciation of a different reality is lacking.

For this reason, in spite of intensive studies of many different systems, I was always very careful not to be in a hurry to transfer knowledge gained from other systems to the realm of healing with crystals. The discovery of 'lifestyles' as a 'basic structure of human reality' and their correspondence to crystal systems was one of those lucky moments during the past 10 years. I now had a system to hand that could be manipulated with a great deal of precision.

Crystal structures and lifestyles

Descriptions of different 'lifestyles' show eight distinct basic characteristics of human behaviour, of personal behaviour and of individual lifestyle. These characteristics are independent of age, background, gender, world view or life experience. They are basic structures out of which we have chosen one as a survival strategy for our entire life or for our present situation. As these basic patterns can be seen in connection with the crystal systems of minerals, those minerals that possess the crystal structure that corresponds to us are particularly suitable for us as healing stones.

The cubic lifestyle

Let us start with the cubic lifestyle, which was already briefly outlined in the earlier example of the 'fluorite collector'. Just as the cubic crystal system is characterized by a square structure and is therefore very regular, the corresponding lifestyle is also characterized by regular structures.

People who lead their lives in the cubic style never leave anything to chance. Order and an overview are very important to you. You will endeavour to create structure in all areas of your life in order to keep everything 'under control': your living space will be structured, for example, by making sure everything has its place. You know, both at home and at your work place, where everything can be found, at least in those task areas that you define or recognize as 'your' areas.

Time, too, has its own structure. Certain habits take up a fixed position in your daily schedule. You keep to daily rituals, whether they be the same sequence of morning hygiene, punctually timed meals, the evening news programme or anything else. You take your commitments seriously and are generally punctual – to the minute or always late by the same number of minutes, which is also a kind of punctuality. You like to plan far in advance so that you can make detailed provisions for later events at an early stage.

Your actions are generally of a very regular nature. You love acting soberly with well-considered plans and are also in a position to anticipate the consequences of what you do, at least, as far as the consequences concern you. You are quickly able to grasp the essentials of a situation and try to create order everywhere – your idea of order – and wherever necessary. Certain events and sequences that you have found to be sensible and effective will be adhered to, just as you prefer to stick to tried and tested ways of doing things instead of engaging in spontaneous experimentation. Security is very important to you.

Logical thinking comes easily to you. You seldom have any difficulty in retaining an overview, even in complex systems, and you are able to look systematically for the causes of phenomena. You are also very precise and exact in all your considerations of whatever will provide security and will strengthen your position in a conflict. You are extremely careful in any overly free associations or risky speculations. For you the inevitable outcome of cause and effect should be recognizable in all circumstances; even a risk should be calculable.

Feelings, too, have their place. You have deep feelings towards people you love, and even, depending on your inclinations, towards animals, plants, stones or even ideas that you feel enthusiastic about. Still, you do not like to allow your actions to be led by your feelings. The terrain is too unfamiliar, lacking any landmarks, and the risk too great that you may allow yourself to be pushed into precipitous actions based on your feelings. Also, objectivity is too important for you to abandon it on a whim. You are, therefore, in a position to control your feelings and remain in charge of the situation.

You also prefer to maintain a constant appearance on the outside. You have certain favourite colours, preferred articles of clothing that you wear even when they are falling apart, and you like to stay in a certain kind of environment. You prefer to appear conservative rather than unorthodox. The same goes for looking after your physical well-being: naturally, you are keen to remain healthy, have regular health check-ups, never miss the half-yearly dental check-up and stick to a regular regime of personal hygiene. Unfortunately, your bad habits are just as persistent! The main cause of illness in the cubic lifestyle is bad habits: poor diet, smoking, alcohol, an unhealthy lifestyle and many things you just cannot give up, no matter how hard you are pushed by your doctor.

Your greatest weakness is your lack of flexibility. On a mental level too, the biggest problems you have are connected with the fact that you cling too much to the familiar and show too little spontaneity if something unexpected happens. The collapse of a well-thought-out plan can create a deep crisis and a temporary sense of disorientation. Defeats like this increase the urge to seek security and control to such a degree that there is a risk of becoming totally 'head-bound', resulting in overemphasis of the rational mind and logic and a suppression of intuition, feelings and emotions, to a degree that their existence can no longer be felt. This is just the beginning of a vicious circle that spirals downwards.

It then becomes utterly impossible to let go of habitual behaviour patterns, as you can now no longer see any other way of acting. Your thoughts and opinions become so rigid that they seem more important than reality itself. Under certain circumstances, you may even be ready to twist the reality of an event to make it conform to your view of it, rather than the opposite. In extreme cases, you will not balk at any means. Depending on your individual character, you may find yourself subject to a strong missionary urge, or even experience a readiness to use violence to promote your own ideas. The desire to uphold your own system of order may lead to unnecessary complications: instead of handling a situation according to the obvious facts, you have to plan, think about it, grasp it, register it, analyse it, structure it, determine priorities, delegate, rule and secure. A simple garden party turns into a state reception ...

All your rules and laws become even more problematical if you overemphasize them so much that you are really only able to live according to these preconceived patterns. Then any change coming from the outside becomes a threat, any criticism is seen as a personal attack, and all other lifestyles or world views become a danger that has to be fought against. Your thinking is, therefore, polarized in an extremely negative way. You see nothing but mistakes, difficulties, failures and dangers, and your faculties for rational thought and logic are used exclusively to support these observations by collecting 'suitable' information that will back up your preconceived notions. Even help offered by others is viewed with suspicion. The opinion that 'the world is not treating me well' can be extended, forcing your own thought and behaviour patterns to be transformed into (small-scale) fortifications.

A climax is finally reached when the 'cubic' person might even be ready to commit suicide, merely in order to uphold an idea, world view or ideology. By this, I do not mean a kamikaze operation or the willingness to die for a good cause, but the daily mistake, repeated a million times over, of throwing away life on account of rigidly adhering to certain patterns of thought and behaviour: for example, being seriously ill and rejecting effective 'alternative' therapies, not going to the doctor in spite of pain, not changing your diet because you do not believe that it will help, driving a car under the influence of alcohol because you are absolutely sure of being in control, working yourself to death because money, position or a career are more important than good health or your life, and so on. Things like this often happen for the simple reason that people of this disposition stubbornly hold on to certain set ways of looking at things, or do not allow themselves a new perspective. This is typically 'cubic'.

Do not despair! You do not need to end up this way if you are a 'cubic' personality. A cubic lifestyle can allow both a negative development, as described above, and development in a positive direction. In the latter case, there is development of precisely those characteristics that will allow you to 'think big' and generously. One of these abilities, for example, is being able to keep an overview of many different sequences: the working connections within a large firm, the complexities of a computer program, or even the many so-called 'coincidences' in one's own life that, seen as a whole, often seem clearly to demonstrate the finger of destiny – if you are able to see the connections. Then you have an opportunity to see yourself as part of a larger plan. Not merely to sense or feel how other lifestyles can make this possible, but to see clearly.

This starts with the possibility of seeing your own life 'pattern' as part of a higher structure. Along with the readiness not to stick stubbornly to your own ideas, you gain the opportunity to fit into the structures of family, community, human life and planetary life, as well as into the laws of a physical and spiritual universe. In this way, forming rigid boundaries, over-protecting yourself, suspicion and violent change become completely unnecessary. Naturally, you do not blindly trust in God and the World, but are ready to allow yourself to be persuaded by new possibilities. You remain open to new experiences. In a typically 'cubic' fashion, you become extremely open to learning. Every new experience, any new piece of information is immediately linked with what is already known, fitted in, connected and is then ready to be applied. Your ability to create order and oversee larger connections can also be employed in a way that is helpful to others. As you are able to see far ahead, you are in a position to 'switch the points' before others are able to see what is coming towards them. Your prognoses are, as a rule, well based and reliable. No matter in what area of work you are involved, you will be concerned with making your work more effective, optimizing actions and improving results. Large goals appear attractive to you, so you rapidly gravitate towards responsible positions and are able to fill them. Difficulties appear as challenges that can be mastered and problems merely help you to learn and grow. You gain fulfilment with the successful realization of each idea and – for a cubic personality who is able to foresee the consequences and results of their actions at the time of acting – success is bound to follow!

The hexagonal lifestyle

Among the seven shapes mentioned above, the hexagon is the one with the smallest perimeter in relation to the area enclosed. This efficient use of space has led bees to construct their honeycombs in hexagonal grid patterns, and this kind of efficiency is also a central theme of the hexagonal lifestyle. 'Hexagonal' humans have a great urge towards success and have plenty of direction. This goes for long-term goals as well as for individual daily stages.

If you are a 'hexagonal' person, anything you aim for you will ultimately reach. Your lifestyle is very consistent. You choose an idea consciously, know exactly who your role models are, and anything you have recognized as being right is made real through a step-by-step process. You love straightforwardness and honesty. The shortest path is your favourite path; diversions and distractions are anathema to you.

Time is one of your most precious commodities. You are anxious to use it as sensibly and usefully as possible; you abhor wasting time. As attaining the goal is more important to you than the path to it, you are able to distinguish very well between the necessary and the superfluous. You devote yourself to the former and ignore the latter. Your days are filled up, idle time or boredom are unknown to you. As a rule, you have a considerable amount ahead of you and once a goal is reached, you quickly look for and find another.

Your actions are well planned and well prepared. You will work tirelessly, with zeal and dedication, both physically and mentally, to achieve your goal, which may be of a personal, social, political or religious nature. You never lose sight of the goal and this is what gives you the strength to carry on, no matter how steep the path or how difficult. Even if there are difficulties and obstacles along the way, the strength to overcome again and again is always available. You like having a career. You are spurred on by wanting to attain something that fills you with pride.

Your thinking processes are clear and analytical. You are quick on the uptake and are very motivated. As a rule, you determine for yourself what you are interested in and will rarely be distracted from it. You quickly understand the sense and usefulness of all matters so they can be incorporated into your plans, if they are appropriate. Even though you are able to change strategies and tactics rapidly if necessary, you remain true to your fundamental persuasions. You are very thorough, sometimes even fussy, and only content if everything is working down to the last detail. As a rule, only the best is good enough for you.

Your life clearly emphasizes the rational side of things. You are able to experience feelings very intensely, but can detach yourself from them instantly if they hinder you or prevent you from acting. Here, too, the inborn faculty to overcome is a great advantage. You are also very individualistic. The fact that you dislike being hemmed in by others and refuse to be slowed down, checked or oppressed is another reason for the urge to reach the top, the desire for a position in life in which you determine your own fate.

It is, however, an interesting fact that you usually stop just one step away from the top. Obviously, it appears more important to continue to have a goal in front of you than to sit at the top without a future prospect. The teacher's best pupil or the boss's right-hand man is a much more desirable position for some than being the teacher or the boss. Many Secretaries of State remain in office when the minister has to leave ... the secret ruler rules longer!

Even your body displays this ideal. You love to have a well-trained, well-functioning body, and engage in just enough sporting activity to keep fit. As a rule, you look after your health and have a good diet, as long as other things do not become more important. If the time left to attain a projected goal is running out, you have no qualms about leaving out a meal here or there (or even several). Drinking coffee standing up and grabbing a quick snack on the hop can rapidly become a habit. Asceticism comes easily if it serves a purpose; you would, however, probably never sacrifice four weeks of holiday to go on a therapeutic diet.

If you do become ill, the main reason is generally overwork, too little self-consideration and too many demands on yourself. You often get very impatient during the get-well phase and the danger of having a lingering illness, suffering a relapse, or using acute suppression that results in an acute illness becoming chronic is far more prevalent with the hexagonal lifestyle than in any other. You also easily become accustomed to taking tablets to combat fatigue or bring sleep, as long as they appear to guarantee that you keep functioning.

Your greatest strengths can at the same time be your greatest weaknesses! You find it too easy to become fixated on a single goal, neglecting to look either to the right or the left. This results in a blinkered attitude that impoverishes your life and you are driven by the feeling that you are constantly lacking the time to do all you want. Hectic behaviour, impatience and stress increase constantly. Then you find you are lacking spiritual nourishment because you have not got enough leisure time, relaxation and variety, as well as the strength that can be derived from these. Even holidays are cut down to a minimum or they are used for another target-oriented and gruelling programme. For a long time this stress will remain hidden, as you can make up for the deficiency in your life for a certain amount of time through sheer willpower, until finally the last reserves are used up. Then, you experience collapse.

The crisis will arrive just as certainly if you succeed in attaining one of the 'great goals' of your life. Suddenly, something seems to be missing: a sense, a task, the feeling of being needed or being important in some way. You need goals in front of you. This means that success is often not celebrated, the fruits of labour are not enjoyed. Instead of relaxing, taking a rest and enjoying peace, you immediately start looking for a new goal, a new direction, the next dimension. If you cannot find it quickly enough, the inner emptiness is bridged by outer activities, at least as long as it takes until your body pulls its emergency brake!

For this reason, 'hexagonal' goals or ideals are often set so high that it is almost certain they will never be attained. This means the risk of that 'great emptiness' arriving is eliminated, but woe betide anything that is in its path. During 'orientation crises', it is high ideals or 'salvation' teachings that will find fertile ground in the hexagonal personality: enlightenment, Nirvana, immortality or eternal bliss. Wherever these ideals are promised, your own critical facilities will suddenly be switched off. You tend to accept the teachings offered without testing them; you lift them up to become a new goal, identify with them and find your way back to your strengths and habitual capacities. You often do not notice at all that it is only the fact that you have a new goal that has set the positive changes in motion, and the goal itself has taken second place.

If you then ascribe the positive changes to the content of this new ideal, fixation upon the new goal becomes very strong. Depending on what kind of content you are committing yourself to, your hexagonal tendency to fanaticism can lead to various different degrees of involvement. In some ways, however, fanaticism is always destructive, as you begin to ignore your own needs and limits. Then it is only a matter of time before you start expecting or demanding it from others too. What was until now voluntary discipline and loyalty to your own principles is confused with ruthlessness and dogmatism. Here, too, in extreme cases, you find the willingness to sacrifice your life, and the lives of others, merely to follow an ideal or a flag.

The positive development of the hexagonal lifestyle begins with the simple principle – do as you say! The consistent way of acting that you have always had will automatically cause you to assimilate experiences while realizing the ideals that will either confirm what you are doing along the way, or send signals that changes are overdue. Here, it is important that you always remain willing to reassess your goals in the light of your experiences. Goals can be changeable. The closer you get to the summit, the more clearly you will be able to see it. Perhaps the goal no longer corresponds to the image you had of it from a distance. This means it is important that you always leave an option open, daily, either to amend this image because new facts have come to light, or to embark on a different path. Both will make you freer.

The second aspect that will make a positive hexagonal development possible is an inner certainty that you will reach your goal. It simply lies in the nature of hexagonal personalities. You do not need to put such a great deal of effort into it. The frequently present feeling of 'being driven', the restlessness and overexerting yourself, often arise from a fear of not reaching the goal you have set for yourself. If you are certain, on an inner level, that you really possess the necessary abilities, you can approach the whole matter in a far more relaxed manner. This 'laid back' attitude is a better guarantee for success than any kind of effort. Naturally, you have to do some work, but you never could resist that anyway!

Freed of blinkers and armed with a consistent approach, inner certainty and a relaxed attitude, you are able to accomplish vast amounts each day. You storm up career ladders and the personal development that you desire moves along splendidly. Individualism and sociability are no longer seen as being opposed, but complement each other. You also find that tolerance and acceptance of others' ways will never get in the way of your own personal self-realization; on the contrary, they will actually encourage it. The combination of foresight and a global view of life will offer such a host of experiences that you will gradually become aware of the truth: the path is the goal!

The trigonal lifestyle

The triangle is the simplest geometric form – likewise, the trigonal lifestyle is basically very simple. If this is your own lifestyle, you will lead a simple, uncomplicated life, very constant and tranquil. You are quite able to appreciate the comforts of luxury, if it is affordable, but you are never prepared to pay an overly high price for wealth or power. Your principles in life are very pragmatic and realistic, the motto 'minimal effort – maximum success' dominate your actions. This is why negligence is much more familiar to you than ambition. Where possible, you choose the path of least resistance but you are able to stick to a certain position or opinion and wait patiently until its hour arrives. Generally speaking, you are more inclined to let things come to you. Hasty action is foreign to you.

The trigonal personality has all the time in the world. You rarely rush and usually approach work and other projects at a comfortable pace, carrying out all necessary tasks with the simple motto: 'One thing after the other ...'. As long as nobody demands impossible things of you, you are usually reliable. You prefer to have a certain rhythm for doing things: there should be breaks – finishing off in time at the end of the day is very important. Nothing irritates you more than unnecessary hectic goings on and people who spread stress around them.

You are also very pragmatic in your actions. You like to learn by observing and are very skilled at simplifying things or procedures. Occasionally, you may be accused of being a bit lazy, but it may be worth remembering here that the greatest inventions were created out of a kind of laziness: the desire to make life easier! For this reason, you are usually completely practical. Complicated theories are not your cup of tea. What counts in the end is whether something works or not. It is precisely with this attitude that you often become a master of your field or career as your results are accessible and applicable.

You do not create unnecessary complications on principle. Usually, you are able to arrive at acceptable solutions to your difficulties and problems without a great deal of thought. As a rule, you are, therefore, much valued by others who like to obtain practical advice or encouragement from you. If an immediate solution is not forthcoming, you are generally convinced 'it will work out', and are still able to sleep peacefully and remain relaxed until the saving idea arrives.

You love to indulge yourself and will occasionally let yourself go. You still try to avoid conflicts and disagreements and you genuinely dislike quarrels and violent emotions. You are happy when domestic peace is maintained and if you have managed to arrange your life in such a way that you can be contented. The atmosphere in which you feel most at home is in one of tranquillity and comfort.

Often your physical self will also display this tendency. Active sports are not usually among your favourites, so you often have a 'rounder' figure than the average person, or at least have a tendency to have a 'spare tyre' or a flabby stomach. Usually, however, you can live with it, as maintaining a dream figure would be just too much effort! On the other hand, laziness and laxness may often become factors in poor health or hinder healing. A complicated diet or a tiring programme of treatment will not exactly fill you with enthusiasm. A leisurely rest cure is quite a different matter.

Generally, there is a tendency to make things easy for yourself. In order to have your peace, you may often retreat into an 'island existence' with a horizon that is bounded by the garden fence. Bad or disturbing news is denied through lack of interest, conflicts are suppressed, complicated people or situations avoided. This results in ever-increasing superficiality that is even encouraged nowadays through 'tele-communications': telephoning is simpler than visiting, faxing less effort than talking, adventures can be experienced on television in the comfort of the armchair, and the horror stories in the news remain at a sufficient distance to avoid spoiling the appetite for chips afterwards.

A quiet type of egotism becomes established: only your own well-being matters any more and only your own interests count, while mutual aid or becoming committed to a 'good cause' become less and less appealing. It is much simpler to donate some money on the doorstep now and then. You tend to be less and less aware of the problems of others. For one thing, these people are nothing to do with you, while at the same time your attention is increasingly taken up by the functions of people you deal with on a one-to-one basis. Instead of feeling that you are surrounded by other human beings, you see them only in terms of the role they play: clients, customers, salespeople, civil servants, bosses, subordinates, or patients. This dehumanizing outlook can be found in some hospitals, where patients may be know only as 'appendixes' or 'fractures', etc.

If this superficiality finally reaches the level of indifference or apathy, things get worse: your feeling side atrophies completely and life becomes uniform, boring and empty. Without feelings, you can only maintain the most necessary of life's functions: eating food becomes merely 'being full'; career becomes occupation; family life becomes a social safeguard; instead of ideas and interests, you have distractions; instead of communication, one-sided conversation; instead of a sense of living joyfully, there is only boredom. This spiritual death starts slowly and stealthily behind locked doors.

It need not be so! As long as you remain open and helpful towards your fellow human beings and retain for yourself an interest in a rich, fulfilled lifestyle, the gift of simplicity will create happiness for you and for others. Your ability to find simple solutions makes you a valued advisor with an effective realism. Experiences and traditions are the foundation of your support. You find it easy to separate fantasy from fact, so where you do provide criticism, it will be well founded; if you recommend something, it can be relied on!

What really characterizes the trigonal personality is great commonsense – natural clarity of thought that is direct and honest and does not allow you to be deluded easily. Indeed, you are able to be neutral. You are able to listen without making value judgements and to understand what someone else is saying. This is precisely what enables you to help others best. It is this neutrality that enables you to grow tolerant and acquire the ability to take others as they are, no matter whether you agree with what they say or do or not. Founded on this tolerance that people are able to sense, many feel they can trust you and your words will weigh more than the statements of enthusiastic proponents of particular opinions.

The result of this developmental process is harmony: actions and thoughts, understanding and feeling harmonize in a very simple fashion with each other. You feel good and are content with your life. Your family life, community life and working life are fulfilled. You enjoy having good friends without having to entertain on a lavish scale, and there is always something to do – you are unfamiliar with boredom. A trust in God or Providence and a relaxed attitude encourage a healthy faith in the future, even in uncertain times, as there is one thing you are certain of: in simplicity lies truth!

The tetragonal lifestyle

The shape of a rectangle is similar to that of the square – but no more than similar. At a superficial glance the tetragonal lifestyle may seem to resemble the cubic lifestyle but at heart they are very different. If you conduct your life in a 'tetragonal manner', it will appear to others that you are always certain about what you are doing and have everything under control. However, what appears as well planned to others is actually spontaneous, but at any time you are quite able to explain everything absolutely logically, even if it was undertaken simply because you felt like it. The 'tetragonal lifestyle' has two faces: an inner one and an outer one.

The tetragonal personality makes detailed plans and then throws them out again at the next moment, partly because of spontaneous changes and partly because of mistaken estimates regarding the actual time required for certain tasks. While endeavouring to bring a certain amount of order into your life, you like to plan well ahead although you are certain from the start that everything will turn out differently from what you think. Personally, you do not find it difficult to make these constant changes, but those around you will often find it quite disconcerting because you appear to radiate such stability and reliability to the outside.

You love the new and the unknown. Every day is different; you dislike constant repetitions. Once something is finished and done with, that is it! This means you are also willing to drop unworkable concepts immediately and replace them with new ones. You are ready to learn from any new action or event and to improve on it next time. For yourself, this characteristic becomes an enormous capacity for personal development, but others often see it as unpredictability.

Your capacity for analytical thought and the volatile nature of your emotional life are at the root of this type of behaviour. You are able to evaluate information very quickly and to interpret, with the interpretation being strongly coloured by your momentary feelings. You do not, therefore, have much difficulty in explaining logically what you feel is right. You will change your mind very rapidly when the need arises, but you will then support the new opinion with the same kind of intensity as you did the old one the day before. Whatever happens, you always have an answer for every question.

In principle, you feel secure, although you prefer always to remain in a position where you can decide whether and to whom you will reveal your feelings and thoughts. If necessary, you are able to cover up feelings and moods in order to appear to address a situation appropriately. You are also capable of conscious deceit and living out several identities side by side without much trouble.

This dual nature is also mirrored in your outward appearance, which can be very variable. Just by changing your clothes and hairstyle, for example, you are able to alter your appearance and your image quite considerably. Even your body weight will rapidly alter, depending on the life situation you find yourself in. You look after your physical body in such a way that desirable features are emphasized and undesirable ones concealed. For this reason, your appearance is generally a statement about yourself, be it an expression of well-being, interest, wealth, power, protest, provocation or whatever.

This calculated way of presenting and expressing yourself does, however, contain a risk: if you are not careful, you will develop an unpenetrable facade that will provide you with a certain amount of protection, but occasionally it will need an enormous effort to maintain. This will make you dishonest, even towards the people who are closest to you. You like to keep your little secrets that you do not wish to share with anyone but run the risk of inner loneliness, although you may appear sociable and friendly on the outside.

The tetragonal lifestyle is predestined to have a double life. Arising from a conflict between on the one hand wanting to give in to your feelings, and on the other hand wishing to keep your own life under control, situations will arise in which you are forced to lie and deceive. In addition, there is a certain cowardice, so a lover is kept secret, a mistake glossed over or a bad habit concealed. As you tend to do things that you yourself do not really agree with, you create shame that has to be hidden.

The day of reckoning will finally arrive when you are forced to confess or one of your secrets is discovered. To begin with, you put a lot of effort into building a new facade, designing a new thought structure that can justify everything, or you use a great deal of artful persuasion to reinterpret all the visible evidence and draw a veil over it. Very often you are successful with this. If you fail, however, you are so overwhelmed that a complete collapse is inevitable. You lose your self-confidence, are ashamed, feel inferior and tend to devalue everything , even the positive achievements in your life.

This 'loss of face' has a destructive effect: repressed aggressions are either directed outward so that you seek revenge on the person who exposed you, wishing them all manner of ills, or inward in the form of depression, self-punishment and, in extreme cases, as a flight into a 'better' world. Schizophrenia may even be the result of such a collapse; this is a 'typical tetragonal' disease – a life lived in several parallel realities. If this low point is overcome in a negative fashion, you are likely to build even thicker walls around yourself in future, which are designed to protect you but instead become oppressive to everyone around you. As long as you do not allow anyone else to be strong beside you, the danger to yourself will be lessened.

The combination of feelings, spontaneity and analytical thinking common to the tetragonal lifestyle makes a positive development in your life possible, in which you no longer invest energy in erecting facades and maintaining them, but in which you penetrate them and discover the secrets lying behind them. As you know from your own experiences that the superficial appearance of things is not everything, you are always endeavouring to find a deeper sense and hidden connections.

Your interest is directed towards the 'Why?', the function and the intention behind all manifestations. When lived out positively, the tetragonal lifestyle can be that of a researcher or scientist. You are not content with what you have accomplished so far but are ready to keep re-examining everything, questioning results, daring to formulate new interpretations and try out new experiments. Your feelings are often the driving force behind this: if you are lucky enough to be on the right path, you stick to it and will not allow yourself to be discouraged by any failures.

The same commitment that you would use to hide things on your negative side is also made during a search for the truth. Imagination proves to be a particular gift here, fantasy – the art of making things visible (Greek *phainein*, 'making visible'). Without imagination, discoveries and inventions would be simply impossible. Your own life will also be included in this search for truth: superficial contentment will not be sufficient as it is the deeper meaning of human existence that interests you. Intuition tells you that you have a task in this life, in whatever fashion this task may appear. Discovering it and fulfilling it provides a challenge to your capabilities and offers you a happy, joyful life.

Because of your versatility, you also find it easy to help others in this. You are able to analyse problems with your sharp intellect and develop creative solutions by using your imagination. Your way of helping may often be imaginative and unconventional but, in the end, new paths are always more attractive than old, well-worn ones. This means that the greater the challenge you are faced with, the more willing you are to accept it!

The rhombic lifestyle

 A rhombus also has a certain similarity to a square, which is why the rhombic lifestyle also appears to outsiders as a condition in which everything appears to be in order. Life is like a long, tranquilly flowing river – this is how you could describe your feelings about it if you were someone who lives in this lifestyle. As a rule, life develops along a continuous line and without special events; only rarely do you experience massive intrusions or 'break-outs'.

A long cycle of daily occurrences that all seem much the same will suddenly bring you to a low point, seemingly for no particular reason. You may experience panic attacks, depression or simply bad moods of an unforeseen extent; just as suddenly as they turned up, these manifestations can disappear again without a trace. 'Break-outs' like this can arise in such a manner that things that seemed important to you until that moment suddenly seem to lose all their value and you are quite easily able to make far-reaching decisions that others find completely inexplicable. Without any regrets, you break off relationships, give notice to leave a job, move house, or throw security overboard. You suddenly start a new life – 'just like that'.

This perverse contrast between long, unchanging phases on the one hand, and unexpected changes on the other, determines your whole life's rhythm. Basically, you adjust yourself to the fact that everything will remain exactly as it is, so you never plan far ahead. There is no need to. For you, Time is a constantly recurring phenomenon; every day the sun rises – it was always so and why should anything about it change? If something does suddenly change, as described above, then the very next day this constant attitude of taking things as a matter of course returns. Admittedly, recently everything was different, but from now on everything will be the way it is now.

Because of this attitude, you find it very easy to make decisions: a lot of money is invested in a new home, even if you do not know how long you will be staying there. A relationship spontaneously turns into marriage, or a task once taken on, often becomes a permanent commitment. In all things, you possess enormous staying power, apart from the occasional intrusions or 'break-outs'. You are thorough and inconspicuous in all you do, and often perform most of the work in team situations without pushing into the limelight. You are very self-sufficient and are not dependent on attention, praise or recognition.

You are ready to be enthusiastic about a good cause and, as a rule, show plenty of social awareness and commitment. You are basically helpful and often able to carry out the small details of a task. The 'big ideas' will often come from others but without your meticulous work on their realization, down to the last detail, very little would be accomplished. Thoroughness and exactness are generally your strong points; you think all courses of action through quietly and objectively, but without falling into un-necessary introspection. You are also very empathetic. You are quick to register the moods of others and find it easy to adjust to them.

You would be popular working in foreign countries and often find yourself engaged in caring work. You are happy if others, too, feel well and happy, and are always keen to create a pleasant atmosphere. You are known as a good listener among your friends, along the lines of: 'A sorrow shared is a sorrow halved. A shared joy is double the joy'. You are, therefore, able to subordinate your own interests to the greater goal of a community, provided that you identify with this community.

As you do not make a great deal of fuss about yourself, your appearance and the way you behave tend to be inconspicuous. You seldom like the limelight but prefer to stay in the background. You run the risk of going unnoticed so that, occasionally, after a party, you may be asked, 'Were you there, I don't remember seeing you?' or you may not climb the career ladder as fast as a loud-mouthed colleague. The other side of this is that, in the latter case, the risk of a 'fall' is also not so great.

The whole business becomes rather more dubious if you fit in too well and give up fulfilling your own interests for the sake of others. Sometimes this urge to fit in can result in an inner emptiness or insecurity that you try to secure through holding on to outer things – a partner, a community or a job. It is precisely this disregard for your own wishes and dreams that reinforces this inner emptiness more and more until the 'intrusion' or 'break-out' occurs.

Intrusions happen when you suddenly become aware of the inner emptiness, but without being able to penetrate to the real cause. Then you find yourself no longer on solid ground; rather you are floundering in a 'mire'. As the cause is not recognized, this state will continue until you once more find your previous lifestyle acceptable and start adapting to your environment again. Suddenly, you begin to 'function' again and you seem to be able to continue with your life at exactly the point where you left off when the 'intrusion'/'break-out' took place. Should you continue to put up resistance to the 'old game', depression will immediately follow. Any kind of help offered will just exacerbate the 'down' feeling. Sympathy, clever advice or psychopharmaceuticals will only succeed in perpetuating this state. Genuine help can only be provided by a recognition of the cause of your problem.

Such a recognition can, however, lead to a 'break-out': if you suddenly realize that you have not been living your own life for a very long time but (depending on circumstances), living through the life of your partner, your parents, children, friends, bosses, colleagues, gurus or whoever, then these bonds will, as a rule, be severed very quickly. The desire to be rid of this outside control can, however, sometimes lead to the 'baby being thrown out with the bathwater'. By turning your life upside down, you also lose the positive things you have worked so hard for. Then you run the risk of fleeing into new (initially unrecognized) dependencies, looking for a new hold until the old game begins anew.

The real way out, or the beginning of a positive development in a rhombic lifestyle, consists of promoting your own life, strengthening your own interests and setting your own goals first. This may begin in the typical 'rhombic inconspicuousness' and is often even recommended: 'a young plant should be protected until its stem is strong enough to hold up to the wind'. Depending on the degree to which this inner hold is created and self-confidence is built up, you will be able to make visible change.

Interestingly enough, attacks from outside will be far rarer than expected. On the contrary, your new way of making decisions will often be admired ('I never thought that you would...') and supported ('It's great the way you have grown...'), and if attacks really do take place, it is now easier to distinguish between friend and foe. Making breaks with people who do not mean well or turn out to be false friends will surely not be harmful!

This new development makes it easy for you to employ your own abilities successfully for yourself and for others. Your capacity for understanding and empathy makes you into a good helper and perhaps even a healer, without having to deny your own identity. You will still be able to enjoy friendships and enjoy the well-being of others. At the same time, all these qualities will also serve your own self-realization. In this way, you will gain permanent stability and fulfilment that is secure enough to stop you desiring more upheavals and changes. In this new state, you may again become inconspicuous, as often happens with people who are clear about themselves: you have no need to seek the limelight as you are happy and content.

The monoclinic lifestyle

A parallelogram often gives the impression of being on the point of tipping to one side. This instability is one of the essential characteristics of the monoclinic lifestyle, which features a continuous up and down movement. Your life changes in almost regular rhythms, moods fluctuate, opinions are changed, even facts appear to keep on showing different facets. Something you really like today will not find favour tomorrow and what will happen next week is something you would rather not think about.

This permanent flux has something almost consistent about it. It appears so certain that you can plan for it. This is why you make arrangements to meet with reservations, never plan exact times but generally time slots for what you are intending to do, and are always ready to change everything at the drop of a hat. You are extremely reluctant to make promises that you might be bound to without keeping a loophole – just in case. However, once you have given your word, you will stick to your promises even if great exertions are necessary at the last minute. You find predictions for the future fascinating, on the one hand, as you would like nothing better than to know exactly what is awaiting you. On the other hand, you do not really believe them. According to your own life's experience, what actually happens is always different from what you thought would happen.

Your ideal would really be to be able to act in a prudent, thoughtful way. Still, you usually act very spontaneously and from a gut feeling. Depending on your moods, some days you are ready to run greater risks while at other times you are over-cautious. In this way, you become completely unpredictable in the eyes of your family and friends, although you are used to it: 'this is me', you say, 'I am the way I am and that means different every day'. If you are told something you can understand, you are easily convinced by another's opinion.

Left to your own devices, you often torment yourselves over making difficult decisions. If you have a choice between two equally valid possibilities, you can usually think yourself into both situations so you are able to recognize advantages and disadvantages in both. The longer you consider the matter, the more difficult the choice becomes. Even your very vivid imagination will not help you; on the contrary, when the decision has finally been made in favour of one thing, the advantages of the other suddenly seem to stand out even more clearly.

Then doubts begin – your constant companions. The changeover from one feeling to another is much more spontaneous: here, often a wrong word (not even meant seriously) is enough to propel you into a downward curve while another event can just as quickly ensure a 'high'. You would never think of yourself as moody as you are aware of very distinct triggers for your changes of mood. Finally, this flexibility does have a positive side: anger and fury will dissolve very quickly, just as sorrow and sadness also disperse rapidly. As a rule you are never one to hold a grudge, certainly not as long as you are able to voice your feelings freely.

Inconstancy is also a feature of your physical state: your sleeping and eating patterns change all the time, sometimes you need more sometimes less. The same goes for your health; sometimes you are in top form, while at other times a gust of wind will knock you over and send you to bed with some ailment or the other. Sporty phases and lazy ones alternate. Your entire appearance can change so much that you are often told by people that that they 'nearly did not recognize you'.

This inconstancy is also the thing that creates the most problems for you. Disagreements with others, in particular with those who find it difficult to understand you, are the order of the day. Depending on how violent these disagreements are, you react in different ways to them: clear, direct confrontations are far more likely to explain your own way of doing things, help you gain trust again and to clarify different points of view (even in you). These discussions are often very necessary for your self-recognition and give you an opportunity, at the same time, to express your feelings. They will help you a great deal.

Constant needling and little intrigues, on the other hand, are pure poison. Because of your ability to be influenced, they gradually whittle away at your self-worth and encourage self-doubt. You begin to lose all feeling of security, start judging the changing sides of character with 'right' or 'wrong', while your fear of making mistakes grows all the time. This causes you to lose all sense of objectivity, which you need to preserve some kind of overview over your life, and you sink into utter confusion. Things seem to become too much for you and growing doubts and difficulties with making decisions cause you to function less and less effectively.

This, in turn, causes ever more things to be left undone, until you are confronted with a mountain of unfinished tasks that appear unsurmountable. This engenders a risk of ignoring things for good while it does not help relieve any of the load. Resignation increases and that puts an end to the fluctuating moods, unfortunately fixing them at the down end of the emotional scale.

The only thing that will help here is to confront the situation as it is. Do not look away, but instead focus directly on it. Conversations with supportive friends are definitely a good idea. If you are then able to regain at least a small part of your self-worth, then it is time to strike and to deal with the unfinished business, step by step. Every small detail that is dealt with takes you another step forward. Finally, your monoclinic nature will even help you: once you can look upon a few small successes, this will give you such a boost that the rest will seem more manageable. Your mood rises rapidly and you now only have to make sure that you keep at it until you have regained that feeling of freedom. The best sign for this is a return of that calm composure that is sure: 'Sunshine always follows after the rain'.

Then you are fully functional again, which is also the best protection against doubts: action brings experience. Experience prevents doubts. Your own experience is a secure island in the changeable world of monoclinic reality – a firm standpoint. If you make a habit of deciding quickly and without hesitation on important decisions, you will soon find that occasional wrong decisions are easier and quicker to correct than omissions caused through holding back. This will strengthen your feeling of self-value again and that, in turn, will make it possible to discover a new aspect of your feelings – trusting them.

Your feelings are often determined by triggers: events for which it is appropriate on the one hand to react with annoyance, rejection and fury or, on the other hand, with joy, trust or enthusiasm. As these triggers are often inaccessible to your conscious awareness, you can learn to use these your feelings as a finely calibrated barometer that will show you exactly whether a person or a situation is trustworthy or not, whether something will be successful or not. If you make a point of looking out for this, you will find that your feelings can be trusted, again and again. This creates security and what is really being developed here is nothing other than intuition! It is intuition that can reach perfection in the monoclinic lifestyle.

The triclinic lifestyle

The trapezium is a shape that has a broad base, symbolizing a stable, fixed nature which does, however, need to be turned upside down again and again to fit in the area to be filled. Turned upside down, the shape looks rather wobbly and insecure. Both realities are properties of the triclinic lifestyle, which manifests even more extremely than the monoclinic lifestyle as a fluctuation between two poles. Volatile, spontaneous and unpredictable, even to yourself, the course of your life is erratic, with fate continuously and unexpectedly taking a hand and presenting new challenges.

This lifestyle contains an interesting phenomenon to do with time: subjective time. Without your being able to ascribe this to a particular cause, time flies on one day and on another appears to drag endlessly. Not only does this make planning of any kind very difficult – it makes it almost impossible! But then planning is not necessary. Because of the lack of an objective means of measuring it, you are used to simply estimating periods of time and points in time and very often hit the mark surprisingly accurately. Those around you often watch this with great astonishment, considering that your estimates often turn out to be more precise – in spite of unforeseen obstacles and upsets – than would any complicated calculations.

A very similar situation exists with respect to your actions: there are days when everything just seems to fall into place, tasks are as easy as never before, everything works, and there are no problems to be seen anywhere. The very next day, however, it may all be quite different. Even breakfast is beset with problems, and the rest of the day follows suit. You have obviously got out of the wrong side of the bed and if you risk leaving the house, in spite of the warnings, at the latest by midday, you will be fervently wishing that you had never even got up that day. It is almost as though fate or providence were doling out good or bad days to you.

Your manner of thinking is just as disjointed and inconstant. Although you are extremely creative and full of ideas, these ideas need to be held on to and realized as soon as they appear. If you hesitate for only a few moments, it may be too late! Here again, days of unstoppable inspiration alternate with those featuring a complete lack of ideas, days on which any kind of effort seems to be for nothing and utterly frustrating. As long as the stream of pictures and ideas continues, you are effortlessly able to cope with many times the usual amount of work without being exhausted afterwards.

Your emotions flow up and down and cannot be influenced. Whereas this apparent fluctuation still manifests as a kind of wave motion in the monoclinic lifestyle, it becomes a strong zigzag motion in the triclinic lifestyle. Every change of mood arrives unexpectedly and without any noticeable trigger or announcement. On the contrary, it seems that moods consistently and suddenly tip over when they have reached a peak: at the climax of your own birthday party, you suddenly become desperately depressed; at the funeral of a dear friend, you suddenly find everything laughable. From agony to ecstasy, apparently without rhyme or reason.

Even your body demonstrates extreme contrasts: you are either tough and strong but appear rather delicate and weak, or you look like 'Mr Universe' but are by no means as sporty and strong as you appear. For the rest, your appearance generally mirrors your mood:

from perfectly turned out to totally scruffy, you are a master of every nuance – something that can make someone who does not know you very well either wonderfully surprised or horrified.

Interestingly enough, all these changing appearances have very little to do with whether your life is happy or not. The basic mood is the really constant part of your existence, the stable aspect of the trapezium. Depending on whether you approach life in a generally positive, friendly manner, or in a negative and denigrating manner, you will experience these daily ups and downs as being wonderfully varied or as a dreadful trip through hell.

The negative aspect often begins with indifference. As everything changes constantly and you apparently have no influence over the happenings within you and around you, you develop a cloak of apathy as a protective mechanism. This does save you from getting too involved in events, but just drives you further into passivity, an attitude where you continue to suffer through everything and have to submit to it.

The result can be that you feel you are a victim: it is just fate that is giving you a bad time, you are unlucky and basically it is others who are nasty to you, wish you ill and are attacking you in some way. All negative things come from outside; you are threatened, struck down by fate or even attacked by evil forces. Finally, you actually need these imaginary enemies in order to justify your pitiable state.

At this point you give up showing any interest in things getting better, if you have not done so already. Any help you are offered is declined as you suspect further bad intentions. Finally, help and healing also appear to you as forms of manipulation and who really knows the motives of a helper or healer? The moment of embitterment is reached: the down points of the original ups and downs stabilize, the high points no longer arrive. This is a truly hellish state.

The only chance of once again attaining moments of high spirits is the decision to make a positive new start. The volatile nature of the triclinic lifestyle can make a leap of faith from the very depths possible. The crucial thing is making a decision to be a doer rather than a victim in your own life and believing the simple notion that 'there is no pure coincidence'. Then you will able to alter a 'triclinic life' quite radically. Unlike the monoclinic lifestyle, the triclinic one does not have difficulties in making a decision. Any spiritual/mental decision is carried out consistently, even the decision to adopt either a negative or positive attitude towards life.

In a positive development, not much will change with respect to the tortuous paths of your life, but it is uncertainty itself that encourages the development of the so-called 'sixth sense' and other gifts. As you are constantly confronted with new things, you remain wide awake and attentive. There are soothing securities in your life and, for this reason, the first thing that needs to be developed again is instinct, a very sure and targeted form of acting that you are often not even aware of but will always lead you to the right place at the right moment. You turn into a 'lucky beggar' and things seem to fall into your lap, once you are prepared to grasp them.

To the extent that you recognize that these moments are becoming much too frequent to be coincidences, you become more and more conscious of your talent. Instinct becomes clairvoyance, to begin with in the shape of vague inklings, but in the course of time these become more like foresight. Provided you nurture these talents, you can develop a fertile, mediumistic talent that will, at the same time, make you more stable.

At last you are able to see a meaning in your eventful life and realize that fate does not mean you any harm. The ups and downs become the winding course of a serpentine path that leads you consistently uphill. You realize you have been led on this path and this, in turn, expands your abilities further: you gain a faith in God that makes miracles possible...

The amorphous lifestyle

Describing amorphism, that is, giving it a 'shape', is not an easy task. Yet it is necessary to try, as there are mercifully few amorphous words in the English language that can describe everything or nothing at once. For example, the word 'versatility'. Versatility is what characterizes a lifestyle that is amorphous. Everything constantly appears new and unrepeatable. You could not call it a change or a transformation, as both terms imply a past and a future, a causal development, a consistent course. All these things do not exist in an amorphous lifestyle. At least – not always.

For the 'amorphous' personality every moment is new. Every moment is unique. You are not interested in the 'Big Bang' or the end of the Universe – the former may never have happened and the latter may never happen, and neither is happening now! Time exists as a point, the very point you happen to be at now. Perhaps Time does not even exist, maybe it is just an invention of physics. In the end, it does not matter anyway.

Spontaneity is, therefore, not merely a feature of the amorphous lifestyle, but is its only way of expression. Between the impulse that motivates you and the action carried out, there appears to be no element of time or duration. Anything you think of is carried out immediately and ended at once if you lose sight of it or forget. This enables you to possess the freedom of the child to enjoy fully the present game you are playing, to live it out and when 'out' is reached, you let go without hesitation. You are one hundred per cent with something.

Every idea is an event. And yet you are still quite capable of thinking anything that can be thought. Your reservoir of creativity is boundless. Sometimes you give birth to ideas more quickly than you can hold on to them, speak them or write them down, and this is the only phenomenon during which you come into contact with Time; thinking seems to be quicker than speaking, speaking faster than acting, and that, paradoxically, all at the same moment.

You are in a position to experience all kinds of feelings but only one at a time. You are one hundred percent certain about this too. In a particular situation, no feeling can exist other than the one you are having right now. You like to show this feeling too; it is impossible for you to hide it because that would mean that two feelings could exist side by side (inside and outside). Amorphism also means being able to get right into any particular feeling. You are able to 'flow into' any situation, identify with it and leave it again. And you can enjoy a particular thing a hundred times over!

Of course, you do have a physical shape, a body, and it is always in motion. At any given moment you are active and busy, 'buzzing' about, like your idol, the butterfly, but you can also be endlessly calm and tranquil, like its close associate, the flower. You love colourful things as they seem to be related to your versatility; you also love freedom and not being tied down.

The only time things get dangerous for you is if you suddenly want to hold on to a particular moment. Then the eternally new is lost and you try to keep the past and future away from you by closing your eyes to them. The effect of this is that you also lose sight of the colourful world of the present moment and become lost in darkness and fog.

You no longer know who you are, and begin to experience the shadow side of the amorphous lifestyle. Ideas no longer come to you, creativity disappears, emptiness arises, nothing motivates you any longer, nothing can make you happy, nothing beckons or seduces you. The rich life in the 'here and now' turns into 'no future', a kind of present you hate and which, for understandable reasons, you do not wish to continue with into the future. You would rather destroy it at once and, in keeping with your amorphous non-structural self, you start this process immediately. You become destructive and aggressive, and in the final stage, apathetic.

Thankfully this is only one of many possibilities that you 'amorphous' beings can fall into, but which you can also leave behind again very quickly, as soon as something turns up that makes you enthusiastic again. The deepest depth lasts only for a moment, quickly supplanted by another moment. Precisely because there is nothing final about the amorphous lifestyle (where there is no development, there is also no end), there is always hope of a new opportunity.

When living positively, the 'amorphous' personality possesses a kind of genius: to be able to think things that have never been thought before, create what has never been seen before, invent what has never been accomplished before. This is only possible if you can be playful and free, not bound to one-way tracks, conventions and rules. You may be looked upon as an eccentric or a loner, but it is very easy to prove that in the history of mankind, far more innovative impulses have come from these people than from the majority of those who adapted themselves to circumstances. But all that is not important for you ....

Note

After all these detailed descriptions of crystal systems and the corresponding lifestyles, please do not expect to meet only people who are one hundred per cent like the types described here. For one thing, 'textbook examples' are always an exception. Then, naturally I was forced to portray the characteristics exaggeratedly, almost as clichés, in order to emphasize the differences clearly. This means you will have to observe very carefully! Often, only single features in the lives or behaviour of a person will give you the right indicator.

Or, to formulate it freely after Samuel Hahnemann, the founder of homeopathic medicine:

▶ Three conspicuous, peculiar or odd features of a personal lifestyle will, as a rule, suffice to support any correspondences with the descriptions given here.

A little experiment

A simple way to make sure about the effect of the crystal systems is to look at one of the geometric shapes or a field of the same shapes for a minute and then read the above text on the description of the corresponding lifestyle. Afterwards, look at different shape or field and read the text again. You will find that after looking at a particular shape or field, you will suddenly be able to identify much more easily with the lifestyle of the relevant crystal system. What an amazing effect these simple structures have!

How crystal structures can affect us

As the descriptions above have clearly shown, each of the lifestyles described is, in principle, neutral. There is no 'better' or 'worse' one, merely a 'different' one. Each lifestyle basically contains two possibilities for development: either a personal development towards negativity, that is the growth of certain difficulties, problems or even illnesses, or a development towards the positive, that is, towards the development of specific capabilities and self-fulfilment.

The difference is very simple: negative development sets in if you are ruled by the relevant 'inner structure', if you are unable to live any other way, that is, when you are totally dependent on a certain lifestyle. Positive development begins once you are the masters of your own life, if you know how to use certain talents and characteristics and are able to handle your life sensibly!

The first prerequisite for positive development is – wanting it! You have to be ready to take responsibility for your own fate and decide consciously to live out the positive side of your life, full stop.

It really is very simple: the effort and energy necessary for the development of all negative phenomena of a certain lifestyle are just as great as the effort and energy necessary for the development of positive phenomena. The question is simply where to direct your attention and your energy. If you identify particularly strongly with one of the above descriptions, then please give a lot of thought and attention to the positive energies described there. Even on its own this will help encourage them.

Luckily you also have your 'helpers': healing stones. Minerals have an enormous effect as they are physical structures. Inconspicuously but nevertheless powerfully, they stimulate the corresponding lifestyle in two ways.

Healing with crystal structures

If you have created certain difficulties or problems based on your lifestyle, or have become ill because of this lifestyle, then minerals with the corresponding crystal structure can help to solve these difficulties and problems or heal the disease. The effects of the mineral can be used to dissolve a blockage within the corresponding lifestyle and you will then become free to handle your life consciously. The mineral works according to the homeopathic principle, 'Like heals like'. The healing process works very quickly. Provided you have found the right stone with a suitable structure, a strong effect may be noted after a few hours or days, or even moments. It will take a while until the newly attained state has become stabilized, but the first changes are very soon visible.

Learning through crystal structures

In addition to the healing described above, there is a second possibility: certain lifestyles will be completely alien to you, something you almost certainly will have noticed when reading the individual descriptions. In spite of this, the relevant lifestyle can offer characteristics or abilities that would be quite interesting or useful for you. With the help of minerals of the corresponding crystal structure, you are in a position to get to know this lifestyle.

The effect of the mineral is to help you develop this unknown lifestyle. Like the crystallization process, during the course of time the characteristics and abilities of the relevant lifestyle become established, the whole process becoming more conscious, the more attention you give to it.

This learning process does take a certain amount of time. Crystals are rarely formed in a single day, and being able to play a musical instrument is rarely accomplished in a single week. For this reason, you will have to allow yourself some time for the process. As a rule, it will take one or a few months until the effect of the mineral becomes noticeable. Then it is like learning to walk – you need to use the newly acquired skill and practise it until it has become a part of you and can no longer be lost again.

The meaning and the goal of healing and learning processes

The prerequisite for a healing process, in which you choose the mineral with a crystal structure that corresponds to your lifestyle, is a situation in which you are no longer in control of your lives. Perhaps you are confronted with difficulties or problems and can no longer see a way out, or you feel ill, either physically, mentally or spiritually. You are the only one who can measure this. If you are no longer content with your life, then healing becomes a necessity.

> The goal of a *healing process* is to bring back the control over your life that you had lost, so you can become well again, are able to solve your difficulties and problems and be content with your life.

The prerequisite for a learning process is that you are happy with your life, but still wish to get to know new perspectives and abilities; you wish to expand your own opportunities and to develop further. As a rule it will first be necessary to get a grip on your own life (to stimulate healing processes, if warranted). Plunging into new experiences before the old ones have been digested can be equivalent to running away and may lead to even greater problems or confusion.

However, it is often necessary to add a learning process onto a completed healing process in order to lead the inner potential that has been released through the healing process in the right direction. If you have spent a long time mentally occupied with certain problems, it may often happen that a kind of peculiar habit causes you create new problems of a similar nature, after having got rid of the old, so that you can continue to be mentally occupied with them. Doctors or therapists often hear something like, 'For a while, everything went well, then the whole thing started up again!'

This can be avoided if you turn to something new right away, thus making the 'old games' superfluous. For this reason, it is also very important to be aware of exactly when a healing process has been completed, so you no longer address the old problem and change over to a learning process.

▶ The goal of a *learning process* is to expand your mental horizon and thereby to expand your abilities and opportunities. In the end, the goal is freedom! Freedom to think, communicate and act unhindered.

Imagine you could choose any of the lifestyles described above according to your preference. You could, for example, be 'cubic' at work if necessary, be 'amorphous' on holiday, 'rhombic' as a host, 'hexagonal' as a student, and so on. You could experience all the possibilities and use them. Nothing would restrict you: you would be free!

Wouldn't that be something?

How to heal with crystal structures

Learning and healing stones

Primarily, the crystal structures described in this chapter and the corresponding lifestyles are intended to help a particular person find the most helpful healing stone for a given moment in time. Determining the crystal structure first will narrow down the choice of minerals to an extent that the analysis of the life situation and the manner of formation, as described in this chapter, will usually offer enough reference points to enable you to choose the right stone. If, nevertheless, there are several available to choose from, then the minerals and colour effects described in the following chapters will give the final guidance in making a choice.

The crystal determined in this way should be worn for a while, shorter or longer depending on whether you are dealing with a healing or learning process, if possible without being influenced by wearing other jewellery. Once the desired result has been stabilized, the stone will no longer be necessary.

During healing processes, it is possible that a superficial structure can be replaced by a 'deeper-lying' one. As a rule, this is displayed very clearly through a marked change in the lifestyle of the person concerned. If the original problems or symptoms of illness do not disappear along with this change, the stone used will lose its effectiveness and a new one suitable for the changed circumstances needs to be determined.

Self-reflection

The characteristics described above can also help you interpret a stone you have chosen intuitively; this may help reflect your own lifestyle and help you become aware of your own weaknesses and strengths. Remember, 'Self-recognition is the first step towards betterment'.

Watching people in their own environments and discovering their structures and lifestyles will also visibly improve your understanding of your fellow human beings. It suddenly becomes clear that another person has his or her own idea of right or wrong, and his or her own idea of how to live their life and be happy. It also becomes clear that this 'other idea' does not threaten your own at all but that everyone is right about their own reality and that it is possible to allow both to stand side by side. Understanding, respect and tolerance towards others become more natural.

Mineral-forming elements

The chemistry of minerals

After dealing with their formation and crystal structure, now is the time to give some attention to the physical nature of minerals. Certain substances or elements in the right proportions and with the right surrounding conditions have to be present to form a certain mineral. Every one of these substances or elements has specific properties that together form the properties of the mineral and will have a noticeable bearing on its healing effects.

In order to understand these connections, first of all we need to take a little excursion into the world of chemistry. Please do not stop reading at this point – it really is all very simple! Unfortunately, chemistry has a very bad name. I can remember exactly how worried I was at the beginning of the year in which we took up chemistry. All I knew about the subject was that it had the reputation of being diabolically difficult, complicated and awful. I was then extremely surprised to discover that it is one of the easiest subjects if you are lucky enough to have a teacher who is able to explain the basics in a manner that is easy to understand. I was very lucky.

Chemistry is absolutely logical and describes the real world. This is great because it is not just a matter of believing what you are told – you can actually try it all out. As a student, I did this with enthusiasm; I set up a small experimental laboratory in my parents' boiler room in the cellar and occasionally made them nervous with explosions, smoke or clouds of chlorine gas. I always managed to placate them afterwards by getting good grades in chemistry.

The word 'chemistry' means 'knowledge of matter', or as described in the dictionary, 'a natural science that deals with researching the properties, connections and transformation of substances and their compounds'. Substances, in this context, are defined as 'matter present in a unified form and characterized by certain properties'. Chemistry is real enough, even in our own lives!

Cooking is a chemical process in which different substances with characteristic properties are mingled, bound and transformed. The same goes for baking, gluing, heating and driving a car (combustion in the engine). So, chemistry is very much an everyday matter.

The structure of matter

Atoms

Several basic principles of matter need to be appreciated in order to understand why substances have different properties; why they can be combined, bound and transformed. All matter known to us consists of three types of 'building blocks', or elementary particles: these are protons (Greek *proton*, 'the first, most important'), electrons (Greek *elektron*, 'amber', used here as a synonym for 'attraction' to other substances') and neutrons (Latin *neuter*, 'neither of the other two'). These three particles form fascinating relationships with each other.

The protons and electrons attract each other, so physics defines them both as having 'electrical charges', meaning both are 'loaded with attraction' (Greek *elektron*, 'attractive force', see above). In order to differentiate between the two opposite types of attraction, a further definition is that protons are 'positively' charged (p^+), and the electron is 'negatively' charged (e^-). To attain a neutral or balanced state together, protons and electrons, as a rule, stand in a special relationship to each other. Should the proton and electron 'lose sight of each other' occasionally, for whatever reason, then their sole aim is to find a new 'partner' immediately. The proton is a heavy, lazy particle. The electron, in contrast, is fast and mobile. For this reason, the proton always forms the quiet nucleus in this partnership, with the electron zipping around it like lightning, rather like a planet being orbited by satellites.

Then there is the neutron (n), which is basically neutral (as the name suggests) and is not particularly attracted either to the proton (p^+) or the electron (e^-). As the neutron is in many ways similar to the proton (almost as heavy and lazy), it tends to stay close to the proton and the dynamic electron orbits both of them.

This is how simple it all is. All substances are built up on this basic foundation: a nucleus composed of protons and neutron, which is orbited by electrons. A particle like this is called an atom

(Greek *atmos*, 'indivisible') and forms the smallest building block of matter.

The elements

In nature, we find no more than 83 different, stable atoms; they are distinguishable from each other only by the number of their elementary particles. These 83 different atoms are also called 'chemical elements' (Latin *elementum*, 'basic matter, original matter'). They form the 'pure matter' out of which all compounds are formed.

The proton only received its name, 'the most important', because the number of protons in an atom determines what element you are dealing with. One hydrogen atom, for example, contains a single proton, oxygen contains eight, iron 26 and gold as many as 70 protons. As soon as there is one more or less proton in the nucleus, you are dealing with an entirely different new element, a new substance with quite different properties. Fluorine, for example, has only one proton more than oxygen, yet this seemingly small difference results in an aggressive, toxic gas instead of the one essential to life.

The neutron, however, may appear in atoms in varying numbers, without changing their chemical properties. It will not influence the nature of an element, so here, too, it displays neutrality.

An atom always has the same number of electrons as protons. This is logical, as each electron is attracted by a corresponding proton. The space in which the electrons orbit around the atomic nucleus is called the electron cloud. It is the particular structure of

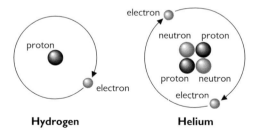

Hydrogen   **Helium**

Fig. 26   *Internal structure of the atom: hydrogen and helium.*

Number of protons	Chemical abbreviation	Name of element	Number of protons	Chemical abbreviation	Name of element
1	H	hydrogen	41	Nb	niobium
2	He	helium	42	Mo	molybdenum
3	L	lithium	44	Ru	ruthenium
4	Be	beryllium	45	Rh	rhodium
5	B	boron	46	Pd	palladium
6	C	carbon	47	Ag	silver
7	N	nitrogen	48	Cd	cadmium
8	O	oxygen	49	In	indium
9	F	fluorine	50	Sn	tin
10	Ne	neon	51	Sb	antimony
11	Na	sodium	52	Te	tellurium
12	Mg	magnesium	53	I	iodine
13	Al	aluminium	54	Xe	xenon
14	Si	silicon	55	Cs	caesium
15	P	phosphorus	56	Ba	barium
16	S	sulphur	57	La	lanthanum
17	Cl	chlorine	58	Ce	cerium
18	Ar	argon	59	Pr	praseodymium
19	K	potassium	60	Nd	neodymium
20	Ca	calcium	62	Sm	samarium
21	Sc	scandium	63	Eu	europium
22	Ti	titanium	64	Gd	gadolinium
23	V	vanadium	65	Tb	terbium
24	Cr	chromium	66	Dy	dysprosium
25	Mn	manganese	67	Ho	holmium
26	Fe	iron	68	Er	erbium
27	Co	cobalt	69	Tm	thulium
28	Ni	nickel	70	Yb	ytterbium
29	Cu	copper	71	Lu	lutetium
30	Zn	zinc	72	Hf	hafnium
31	Ga	gallium	73	Ta	tantalum
32	Ge	germanium	74	W	tungsten
33	As	arsenic	75	Re	rhenium
34	Se	selenium	76	Os	osmium
35	Br	bromine	77	Ir	iridium
36	Kr	krypton	78	Pt	platinum
37	Rb	rubidium	79	Au	gold
38	Sr	strontium	80	Hg	mercury
39	Y	yttrium	81	Tl	thallium
40	Zr	zirconium	82	Pb	lead

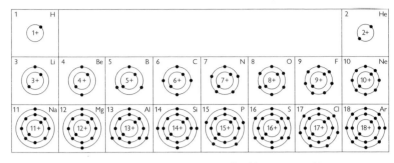

Fig. 27   The electron 'shells' have a structure rather like an onion skin.

this 'cloud' that is responsible for allowing atoms to combine with each other. The 'cloud' consists of different 'shells' where only certain numbers of electrons can be accommodated. In most atoms, the outer shell contains a maximum of eight electrons, although the inner shells can contain other fixed numbers of electrons.

Chemical compounds

Once an electron shell possesses its full complement of electrons, the shell is stable. Consequently this shell cannot accept any more electrons, nor will it release any. If the outermost shell of an atom has exactly eight electrons, the atom itself is also stable and it will not display any chemical reactions. This state occurs naturally only in the noble gases (helium, neon, argon, krypton and xenon). These elements are never found in any chemical compounds (they are too 'noble'). As long as an atom has less than eight electrons in its outer shell, it will form compounds with other elements that will allow it to achieve the stable state described above. It will try to fill up its outer shell with 'foreign' electrons, or shed electrons from its own outer shell so that the next shell in (which will already be completely filled) becomes the outer shell. The three main types of bonding between atoms are ionic, covalent and metallic bonding

Ionic bonds

Ionic bonds are formed when electrons are transferred from one atom to another. The ions created in this way are held together by electrical attraction. The bonding of chlorine and sodium is an example of ionic bonding. The chlorine atom has only seven electrons in its outer shell, exactly one electron short of the stable state. The sodium atom, on the other hand, has only one electron in its outer shell, so its aim is to get rid of it. If sodium and chlorine meet, a simple barter takes place: the sodium releases one electron to the chlorine so that both achieve the desired eight outer electrons and both are happy. This trade does have certain consequences, however, as the attractive force of the exchanged electron remains. The sodium is now positively charged and the chlorine negatively charged. The electrical attraction between the two holds them together in a compound, sodium chloride, more commonly known as ordinary cooking salt!

As the atoms in these compounds now possess electrical charges ('attractive forces'), they are called ions ('charged particles'). Sodium chloride consists of one positively charged sodium ion (Na^+) for each negatively charged chloride ion (Cl^-). This information can be found, for example, on a mineral water bottle; the first item listed is usually the positively charged ions (the cations), followed by the negative ions (the anions). The bond that exists between cations and anions owing to their electrical attraction is, therefore, called an ionic bond.

Covalent bonds

Another kind of bonding occurs if two atoms meet, both of whose outer shells are lacking very few electrons, and when neither is 'ready' to release any electrons to form ions. In this case, the trade occurs in such a way that both atoms 'agree' to utilize certain electrons mutually, so that both can enjoy having eight electrons in the outer shell. The mutually shared electrons then occur in pairs between the atoms and become attracted equally to both. This sharing of electrons creates a bond, called an electron pair bond or covalent bond. No ions (charged particles) are created, but rather both atoms remain neutral and merely bond together with their 'mutual possessions'.

An example may make this clearer: the chlorine atom with its seven outer electrons is lacking just one electron to be stable. If two of these atoms meet, both lacking just one electron, they agree that each will put one electron at the disposal of the other, so that there are two electrons shared between the atoms. The result of this is to give both a complement of eight electrons, and a stable state is achieved. The mutually shared electron pair does, however, result in both atoms remaining wedded (until 'another chemical interaction shall part them').

Metallic bonds

A third possibility that certain elements, the metals (Greek *metallon*, 'mine, vein of ore'), like to use to achieve the desired stability is the metallic bond. Here, the excess outer electrons are simply generously put at the disposal of the general community. The atom distances itself from its outermost 'appendages', feels stable, and the freed electrons can move around between the atoms. The bonding here occurs via a shared 'cloud' of electrons. The bonding is not as rigid as in ionic and covalent bonds, as no single atoms are joined together – instead, it is the entire structure that is held together. For this reason, metals can be bent and formed, and because of the 'free electrons' they are able to conduct electric current. (Electrical current is merely a 'current' or 'flow' of electrons.)

Metals and non-metals

Based on the bonding properties described above, all elements can be categorized into two main groups. The larger group, the metals, consists of elements that release electrons (can and will). In ionic bonds with non-metals they provide the 'cations' (positively charged ions), they create metallic bonds with each other, and they are only rarely found in covalent bonds.

The other group consists of the non-metals. These can accept electrons, provide 'anions' (negatively charged ions) in ionic bonds with metals and, as a rule, form compounds with each other via covalent bonds. Non-metals do not form metallic bonds.

In-between these groups there are a few elements that are neither distinctly metals nor non-metals, but have a mixture of properties. These are called metalloids. Depending on the circumstances they are capable of sometimes releasing electrons and sometimes accepting them, and they show the entire range of different bondings.

Mineral-forming elements

Not all of the elements in a chemistry book can be found in minerals. Some are missing because they do not form bonds (noble gases), and some because they were created by humans in laboratories and atomic reactors (plutonium, etc.). In order to limit ourselves to those elements that actually form minerals, they will be called mineral-forming elements from now on. After dividing them up again into the classification of metals and non-metals, the following list presents the most important mineral-forming elements.

Metals: aluminium, antimony, beryllium, lead, calcium, chromium, iron, gold, potassium, cobalt, copper, lithium, magnesium, manganese, sodium, nickel, silver, titanium, vanadium, bismuth, zinc, tin and zirconium.

Non-metals: boron, chlorine, fluorine, carbon, phosphorus, oxygen and sulphur.

Metalloids: the most important in this group, and in the entire mineral kingdom, is one of the most important and abundant of all elements, silicon. Other metalloids are boron, germanium, arsenic, selenium and tellurium.

From the compounds of these few elements, the overwhelming majority (over 95%) of the 4000 known minerals are formed. Quantitatively, these elements actually make up over 99.9% of the Earth's crust. Each of them has its own special properties and the compounds of these elements create the characteristic features of minerals. These properties are also extremely important in healing for the effect of the minerals on the human body, soul, mind and spirit.

The properties of the mineral-forming elements

As a rule, minerals consist of two components, a metallic and non-metallic portion – only very rarely do we find a metal or non-metal 'alone' in nature. This polarization is a determining factor both in the mineralogical and healing properties of a mineral. One fact that stands out from the start is that nature has far more metals than non-metals to offer. Looking more closely, we will also see that the non-metallic proportion of a mineral determines its basic qualities, while the metallic portion produces individual variations.

With all minerals that contain the same non-metallic proportion, we find common features as in a kind of relatedness. Using a rather free analogy from the human world, we can liken the non-metallic portion to the 'family name' of the mineral (in a chemical formula it always appears at the end).

Following this analogy through, the metals in a mineral correspond to the first name. The metals serve to distinguish the various members of the family from each other and visibly alter the basic properties of each mineral. The metals are also the part of the mineral that give it its characteristic colour, as we shall see later on.

The mineral classes and their properties

Just as biology distinguishes by groups such as genera or species, mineralogy proceeds as follows: all minerals are divided up into eight large classes, determined by the most frequent non-metallic proportions and the similarities that result from them. These classes of minerals also demonstrate the first spectrum of effectiveness of minerals for healing purposes so, in the following text, mineralogical and healing aspects will be shown alongside each other.

Mineral classes		Non-metallic portion	Chemical symbol
I	natural elements	consists of only one element	element's symbol
II	sulphides	sulphur	S
III	halides	fluorine, chlorine, bromine and iodine	F, Cl, Br, I
IV	oxides	oxygen	O
V	carbonates	carbonic acid	CO_3
VI	sulphates	sulphuric acid	SO_4
VII	phosphates	phosphoric acid	PO_4
VIII	silicates	silicic acid	Si_nO_m

Class I The minerals of the class of **natural elements** consist of only a single mineral-forming substance, a single element. This is very rare in nature, as only very few chemical elements are able to remain uncombined with other elements. Among the non-metals only carbon, which can be found in the form of graphite or diamond (formula: C_n), and sulphur (S_8) appear as natural elements. Among the metals, only the precious metals gold (Au), silver (Ag), copper (Cu), etc. sometimes occur in a pure form.

The natural elements represent purity and the ability to remain uninfluenced. They help us to develop our personalities without interference from outside. They also stimulate us to distance ourselves from anything in life that is not really part of our essential nature. They help us recognize what will harm or help us. Depending on which element is involved, certain corresponding areas of life will be particularly addressed (more on this later on).

Class II The minerals of the class of **sulphides** are derivatives of sulphur, or to be precise, of hydrogen sulphide. This highly toxic gas is often a product of decay and produces the well-known odour of 'rotten eggs'. Hydrogen sulphide is formed during volcanic activities and during the decay of organic matter, and is present almost all over the Earth in varying quantities. The sulphides arising from its compounds with metals are generally opaque and are characterized by a metallic sheen, rather like the surface of a mirror. Their chemical formulas end in S (sulphur), for example pyrite is FeS_2 (iron sulphide).

Sulphides are the mirrors of hidden things. They help uncover repressed and forgotten matters and get rid of confusion and muddle, with precisely that area of our lives coming under scrutiny where something 'stinks' or is 'bad'. Sulphides are also known as the 'merciless awareness-makers', as they will, on the one hand, guide our attention to where changes are drastically necessary but, on the other hand, will not give any kind of help in setting these changes in motion. But then, knowing oneself is the first step towards bettering oneself.

The following sulphides are currently used as healing stones: antimonite, boji stones, chalcopyrite, covellite, jamesonite, marcasite, pyrite and sphalerite.

Class III The minerals of the class of **halides** (Greek *halos genes*, 'salt-forming') are derivatives of a group of elements called halogens, which include fluorine and chlorine. In the pure state halogens are toxins, but they readily form compounds with other elements to become valuable salts (hence the name). Combined with hydrogen they form, for example, hydrofluoric acid (HF) and hydrochloric acid (HCl). Both acids are extremely aggressive; hydrofluoric acid is even able to corrode quartz and dissolve glass. When these acids come into contact with metals they form transparent minerals, such as fluorite (CaF_2) or rock salt (NaCl).

Halides have a dissolving property, in accordance with the properties of acids from which they arise. Just as they are able to dissolve metals with which they would like to form compounds, so they can also help us to end restrictions and break down barriers. Patterns of thinking, behaving or living that are no longer any good for us but merely hinder us can be dissolved with their help. In the Middle Ages salt was thought to be capable of driving out demons! And what are demons, but circumstances in our lives that we cannot control but that control us?

Of the mineral class of halides only fluorite and halite (rock salt) are currently used as healing stones.

Class IV The minerals of the class of **oxides** are derivatives of oxygen (Greek *oxys genes*, 'oxygen, the acid-former'). They can occur anywhere as oxygen is contained in magma, in water and in abundance in air. The formation of oxide minerals can take place in front of your very eyes – for example the formation of rust (iron oxide) on the bodywork of cars owing to oxygen in the air. Oxygen is the most prevalent mineral-forming element on Earth: 50% of the solid crust consists of this element. The formula for oxides ends with oxygen, for example haematite is Fe_2O_3 (iron oxide).

Oxides have a transformative effect, and will convert unstable states into stable ones. Oxygen is the element that feeds combustion processes: anything from a campfire to energy consumption in our body cells. During this process, energy-rich unstable compounds are converted into energy-poor but more stable compounds (wood turns into ash). Wherever we need to invest energy constantly, in order to maintain an unstable state, oxides will become active to transform this state into a stable one. The energy bound up in this transformation (and therefore not available for use) is released and can be used. Hence oxides also advance all unfinished things in our lives that would otherwise be constantly draining away energy.

The most important healing stones from the class of oxides are hematite, magnetite and tiger iron, alexandrite and chrysoberyl, spinel, the corundum group containing ruby and sapphire, the quartz-related minerals obsidian and opal, and naturally also the actual quartz group itself. This includes crystalline quartzes: amethyst, rock crystal, citrine, smoky quartz, rutile and tourmaline; rough quartzes: aventurine, dendritic agate, blue quartz, prase, rose quartz, falcon's eye and tiger's eye; fibrous quartzes: chalcedony, chrysoprase, carnelian, heliotrope, moss agate, onyx, sardonyx and fossilized wood; grainy quartzes: jasper and mookaite; and agate that combines different quartzes in layers.

Class V The minerals of the class of **carbonates** are derivatives of carbonic acid (Latin *carbo*, 'coal'). Carbonic acid (H_2CO_3) is a very unstable compound of liquid (water, formula H_2O) and gas (carbon dioxide, CO_2) that very easily breaks down in its liquid form. We can readily observe this: when a bottle of carbonated mineral water is opened carbon dioxide is released and immediately escapes. When carbonic acid reacts with metals more stable compounds are formed – the bonds are firmer. Even then, a certain amount of reactivity is retained: carbonates are rarely a stable end product, rather a temporary transitional phase that is further developed when new influences begin to become effective. Their chemical formulas end in CO_3 (carbonate), for example calcite is $CaCO_3$ (calcium carbonate).

Carbonates influence developmental processes. During these processes carbonates that contain water, such as azurite and malachite, have an initiating effect, which means they stimulate new developments. Just as carbon dioxide gas escapes from the liquid in mineral water, unfamiliar thoughts may suddenly rise up into our conscious awareness. In contrast 'dehydrated', dry carbonates stabilize developmental processes that have got out of balance, either because they were too fast (e.g. aragonite) or too slow (e.g. calcite) The shared theme in all cases is a permanent change.

Of the carbonates the following are currently used in healing: aragonite, azurite, azurite-malachite, calcite, dolomite, magnesite, malachite, rhodochrosite and smithsonite.

Class VI The minerals of the class of **sulphates** are derivatives of sulphuric acid (not to be confused with sulphides). Sulphuric acid is a compound of hydrogen and a sulphide (H_2SO_4) and is a very dense liquid that flows much more slowly than water, for example, and hardly evaporates at all if it is kept in an open flask. Sulphuric acid compounds are very stable and persistent. This property is used in pharmacology when, for example, unstable medications are crystallized out as sulphates. This makes them more persistent and they keep longer. The formulas of sulphates end in SO_4 (sulphate), for example anglesite (anhydrite) is $CaSO_4$.

Sulphates make things constant or lasting. They fix a certain state and can maintain it over a long period of time. They also have an insulating effect, so they form a protection against outside influences. Depending on whether the fixed state is pleasant or unpleasant for us, this may represent heaven or hell. They have a dampening effect on developmental processes; this means they may afford us a period of rest, but using them for a long time requires caution!

Among the sulphates, anglesite (anhydrite), celestine and gypsum in the form of Mary glass and selenite are currently used as healing stones.

Class VII Minerals from the class of **phosphates** are derived from phosphoric acid (H_3PO_4), the central element of which is phosphorus (Greek *phosphoros*, 'light-carrying'). Phosphates are in fact carriers of energy in our own bodies (see below). In addition, phosphates are an important 'buffer'; that is a substance that is able to neutralize both acids and bases (alkalis). The formulas of phosphates end in PO_4 (phosphate), for example variscite is $AlPO_4$ (aluminium phosphate).

Phosphates have a balancing effect and can mobilize energy reserves. The buffering effect of phosphates helps to preserve neutrality in our body fluids, thereby promoting stability in terms of health and a balance of mood. In addition, when phosphates are deposited in our bodies in the form of certain organic compounds, their energy levels are raised; when these phosphate compounds are broken down, energy is released. Phosphate compounds are the energy carriers in our cells. Energy turnover is increased through the use of phosphates and this makes us awake, lively, active and ready for action.

From the mineral class of phosphates, apatite, turquoise, variscite and vivianite are currently used in healing.

Class VIII Minerals from the class of **silicates** are derivatives of silicic acid ($H_xSi_yO_z$). Silicic acid is one of the most versatile of acids, which is why its structure cannot be expressed in a single formula. The smallest unit of silicic acid consists of a single silicon atom surrounded by four oxygen atoms and to which, in turn, four hydrogen atoms are bound (H_4SiO_4). Several of these units can be bound in groups, chains, rings, layers and lattice-like structures by splitting off water, which means that, in principle, there is not just 'one' but 'several different' kinds of silicic acid. For example:

$$2\ H_4SiO_4 \rightarrow H_6Si_2O_7 + H_2O$$

$$3\ H_4SiO_4 \rightarrow H_8Si_3O_{10} + 2\ H_2O\ \text{etc.}$$

Silicates, therefore, possess the most versatile crystal lattices, which makes it impossible to give a general description of their properties and also makes further distinguishing features very necessary.

Class VIII – 1 The crystal lattice of **nesosilicates or island silicates** contains individual silicate molecules, single tetrahedrons like 'islands' between the metal ions. Their formulas end in SiO_4, for example zirconium is $ZrSiO_4$ (zirconium silicate). The way the island silicates are structured results in very compact minerals with a high density.

Island silicates strengthen resistance and the desire to structure one's life according to one's own wishes. The individual island silicates represent individuality, the path one can travel alone. Island silicates also fortify one's health and are helpers in crises and emergencies so we are able to remain true to our convictions, even when under great stress.

At present the following island silicates are used for healing purposes: andalusite and chiastolite, disthene (kyanite), dumortierite, the garnet family with andradite, almandine, hessonite,

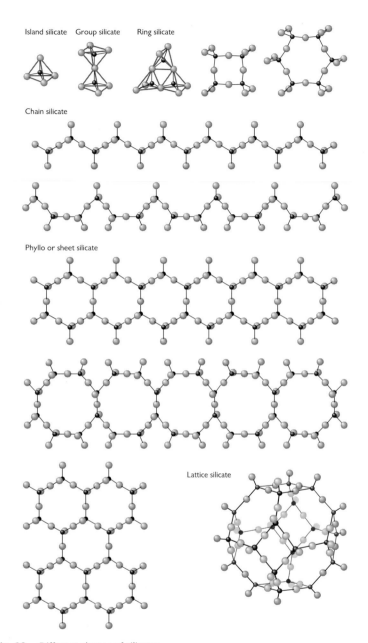

Island silicate Group silicate Ring silicate

Chain silicate

Phyllo or sheet silicate

Lattice silicate

Fig. 28 *Different shapes of silicates.*

grossular, melanite, pyrope, rhodolite, spessartite, tsavorite and uvarovite, as well as peridot (olivine or chrysolite), sillimanite, sphene (titanite), topaz and finally, the zirconium family with the variety called hyacinth.

Class VIII – 2 The crystal lattice of **sorosilicates or group silicates** contains silicate molecules that are bound together in pairs or small groups, as a rule, two to four connected tetrahedrons. The end of the formula can be derived as follows: Si_nO_{3n+1} where n is the number of silicon atoms, or the number of silicon tetrahedra. For example prehnite has the formula $Ca_2Al_2[(OH)_2/Si_3O_{10}]$; this is calcium aluminium hydroxide silicate, an alkaline (OH) group silicate comprised of three connected silicate tetrahedrons.

Group silicates strengthen the power of regeneration. They encourage the healing process after an illness and help one find one's way back to the original wishes, goals and intentions that inspire us. They are helpful whenever we have to orientate ourselves again or are faced with a new beginning. They stimulate the energy flow inside and the increase the speed of the healing process.

Of these group silicates at present only epidote, prehnite, vesuvianite (idocrase) and the zoisite family with tanzanite, thulite and zoisite are used for healing. The zoisite minerals contain both island silicates as well as group silicate molecules and therefore beautifully combine the properties of both classes.

Class VIII – 3 The crystal lattice of the **cyclosilicates or ring silicates** contains rings of three to twelve closed circles of silicate tetrahedrons. The end of the formula is Si_nO_{3n}, for example beryl: $Al_2Be_3[Si_6O_{18}]$ = aluminium beryllium silicate. Whenever these rings are arranged in 'pillar-like' structures in the mineral, the ring silicates become extremely good electrical conductors. If the rings are not in regular arrangements, the structure is 'sponge-like' and results in opaque minerals.

Ring silicates with a pillar structure conduct and direct energy flows; ring silicates with a sponge-like structure have a strongly absorbing effect. The former can be used when energy flows in our bodies are blocked or if there is a general lack of energy. Ring silicates with a pillar-like structure have a stimulating effect, making one active and dynamic. Ring silicates with a sponge like structure will absorb excess energy. They have a calming, sobering effect and will lower a fever or reduce heat and pain.

Ring silicates with a pillar structure used as healing stones are: the beryl family with aquamarine, beryl, bixite, golden beryl, heliodor, morganite and emerald, as well as cordierite (iolite), dioptase and the tourmaline family with dravite (brown tourmaline), indicolite (blue tourmaline), rubellite (red tourmaline), schorl (black tourmaline), verdelite (green tourmaline) and all their colourful mixed crystals. Among the ring silicates with a sponge-like structure, only the healing stones chrysocolla and sugilite are used.

Class VIII – 4 The crystal lattice of the **inosilicates or chain and band silicates** contains silicate tetrahedrons that are linked together in long chains. Their formulas show the same relationships as those of the ring silicates, Si_nO_{3n}, but owing to the length of the chains (which often cannot even be determined) only the quantity ratio between silicon and oxygen is given (2:6). This helps distinguish the chain and ring silicates by their formulas. An example of a chain silicate is kunzite: $LiAl[Si_2O_6]$ = lithium aluminium silicate.

Chain silicates stimulate energy flows in us and increase the speed of healing and developmental processes. They provide for a balanced distribution of energy in the organism and, in this way, they also have an emotionally balancing and harmonizing effect. At the same time, they improve spiritual and physical flexibility and encourage a spiritual movement towards goals and ideals.

Among the chain silicates the following minerals are used as healing stones: actinolite and nephrite, bronzite, chloromelanite, diopside (also chromium diopside), jadeite, the spodumene family with hiddenite and kunzite, as well as rhodonite.

Class VIII – 5 The crystal lattice of **phyllosilicates or sheet silicates** consists of silicate tetrahedrons that are connected in sheets. Their formulas end in Si_nO_{2n+2}, for example apophyllite: $KCa_4[F/(Si_4O_{10})_2] \cdot 8\ H_2O$ = potassium calcium fluoride silicate containing water. These layers are very cohesive. They can be separated easily but it is very difficult to cut through them. The structure of the layers means that sheet silicates are easy to split but difficult or impossible to slice!

Sheet silicates have a protective effect and strengthen boundaries. These minerals display poor energy and warmth conducting properties at right angles to the layers or sheets (they are used as insulators in technology). They are able to shield us from energy forms affecting us from outside, while the flow of energy in ourselves is unaffected.

Healing stones used from the group of sheet silicates are apophyllite, biotite, charoite, lepidolite and serpentine.

Class VIII – 6 The crystal lattice of **tectosilicates or framework silicates** forms three-dimensional grids of silicate tetrahedrons, usually incorporating of further elements such as aluminium (Al), beryllium (Be) or boron (B) in the crystal lattice. These lattice structures are too complex to be reduced to a simple, generally applicable summary formula. Where there is doubt, we recommend consulting mineralogical specialist literature on the particular stone involved.

Framework silicates have a filtering effect that will absorb certain things and reflect others. Their three-dimensional structures can have an absorbing effect, producing opaque minerals that have absorbing properties, as in the 'unstructured' ring silicates. They also have a calming and sobering effect and reduce fever, heat and pain. Among these are the healing stones amazonite (feldspar family), lapis lazuli and sodalite.

If the mineral remains transparent, we often see partial absorption and light reflections that result in a change in our perception: our usual 'filters' are adjusted and suddenly we see the world with 'new eyes' and are able to adopt new perspectives we could not have imagined possible until now. Framework silicates promote a broadening of our horizons. Among these healing stones are the minerals gold-orthoclase, labradorite, moonstone and sunstone (all of the feldspar family).

The metabolism of minerals

The second important range of effects of mineral-forming elements results from the direct influence they have on our bodies. Many mineral-forming substances have important key functions in the body: they are vital to the formation of many enzymes, which are substances that make chemical processes in the body possible and guide them, thereby regulating our entire metabolism. Also some play an important role in the stimulation and conduction of our nerves, that is, in conducting sensory impulses, regulating the activity of the brain, and directing the function of the muscles and organs. Regulation of the water metabolism is also directly connected with these substances, as is the quality of the blood and body fluids.

Minerals cannot be produced by the body; they have to be absorbed through food. They could be looked upon as 'inorganic vitamins' – vitally important substances whose continuous supply from outside has to be ensured at all times. Mineral deficiency can arise if too few minerals are present in the diet, for example through poor eating habits with too many processed foods, fast foods and preserved foods, or if the small intestines are unable to absorb the necessary minerals. The last example is the most frequent cause of mineral deficiency.

The small intestine is a sensitive organ. The stress of a permanently bad diet will give it a hard time, as will emotional stress, traumatic experiences or negative attitudes towards life – in short, an unhealthy quality of life. These influences will perceptibly and negatively affect its function of absorbing vitamins, nutrients and minerals. As long as it is able to function without interference, the small intestine possesses a complicated system of many biochemical mechanisms that are responsible for absorbing precisely those substances into the bloodstream that are needed by the body while all superfluous or even harmful substances are kept out. Under the type of stress described above, these mechanisms get muddled up. Vitally needed substances are no longer absorbed and others are absorbed in excess. The kidneys are often able to work against the excess substances by excreting more of these, but where vital substances are not absorbed in sufficient quantities there will be a deficiency that gradually uses up the reserves in the body and in the long term there can be no balance!

The consequences are fairly inconspicuous to begin with, the first signs being certain repetitious thoughts, ideas, feelings, moods and emotions, tiredness or hyperactivity and nervousness. Gradually the deficiency leads to more serious physical manifestations through to physical illness. The effect of lack of particular minerals may appear anywhere in the body; the importance of minerals to the whole body is clear from the description given above of the areas of function of minerals. It has been found that minerals that contain certain mineral-forming substances stimulate their absorption via the small intestine and encourage their metabolism within the organism. The problem of disruptions to absorption from the small intestine can be solved with their help. As long as the food intake offers the necessary substances, the body should be in a position to absorb them adequately. In this way minerals fundamentally support our health.

Minerals stimulate all metabolic processes that are connected with the relevant mineral-forming substance and this activates the elimination of excess or harmful substances from the organism. Typical symptoms of irritation or toxicity right through to allergic reactions can be healed in this way. This aspect is very important as healing with crystals and stones opens up the possibilities of employing minerals whose compounds are not present in the human organism.

Acids and alkalis

Minerals are rarely formed directly from pure elements. In general they first form acids and alkalis (also called bases) and then comes a reaction with the mineral. Acids and alkalis arise from the bonding of a mineral-forming substance with water (H_2O) that is first split into the ions H^+ and OH^- ($H_2O \rightarrow H^+ + OH^-$). If the compound thus formed now contains H^+ ions, or if it is able to release these, it is called an acid, for example:

$$\text{hydrochloric acid } HCl \rightarrow H^+ + Cl^-$$

$$\text{carbonic acid } H_2CO_3 \rightarrow 2\,H^+ + CO_3^{2-}$$

$$\text{phosphoric acid } H_3PO_4 \rightarrow 3\,H^+ + PO_4^{3-}$$

If the compound formed contains OH^- ions, or is able to absorb H^+ ions and bond them, it is called an alkali, for example:

$$\text{sodium hydroxide } NaOH^- + H^+ \rightarrow Na^+ + H_2O$$

$$\text{calcium hydroxide } Ca(OH)_2 + 2\,H^+ \rightarrow Ca^{2+} + 2\,H_2O$$

The reaction of an acid with an alkali is called a neutralizing reaction as a neutral substance is formed if both are present in the right quantities:

sodium hydroxide + hydrochloric acid → salt + water

$$NaOH + HCl \rightarrow NaCl + H_2O.$$

Nature is no sterile laboratory. This is why it rarely happens that acids and alkalis meet in exactly the right quantities necessary for complete neutralization. Usually, a certain quantity of one remains, and it is then often built into the crystalline lattice of the mineral being formed. The mineral then acquires an acidic or alkaline character. Acidic minerals tend to look transparent, while alkaline ones are more often dark or opaque.

This properties of a mineral are very important for healing as there are areas in our bodies that are more acidic (stomach), alkaline (small intestine) or neutral (blood). Minerals work according to their character on the milieu of the body fluids and make them either more acidic or alkaline. This determines, among other things, what diseases can in fact develop in the body, as they usually need a certain environment to 'flourish'. Rheumatic diseases or viruses, for example, require an acidic environment, bacteria a neutral one, and fungi an alkaline one.

In addition, our spiritual health also corresponds to the milieu of liquids. Not for nothing has the word 'humour' been derived from the Latin for 'moisture' and the word 'temperament' from the Latin *temperamentum*, 'the right proportion of a mixture', concepts which, in the Middle Ages, dealt with the 'mixing or balancing of the four humours or liquids in the body'. These corresponded to the four temperaments: choleric, sanguine, melancholic and phlegmatic. In fact a more acidic metabolism tends to promote a choleric temperament (a sour disposition!), while an alkaline metabolism promotes a phlegmatic temperament. In accordance with this, acidic minerals are more stimulating, alkaline ones more calming.

Substances such as phosphates, for example, are particularly interesting as they are able both to absorb H^+ ions and release them. They are called buffers as they are able to keep acids and alkalis in a balance for a long time through the following reactions:

$$NaH_2PO_4 + OH^- \rightarrow NaHPO_4^- + H_2O$$

the buffer reaction if an alkali is introduced

$$NaH_2PO_4 + H^+ \rightarrow H_3PO_4 + Na^+$$

the buffer reaction if an acid is introduced

With these properties, minerals that contain buffers are able to stabilize the acid–alkali equilibrium in the body and promote a balance of emotions and temperament.

The principles of the effects that mineral-forming elements have on us

▶ The absorption and metabolism of mineral-forming elements that have an important function in our bodies are stimulated by minerals that contain the same mineral-forming elements. Deficiencies can be removed and the functioning of the organs improved.

▶ Mineral-forming elements that are in excess or harmful in the body will be increasingly eliminated under the influence of minerals that contain these or similar substances. This stimulates purification and detoxification which, in turn, alleviate or heal symptoms of irritation or poisoning, as well as allergic reactions.

▶ The alkaline or acidic character of a mineral will influence the milieu of body fluids in a corresponding manner. As physical illnesses as well as mental perceptions correspond directly with the milieu of body fluids, minerals will influence the general tendency towards illness, and will also influence emotions and temperament.

These three principles are not limited to the body. Just as the mental and spiritual state have an effect on physical well-being, so physical changes also stimulate certain emotions, inner visions, thoughts and intentions. 'As above, so below' is an ancient saying derived from Hermetic wisdom, which is just as valid today.

Mineral-forming elements also activate spiritual and mental experiences, encourage the necessary processes of accepting, both an inner 'digesting' as well as the 'elimination' of thoughts, ideas, constructs, moods and emotions that bother us or harm us. Whether a mineral will be effective primarily on the physical, the mental/soul or spiritual level, will be decided for the most part by one important factor: the amount of mineral-forming substance contained in the mineral

The principle of dilution

We make a distinction here between 'large or frequent' quantities, 'smaller' quantities or trace amounts. The larger the quantity of a certain mineral-forming element within a mineral, the more extensive its effect, extending from the material to the spiritual levels. The smaller the amount and the finer its distribution, the more discretely levels of effectiveness can be attained. This distinction helps, on the one hand, to choose more precisely the suitable mineral for a particular situation, while on the other hand, it shows on which level an initial reaction to the use of the mineral can be expected. The emphasis here is on the 'initial reaction' as, in the end, all levels correspond with each other and holistic healing is aimed for in the long run.

We speak of a **frequent** component if the relevant mineral-forming element (X) is present in such large quantities in the mineral that it acts as one of the mineral-forming elements and can also be represented in the chemical formula (X_nY_m). Rose quartz (SiO_2), for example, contains silicon and oxygen as its most abundant components. The mineralogical formula does not take account of all the minerals present as every mineral contains a number of inclusions and 'foreign substances'. Including these would only lead to confusion. This circumstance can be used in healing with crystals and stones through looking at the formula to see which mineral-forming elements are particularly 'frequent'. Their effect then takes place primarily in the body, corresponding to the incidence in one's own metabolism, for example, in the momentary stress created by toxic or waste products. But it also includes mind/soul and spiritual effects.

We speak of the '**smaller**' component when a certain substance (Z) is present in such minute quantities that it is no longer part of the formula but can still be proven to be present. Here, too, we have an appropriate distinction taken from mineralogy: 'well proven' means the substance can be identified through chemical analysis. It has to be present in sufficient quantities to have a visible effect (energy levels) and to take part in the chemical reaction. These components, present in minute quantities, are only rarely mentioned in the mineralogical literature; they are added as follows to the chemical formulas of stones in this book: X_nY_m + Z. Rose quartz (SiO_2 + Fe), for example, contains iron in very small quantities. Its effect then takes place primarily on the mental/soul level. For every mineral-forming element, certain typical emotional, mental and spiritual properties are displayed.

A component is only present as a **trace** when the amount of mineral-forming element (A) is only just detectable on the borderline. 'Borderline' means that many chemical methods can no longer identify this substance; it may only be detectable using procedures in modern physics (spectral analysis, X-ray analysis, electron probe microanalysis). Nevertheless, these substances are often of great importance as it is often these very trace elements that are responsible for the colour of crystals and stones, for example. In older mineralogical literature we often have no indications of these mineral-forming elements, as certain discoveries have only been made during the past few years. The trace element components have therefore been added to the end of the formulas in this volume: X_nY_m + (A). Here again, the example of rose quartz: SiO_2 + Fe + (Mn), in which manganese is present as a trace element. The effect here takes place only on the spiritual plane through changing patterns of life, thought and behaviour, spiritual structures and character.

The healing properties of mineral-forming elements

The effects described below can be observed when a mineral that contains the relevant mineral-forming element is worn close to the body (ideally next to the skin). On no account should the properties listed here be attributed to the pure chemical substance without checking. Also, we strongly recommend you do not take many mineral-forming elements internally as high doses are toxic and would have exactly the opposite effect to the one desired. A healthy, balanced diet can supply the body with enough of the necessary mineral-forming elements and in exactly the right form for the body to deal with them, organically constituted. In order to achieve the desired effects, it will be quite sufficient to wear the appropriate mineral!

The chemical abbreviation for the mineral-forming element in the chemical formula of a mineral is given again for identification purposes. For those interested in chemistry, we also give the number of positive or negative charges of the element in the ionic bonds of the minerals.

Aluminium (Al^{3+})

Physical Aluminium promotes alkaline metabolic processes. In this way, it will help with all problems that arise through over-acid conditions, for example rheumatism and gout, and will decrease excessive acid formation in the stomach. Aluminium supports the absorption of iron in the intestine and normalizes conductivity in the nerves. In this way, it helps with symptoms of weakness, slowed down perception and even with paralysis.

Psychological/mental Aluminium has a very calming effect on nervousness, fears and feelings of guilt. A typical indicator is a feeling of impending madness. Aluminium encourages the facility to express feelings, and to release behavioural patterns of holding onto things and holding back. It also stimulates a desire for change and alteration.

Spiritual Aluminium can help with a loss of identity, finding out again who we really are and what our task is in life. It encourages a sense of reality, soberness and alertness at any given moment. Aluminium aids the recognition of the seductions of modern life as the illusions they are and helps us to deal with them.

Antimony (Sb^{3+})

Physical Antimony supports the digestion and helps with stomach problems, particularly heartburn, nausea and vomiting. It helps with skin diseases, dry, cracked skin, all kinds of rashes and spots, eczema and persistent itching. Antimony regulates all elimination through the skin and the gut.

Psychological/mental Antimony promotes objective, logical/ rational thinking and helps overcome anger, dissatisfaction, sadness and oppressive feelings. It helps with a retreat from senti-mental emotions, love-sickness or world-weariness. Antimony dampens excessive sexual desire and helps us to give up habits that are merely substituted gratification for unfulfilled desires (for example, overeating out of frustration).

Spiritual Antimony encourages a creative lifestyle. It facilitates following one's own inner voice and in overcoming limiting ideas. Antimony helps balance and harmonize personal interests and higher ideals, and makes life appear more meaningful and happy.

Beryllium (Be²⁺)

Physical Beryllium helps with allergies, eczema and ulcers; also with rheumatic complaints and hormonal problems.

Psychological/mental Beryllium encourages a far-seeing perspective, clear perception and concentration.

Spiritual Beryllium helps create goals and encourages discipline and consistency in attaining these goals.

Bismuth (Bi³⁺)

Physical Bismuth has disinfectant and contracting properties, so it is used for injuries and the healing of wounds. In its mineral form, it enhances the ability to regenerate the mucous membranes and is helpful with gastritis and stomach ulcers.

Psychological/mental Bismuth enhances a natural, child-like lack of inhibition and a playful attitude towards life. It helps us accept our mortal existence when strong aversion to it exists and there is a predominant feeling of being lonely and not really at home on this planet.

Spiritual Bismuth helps us to take up again forms of spiritual development that had been abandoned owing to external circumstances and bring them to completion.

Boron (B³⁻)

Physical Boron helps with many diseases of the stomach and intestinal tract: nausea, vomiting, cramps, colic and diarrhoea. It dissolve energy blockages and leads to relaxation of the affected organs. It helps with skin problems, for example those caused by contact with irritating or toxic substances, and with problems of the nervous system, for example epilepsy or perceptual problems.

Psychological/mental Boron has a balancing effect on nervousness and jumpiness, promotes equilibrium and prevents us from stumbling or dropping things. It helps with panic attacks and great fear, promoting harmony and trust.

Spiritual Boron helps us gain control over our own life, that is, to get a grip on our life.

Calcium (Ca²⁺)

Physical Calcium encourages the metabolism of the cells, absorption of nutrients by the cell membranes, and energy use in the cells. It is necessary for the formation of DNA (the carrier of genetic information) and RNA (the messenger that passes on information on proteins, enzymes and hormones).

Calcium supports the growth, firmness and flexibility of bones, teeth and tissue. It is important for the regulation of the acid/alkali balance and encourages the elimination of fluid (the antagonist of sodium). It supports blood clotting (the antagonist of magnesium).

Finally, calcium is important for the formation of transmitter substances in the sensory system from nerves to organs or muscles. It regulates the heart rhythm and strengthens the heart.

Psychological/mental Calcium encourages receptivity, discrimination and memory. It has an emotionally stabilizing effect, lends self-confidence and helps to eliminate fear, particularly of accidents and illness. Calcium gives inner drive in cases of lethargy and clears up confusion.

Spiritual Calcium regulates the development of the personality. It speeds up a development that is slowing down and normalizes situations where developmental processes have become over-accelerated and chaotic. Calcium promotes mental growth.

Chlorine (Cl-)

Physical Chlorine helps with all feelings of weakness, including fainting and blackouts. It raises the blood pressure and regulates elimination through the kidneys. In addition, it encourages retention of water in the tissues and helps make them more elastic (works against 'stiffness') and encourages detoxification and the elimination of waste products in the cells. Chlorine encourages production of hydrochloric acid in the stomach and stimulates the digestion. Together with sodium and potassium it regulates the transmission of impulses in the nervous system.

Psychological/mental Chlorine dissolves tension and illnesses caused by stress, constriction, sorrow or fear. It makes us less sensitive to outer influences and reduces irritability. Chlorine gives us tranquillity and encourages deftness.

Spiritual Chlorine causes or promotes a positive, optimistic attitude towards life. It helps make us freer and able to unfold on an inner level without being bound.

Chromium (Cr^{3+}, Cr^{4+}, Cr^{6+})

Physical Chromium helps diabetes in its early stage as it assists the insulin in maintaining an equilibrium in blood sugar and storing sugar in the muscles. Chromium stimulates the fat metabolism, lowers the cholesterol level and prevents arteriosclerosis. It encourages growth as it influences the formation of growth hormone.

Chromium has anti-inflammatory properties, particularly in the central organs (the liver, heart, stomach, intestine and kidneys), as well as in infections of the nose and nasal passages (sinuses). It stimulates detoxification of the organism, lowers acidity and encourages fever as a healing reaction. It regulates the energy and heat levels in the body and soothes pain, particularly in the case of 'wandering' pain or headaches caused by weakness. Chromium helps clear cloudiness in the cornea.

Psychological/mental Chromium encourages mental regeneration and healing. It takes away the feeling of being under pressure. The richness of the world of ideas and creative imagination can be discovered and versatile ideas and enthusiasm are the result. Chromium brings colour into our life (Greek *chromos*, 'colour')!

Spiritual Chromium encourages the desire for self-determination and individuality. It stimulates us to discover and develop our own capabilities and to realize those important dreams in life. Chromium promotes all processes of mental healing.

Cobalt (Co³⁺)

Physical Cobalt increases the formation of red blood corpuscles in the bone marrow through the creation of a hormone in the kidneys. It accelerates maturation and extends the lifespan of blood cells. Cobalt also increases the ability of the small intestine to absorb iron.

Psychological/mental Cobalt, like chromium, enhances a desire for change and new experiences. It awakens curiosity and joy in living, removes melancholy and strong yearnings, and promotes wit and cunning. Not for nothing has it been named after the German *Kobold*, a clever and mischievous type of gnome.

Spiritual Cobalt helps to develop the view that all spiritual things are imbued with invisible being. It also promotes recognition of the spiritual universe.

Copper (Cu, Cu²⁺, Cu³⁺, Cu⁴⁺)

Physical Copper promotes absorption of iron in the small intestine and triggers the transformation of stored iron into a form that can be transported by the blood. It is a catalyst in the formation of haemoglobin and is responsible for the formation of enzymes that keep the blood vessels elastic. Copper promotes the development of the female sexual organs and helps with menstruation problems.

Copper promotes cell growth, cell respiration and pigmentation of hair and skin. The greatest concentrations of copper are in the liver, brain and blood and it stimulates all their activities. Copper is effective in lowering a temperature and loosening cramps; it is anti-inflammatory and detoxifying.

Psychological/mental Copper increases dream activity and promotes the inner world of pictures and imagination and the creative potential resulting from it. Copper helps develop creative imagination and dissolve confusion. It creates neutrality and a balancing of mood and also promotes free expression of feelings. Copper makes it possible to live out and enjoy the senses and sexuality.

Spiritual Copper encourages a sense of aesthetics and beauty, as well as the development of a spiritual culture. It fortifies a sense of justice and promotes friendship and love towards all beings.

Fluorine (F-)

Physical Fluorine promotes firmness of bones and teeth and improves stiffness and problems with joints, even with arthritis (inflammation of the joints). It promotes the regeneration of the skin and mucous membranes, particularly in the respiratory tract and the lungs. Fluorine promotes the activity of the nervous system, particularly that of the cerebral cortex, and helps tone down allergies of psychological origin.

Psychological/mental Fluorine helps us get rid of fixed behavioural patterns, fixed ideas, small thinking, narrow-mindedness and a generally uptight manner. It promotes flexibility, quick thinking, concentration and the ability to learn.

Spiritual Fluorine promotes spiritual freedom.

Gold (Au)

Physical Gold promotes the distribution of energy and vitality in the body. It is 'warming' and promotes a well-functioning circulation. It helps with problems and diseases of the sexual organs, generally supports the functioning of the glands, and helps heal damage to bones and tissues. Gold regulates conduction of impulses in the nervous system.

Psychological/mental Gold helps us out of depression, fear of death and, in severe cases, inclination to commit suicide. It confers self-confidence and self-consciousness and releases us from destructive influences.

Spiritual Gold brings our innermost core, our essence, to light. It helps give meaning to life and enables the realization of great deeds and projects. Gold represents generosity and magnanimity.

Iron (Fe^{2+}, Fe^{3+}, Fe^{4+})

Physical Iron promotes the absorption of iron through the intestine, as well as the formation of haemoglobin and red blood corpuscles. This ensures transportation of oxygen to the cells of the muscles and organs, good energy transfer and physical vitality. It helps in cases of weakness, tiredness and exhaustion. The functions of the liver, spleen, intestine and bone marrow are stimulated by iron. In addition, it fortifies the immune system – in silicon compounds mainly unspecifically, in oxides specifically the immune response.

Psychological/mental Iron has a stimulating, activating effect, encourages activity, initiative, dynamism, endurance, willpower, the ability to assert ourselves and the ability to be enthusiastic about something. Iron promotes the warrior side of us, the urge to research and discover and to conquer. It also promotes an upright attitude and honesty.

Spiritual Iron promotes inner calm and makes us unchallengeable. It will purify consciousness of painful and unpleasant contents, gives alertness and deepens meditations. Iron also stimulates the mental processing of perceptions and experiences and thereby helps to complete unfinished cycles.

Lead (Pb^{2+})

Physical Lead stimulates the elimination of heavy metals in the body, in this way helping with disease in organs affected by harmful substances, particularly the stomach, the intestine, blood and nerves. It helps with dehydration, sclerosis, stone formation in organs, loss of weight, muscular atrophy and severe localized pain.

Psychological/mental Lead promotes joy in living, particularly when we are depressed by a personal or social situation that seems to be hopeless (the feeling that everything is 'heavy as lead'). It stops hallucinations and obsessions and helps us to release ourselves from restricting habits and oppressive dogmas.

Spiritual Lead provides life with structure and encourages self-control, a sense of duty, constancy and loyalty.

Lithium (Li+)

Physical Lithium reduces blood pressure and dampens over-sensitivity in nerves and the motor nervous system, thereby alleviating restlessness, trembling and neural pains, for example in sciatica or neuralgia. It reduces the cholesterol levels and helps to prevent deposition of plaques in the blood vessels and joints. In this way, lithium also helps with kidney disorders, rheumatism and gout.

Psychological/mental Lithium has a generally calming effect, is an effective anti-depressant and improves the memory. It also encourages self-confidence.

Spiritual Lithium promotes devotion and humility, acceptance of what is unalterable. It teaches us to be able to bend and give in and still remain true to ourselves.

Magnesium (Mg²⁺)

Physical Magnesium dampens irritation of the nerves and muscles. It loosens cramp and relaxes muscles, for example in migraine, cramp-like headaches, cramp in the circulation, stomach and intestinal cramps and gallbladder colic. It is the antagonist of calcium.

As such, it hinders blood-clotting and all kinds of processes connected with stimulation and secretion. It increases blood circulation, makes the walls of the blood vessels tough and elastic, and expands the blood vessels surrounding the heart, thereby improving the functioning of the heart muscle. Magnesium promotes the toughness and hardness of the bones and is also involved with the metabolism of carbohydrates, fat and proteins and prevents sclerosis of tissue and vessels.

Psychological/mental Magnesium is calming and relaxing. It promotes a peaceful disposition and is effective against nervousness, fearfulness, hypochondria, schizophrenia and dampens excitability, irritability and aggression. Magnesium makes us more resilient towards stress.

Spiritual Magnesium promotes a positive attitude towards life. It helps us accept ourselves for who we are and to love ourselves. This gives us the gift of cheering up others and encouraging them, solely through the atmosphere we create.

Manganese (Mn^{2+}, Mn^{3+}, Mn^{4+})

Physical Manganese has a pain-relieving effect and fortifies the body's own defences by activating immunological and detoxifying enzymes. Fertility is increased as manganese stimulates the formation of the sexual organs. It influences the heart and the heart function, stimulates growth and the development of the skeleton. Manganese promotes fat metabolism and lowers blood sugar levels. It hinders the absorption of iron (and vice versa).

Psychological/mental Manganese encourages empathy, and sometimes sensitivity. It brings out warmth of heart and generosity. Manganese allows psychological wounds and injuries to heal, reduces strife, feelings of revenge and grudges, promotes trust and affection, as well as inner growth and maturity.

Spiritual Manganese promotes understanding of our own reality and of the reality of our environment. It stimulates a clearing of consciousness and of our relationships.

Nickel (Ni^{2+}, Ni^{3+})

Physical Nickel promotes the absorption and utilization of iron. It promotes the activity of the liver and detoxification of the organism. Nickel helps with pain that arises periodically, for example, headaches.

Psychological/mental Nickel promotes a feeling of security within us and helps with fearfulness, sadness and irritability. It helps us let go of oppressive images, particularly in the case of recurring nightmares. Nickel also fortifies the power of regeneration.

Spiritual Nickel promotes creativity and inventiveness. Nickel keeps us young mentally and encourages a playful nature.

Oxygen (O^{2-})

Physical Oxygen is the element that feeds all combustion processes in the body. It is, therefore, the energy supplier in all cells, tissues and organs. Oxygen is obtained from the air via the lungs, transported in the blood bound to iron (in haemoglobin), and is finally released to the cells. In this way, oxygen is the prerequisite for all metabolic processes.

Psychological/mental Oxygen supplies vitality and alertness, promotes creativity and the desire to turn ideas into reality. It mobilizes states of mood that have become rigid or frozen and provides the possibility for change.

Spiritual Oxygen represents the life principle. It promotes joy in living and the ability to be creatively active. Oxygen ensures survival in the sense of continuous further development towards optimal conditions.

Phosphorus (P^{3+}, P^{5+})

Physical Phosphorus is the building block of bones and teeth. Calcium always occurs with phosphorus in compounds and can only be absorbed through the small intestine with its help. It is involved in the formation of the genetic carriers DNA and RNA and of the cell membranes. In this way, it fundamentally increases the ability to regenerate all cells, tissues and organs. In lecithin, phosphorus promotes the functioning of the brain and the nerves.

Phosphorus compounds play an important role in the energy metabolism of all cells. Without this substance, there could be no growth, procreation, no muscular strength, heat formation or perception through the senses. The latter, in particular, is very important: phosphorus helps with many eye and ear complaints and the sense of smell. Phosphoric acid provides the buffer in blood to maintain the balance between acid and alkali.

Psychological/mental Phosphorus has a mood-lightening effect and is enlivening in cases of tiredness, dejection or despondency and states of exhaustion. It has a balancing effect on anger and irritability and protects from heightened sensitivity towards outer influences. Wherever complacency and lack of sensitivity have been developed as safety mechanisms, phosphorus brings openness and sympathy.

Spiritual Phosphorus is the bringer of light. It promotes consciousness, perception and extrasensory perception. Phosphorus helps us to realize our life through self-determination.

Potassium (K+)

Physical Potassium improves the solubility of nearly all compounds in body fluids; it influences metabolic processes in the cell membranes and thereby determines the pressure in the cells and blood. In this way, it also stimulates the function of the kidneys. It further encourages (together with sodium) electrical conduction in the nervous system, as well as stimulation and contraction of the muscles. Stimulation of the heart muscles is particularly influenced by potassium. It is also concerned with transportation of nutrients (glucose) to the cells and is important for the synthesis of proteins. The functioning of the pineal gland is supported by potassium in its activity of 'translating' outer light (qualities) into inner, hormonal impulses.

Psychological/mental Potassium helps to free us from fears, melancholy, depression and a feeling of failure. It promotes contentment and tranquillity, particularly with sensitivity to pain, noise and restlessness (a secret tip for morning 'grumps'). Potassium promotes a feeling of self-worth and removes the impression of being a victim of fate or of outside enemies.

Spiritual Potassium improves perception, particularly with perceiving light. This promotes intuition and helps us to recognize illusions and imagination as such. Potassium helps develop a freer attitude towards religious matters without dogma and suppression.

Silicon (Si^{4+})

Physical Silicon fortifies the skin, hair and nails and toughens up the connective tissues and the bones, the latter through stimulating the calcium metabolism. It fortifies the immune reactions in the blood and body fluids and encourages the activity of the lymph nodes, the spleen and the lungs. It is particularly helpful with a tendency to persistent colds.

Silicon has a stimulating effect on cell metabolism and cell division, promotes the healing of wounds or injuries, prevents scar formation and generally prevents premature ageing. It improves the elasticity of the blood vessels and has an anti-inflammatory effect. Silicon enhances the sensory organs.

Psychological/mental Silicon makes us warm-hearted and generous. It promotes a feeling of inner well-being that makes us less affected by external difficulties. It also works against fearfulness, oversensitivity and exhaustion. Silicon gives us inner stability, security and determination. It helps us to let go of fixed ideas and to open ourselves to inspiration and new impulses.

Spiritual Silicon helps us to be alert and ready to react in all situations. It enhances the facility to fit in with the rules of the physical and spiritual world and to work creatively in harmony with them.

Silver (Ag, Ag⁺)

Physical Silver appears cooling and directs heat and pain away (a typical indication, for example, is the inability to cope with heat). It stimulates the vegetative nervous system, helps harmonize the functioning of the inner organs and encourages fertility in women. By balancing the functioning of organs, many types of headache, particularly left-sided ones, are dissolved. Silver stimulates the activity of body fluids, improves the skin's ability to cope with light, fortifies the ability to see and the sense of balance, and gets rid of dizziness.

Psychological/mental Silver releases the emotions and encourages proper expression of feelings. It promotes generosity and empathy. Silver helps us to become more flexible mentally or to remain so and to let go of influences and dependencies, particularly if these go hand in hand with feelings of helplessness. The imagination and the ability to visualize are all stimulated by silver. Somnambulism (sleepwalking) is helped. Silver also helps maintain control and balance on a psychic level.

Spiritual Silver promotes the receptive, mediumistic side of our nature. It encourages a sense of community and an interest in traditional values. Silver also enhances the ability to see varying qualities of light and to harmonize inner life rhythms with the cycles of nature.

Sodium (Na⁺)

Physical Sodium regulates the water metabolism; it helps store water in the body and thus controls the osmotic pressure in the cells and body fluids. In this way, it increases blood pressure, stimulates the metabolic processes and the circulation, and eliminates dizziness and vertigo. Sodium stimulates functioning of the kidneys, thereby balancing the acid/alkali metabolism. Together with potassium, it ensures the correct stimulation of muscles and nerves.

Psychological/mental Sodium provides structure. It binds free energy in fixed goals, in regular processes and inner order. Sodium helps us not to squander our own potential and inner strength, but to channel it properly. It helps us to grasp situations, conclusions and inner pictures and to preserve them.

Spiritual Sodium promotes a sense of tradition, constancy and steadfastness.

Strontium (Sr²⁺)

Physical Strontium is related to calcium, but forms stronger, unbreakable bonds, and so tends to have a harmful effect on the body. In the mineral form, however, it tends to have a dissolving effect in bones, tissues and organs; also in the case of contraction of the blood vessels. Strontium helps with inflammations of the nerves and post-operative shock, relieves chronic muscular tension and accelerates the healing of sprained joints.

Psychological/mental Strontium helps counteract a feeling of constriction, also feelings of asphyxiation. It brings relief when everything in life seems to be in disarray. It helps overcome feelings of helplessness and with gaining a more positive outlook on life.

Spiritual Strontium helps build healthy, spiritual structures that stabilize life without restricting it.

Sulphur (S²⁻)

Physical Sulphur is the formative building block of many proteins, enzymes and hormones. It is a component of keratin, a protein vital to the formation of hair, nails and the external layer of skin. It develops healing effects when used for skin diseases, psoriasis and fungal infections.

Sulphur compounds (sulphates) are vitally involved in the formation of connective tissue and in detoxification processes. This is why sulphur is so helpful with rheumatic disorders, gout and liver problems. Sulphur is a particular antidote for heavy metal poisoning, encourages elimination processes and strengthens the body's defences.

Psychological/mental Sulphur uncovers confusing and muddled matters, illusions and hidden contents of the consciousness. It clarifies symptoms of illness by eliminating secondary symptoms and emphasizing the causal psychological/mental background symptoms. Sulphur helps with forgetfulness, laziness, lack of interest and a moody nature.

Spiritual Sulphur wakens our shadow sides and helps us confront them and overcome them. Then we find the shaft of light that makes it possible for us to accept things we rejected before and to integrate them.

Tin (Sn^{4+})

Physical Tin encourages the development and activity of the cerebrum and harmonizes the nervous system. It encourages the healing of spasms, states of weakness and paralysis that can be traced back to disturbances in the nervous system. Tin helps greatly with chronic problems, particularly in the area of the respiratory tract, secondarily also with liver and gallbladder problems (colic). Tin controls the sense of taste.

Psychological/mental Tin helps us transform emotions into a concrete form; it helps us to put feelings into words. Tin encourages enthusiasm, tolerance, trust and a friendly attitude and gives us the courage to master everyday difficulties. It dissolves sorrow into relief.

Spiritual Tin encourages us to realize our own life's dream. It has an inspiring effect and helps develop our innermost talents and abilities. Tin brings sociability and generosity to guests. It encourages musical talent, particularly the playing of music.

Titanium (Ti^{4+})

Physical Titanium is found in its highest concentrations in the muscles and bones. There it promotes growth and an upright posture. It also has anti-inflammatory properties, particularly in the case of colds, bronchitis, pneumonia and kidney infections.

Titanium fortifies the heart and the ability to regenerate the organism.

Psychological/mental Titanium has an enlivening and freeing effect in the case of claustrophobia, fear and oppression. It promotes sexual fulfilment and is helpful with problems of impotency and premature ejaculation.

Spiritual Titanium confers honesty, independence and spiritual greatness.

Vanadium (V^{5+})

Physical As vanadium itself is a severe irritant toxin in its mineral form, it has a strongly anti-inflammatory effect, particularly in skin diseases, eye problems (for example, inflammation of the cornea or conjunctiva) and with inflammatory illnesses of the respiratory organs.

Psychological/mental Vanadium helps us express feelings freely and to get rid of undue restraint and caution.

Spiritual Vanadium makes it possible to transform destructive attitudes into a constructive way of life.

Zinc (Zn^{2+})

Physical Zinc activates all kinds of different hormones and enzymes. It enhances the effect of insulin and helps with diabetes, supports the immune system and promotes production of growth hormones and sex hormones. The function of the male sexual organs (formation of the seminal vesicles) is stimulated; prostate disorders and problems with the ovaries are improved.

Zinc also regulates the development of the brain and sensory perception. It is extremely important for the retina (especially for vision in bad light) as well as for the senses of taste and smell. It encourages regeneration and healing of wounds, bone formation and toughening of the outer layer of skin, hair and nails. Zinc protects the organism against harmful substances and radiation.

Psychological/mental Zinc promotes the development of intelligence (abstract thinking). It helps with exhaustion, weakness, loss of courage and fearfulness, restlessness, lack of concentration and sleep disturbance, particularly with difficulties sleeping because there are too many ideas and thoughts running through the mind. Zinc encourages spontaneity and intuition.

Spiritual Zinc initiates great changes in life. It breaks up outworn structures and helps us use these upheavals in a meaningful way for creating better circumstances in our life. It brings idealism and intensifies our lives. Zinc encourages the ability to communicate.

Zirconium (Zr^{4+})

Physical Zirconium has an antispasmodic effect, particularly with menstrual problems that are connected with delayed menstruation. It also stimulates the liver's synthesizing function.

Psychological/mental Zirconium helps with the release of material worries and blocks and with letting go of suppressed and retained fears. It encourages symbolic and pictorial thinking and brings deep insights in dreams.

Spiritual Zirconium reminds us of the meaning of our existence. It helps with developing a spiritual view of things and with seeing through the illusory values of materialism as such.

How to use mineral-forming elements

Knowing the mineral-forming element content of a precious stone or mineral will immediately give a clear picture of its healing properties. Which aspects will be prominent in each individual case, however, will be determined by the relevant correspondence to those properties that derive from the way the mineral was formed and from its crystal structure. A mineral can be formed from a whole range of mineral-forming elements. Usually, only those that we actually need for a physical, psychological/mental or spiritual situation in our lives will be effective in their use for healing. A prior investigation of the life situation (manner of formation) and the lifestyle (crystal structure) is definitely a good idea when choosing the right stone for healing purposes.

If this is not possible for some reason, or if you are going to use a mineral primarily for its material properties, the following procedure is recommended in making your choice:

1. Determine the suitable mineral class – this helps the initial choice by matching the mineral to the dominnat theme of the person's life.

2. Find a correspondence between the acid or alkaline character of the mineral and the person's temperament – this helps narrow down the first choice.

3. Determine the degree of dilution - this will define whether you should target mineral-forming elements with a stronger or weaker concentration, or even look for trace components.

4. Consider the mineral forming-elements themselves – this will finally will give you information on the essential properties of the minerals in question. Then you can choose the most suitable one.

This mineral – it is recommended to choose only one initially - should, as far as possible, be worn or carried for several weeks. As substantial changes on all levels are involved with the effect of mineral-forming elements, a certain amount of time will be needed for it to work. The use of the mineral can be terminated at the moment when the original problem is clearly solved or if there appears to be a sudden aversion to continuing to wear it.

If no change is noticed, it is recommended to switch to another mineral containing the same mineral-forming elements or to check whether another, similar mineral-forming element would not be better.

Finally, if there are several colour variations of a chosen mineral, the next chapter will help you to make the right choice.

The colour of minerals

It is a strange fact that such colourful things as minerals and precious stones can be produced from the depths of the Earth, in what we think of as eternal darkness. This is precisely what has fascinated people over the centuries, in so far as minerals are in no way less colourful and spectacular than flowers. On the contrary, while the latter are ephemeral, and will wilt and decay, the colour of precious stones is (usually) permanent. In ancient times, not only the inexplicable shapes of crystals but also their remarkable colours were looked upon as direct, divine manifestations. Countless mythological descriptions, assignments to groups of elements and powers, as well as manifold effects, were ascribed by the ancients to these colours.

Modern life has destroyed even this veil of magic. Today, colours are seen as specific parts of the spectrum of light and are defined as radiation of a certain frequency and wavelength. They are analysed according to their shade and nuance, saturation point and brightness, divided up in standardized colour systems, and can be produced at any time, in any variation; colours are just not that special any more. Or are they? When the trees start sprouting in the spring, then those shades of green are not merely a shade of a colour, but an experience! Whenever we gaze at a harmoniously composed picture with glowing colours, this is not just perceived through the eye but felt with the entire soul. If you observe someone who is holding up a sparkling precious stone to sunlight, you will suddenly be able to see the glowing eyes of a child, even in the face of the very old!

This is something to contemplate before we turn to the physical/scientific side of colours. Colours provide us with wonderful experiences, the depth of which risks being played down if we talk about it too much. Colours belong to the reality of the soul, rather than to the intellect, so I will endeavour to keep my remarks brief in this chapter.

Colour and light

Simply expressed, colours are part of light. Or put another way: our sunlight contains all the colours of the spectrum. 'Light' in its original meaning is 'the enlightening, vision giving', and is a name for the phenomenon that allows us to see. This is so taken for granted nowadays that we never think about it any more. It seems logical: in order to see, we need light – if the light is switched off, it becomes dark....

According to modern thinking, light is an energy form that spreads in all directions in the form of radiation from a source of light. If a ray of light meets a solid body, it is reflected ('radiated back') or absorbed ('swallowed'). The reflected light is what makes it possible for us to see things that do not themselves radiate light. There is always something that radiates of its own accord (sources of light like the sun, stars, a candle, a light bulb) and something else that is illuminated (everything else, the visible world). The statement that initially sounds fairly simplistic will become enormously important a few lines on, when we attempt to understand the various forms of colour play.

In German, the word 'colour', *Farbe*, and the Old High German word, *farawa*, originally meant the 'property of a being or thing'. This can still be found in the expression 'to show one's true colour' (to tell the truth). Light is a prerequisite for seeing something. Colour, on the other hand, conveys a content, determines what we see. The connection is fairly simple: if we break down a ray of sunlight into its spectrum, we obtain beautiful colours, ranging from red, through orange, yellow, green, blue to violet. Nature presents these as a rainbow (rays of light are broken in the atmosphere by finely distributed droplets of water and displayed 'fan-like'). We can recreate this process by using a glass prism.

The reverse happens if the coloured rays are bundled together again, and we see white light. White light is the sum of all the colour rays and contains all colours.

Black is, therefore, the absence of all light (light off = darkness) and the absence of all rays of colour.

Colours are formed on a material object by the object absorbing a portion of the white light falling on it and reflecting the rest. We see the reflected light and this is what is perceived as the object's colour. This is how we perceive the colour of a mineral or precious

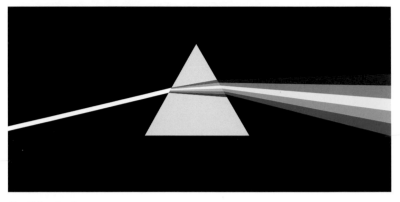

Fig. 29 *A prism.*

stone, and this is how we see the colours from our paintbox, from painting pictures or painting the walls in the house.

However, there is a very different effect when we mix colours. When you mix together pigments (Latin *pigmentum*, 'colour') of all the colours in a paintbox, the result will be black, not white. This is because all the colours are combined in the pigment substances and, therefore, absorb all the light. Not much light is reflected, we cannot see much and the absence of light is recognized as black.

White colour is, therefore, a substance that does not absorb any light but reflects it all. White objects do not contain any colour substances; black objects contain all colour substances.

This seeming paradox to the above can be explained with the simple statement that we have to distinguish between bodies that actively illuminate and are sources of light and those that are illuminated. Here is a brief summary:

> When coloured rays that are transmitted from sources of light are 'gathered' together, we get white light (an additive mixture). White light contains all colours. Black arises through a complete absence of light.

> By mixing all the colours on an object we obtain the colour black, as it absorbs all the light falling on to it (a subtractive colour mixture). White is created through the absence of all colour pigments and reflection of all the light falling onto the body.

These simple laws of physics are illustrated in Figure 30.

On the left, you can see an overlapping of coloured light rays and the resulting colour of the combined rays. On the right, you see the colours that are formed when coloured pigments are mixed. Based on these simple laws of physics, we have to look upon the colour rays of a source of light and the reflected colours of a solid object as two very different phenomena. In the case of the visible colours of minerals and precious stones, we are dealing with the second phenomenon. In minerals, the colour is created through by absorbing certain portions of the light and reflecting the remainder.

This is also why we cannot find immediate correspondences between the colours of minerals and the colours of the human chakras and the aura, where we ourselves represent the source of light. These manifestations of colour are colour rays that are released through inner processes within ourselves and are not influenced by the reflected colours of a precious stone! Even though appropriate tables of colours are widely published throughout the relevant literature, I would strongly recommend that you try out these tables: you will find out for yourselves that they do not work. There is a very different connection between stones, chakras and the aura which is our 'own light', light radiation from the stones (cf. Chapter 2.1 in Part 2). This connection will be discussed in more detail in a later book.

Colour variations

As shown in the graphic illustration of subtractive colour mixtures below, there are three basic colours, or primary colours, which yield

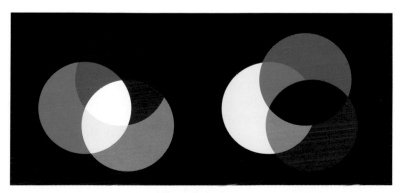

Fig. 30   *Left: additive colour mixing, right: subtractive colour mixing.*

Fig. 31 The colour sphere.

all other colours through mixing. The three primary colours are red, yellow and blue, from which derive the mixed colours orange (red + yellow), green (yellow + blue) and violet (blue + red). These six colours produce a circle that can also be used as a basis for discussing mineral colours. Now, in nature, we do not usually just come across pure colours, but most of the time a huge range of different variations of every colour, depending on how much white or black (or other colours) are mixed in. Red with a large proportion of white becomes pink, with a large proportion of black, it turns brown. This turns the colour circle into a sphere.

Imagine there was a planet of colours with its axis running from north to south continuously from white through all shades of grey to black. Around the equator, we would find the 'pure' colours corresponding to a colour circle: red – orange – yellow – green – blue – violet. The colours of the equator are pure and undiluted as they are furthest away from the axis. The closer the colours approach the axis in the north and the south, the more they are mixed with light grey or white (north), or dark grey or black (south). Thus we have pastel shades around the white north pole and darker shades around the black south pole.

The illustration in Figure 31 shows this colour distribution, on the left dealing with the 'warm' colours (red – orange – yellow), and on the right with the 'cold' ones (green – blue – violet). For our use in healing with crystals and stones, this pair of three-dimensional models can be radically simplified into a two-dimensional one with the 'north pole' moved to the centre and the 'south pole' represented as a dark ring around the 'equatorial' colour circle. This representation will be referred to in what follows as a colour wheel (Figure 32).

The colour wheel

The colour wheel provides a simplified overview of colour development as we find it among minerals: from black on the outside that absorbs all colours, via dark grey to the middle colour circle and further to silver, colourless, white and clear, that reflect all colours. The upper half of the middle circle displays the 'cold colours' green, blue and violet, while the lower half represents the 'warm' colours red, orange and yellow. These colour appearances are quite real: a red room that is the same temperature as a blue one will be felt to be warmer. This is already a small indicator that colour is not merely perceived with the eyes.

The complementary colours

Further, the wheel shows us that complementary colours are always situated opposite each other (Latin *complere*, 'to make

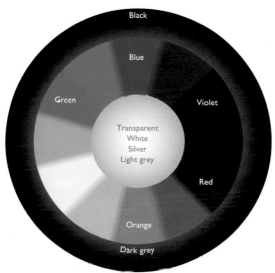

Fig. 32 The colour wheel.

complete, to add'), these being the colours that taken together as colour rays will produce white light, or when mixed as pigments, will produce black. For example, a mineral that appears violet actually absorbs yellow light and reflects violet light. An orange-coloured stone will absorb the colour blue and reflect orange, and so on. The complementary colour plays an important part in healing with crystals and precious stones and when treating someone with minerals. It will be discussed again in more detail at a later stage.

How mineral colours are formed

In order to produce a certain colour, a mineral has to be able to absorb certain portions of white light. This possibility exists when so-called colour centres are present in a mineral. Colour centres are formed through mineral-forming elements that are electrically charged (usually metals), through free electrons trapped in the crystal lattice, or through a certain structural consistency, which ensures that incident light rays are broken up and partially absorbed. In all cases, the light energy of the incoming light is taken up by electrons that are stimulated and then transform the light energy into kinetic energy.

When the excitation of the electrons calms down again, the energy is released and given off in the form of warmth (infrared radiation), visible light and microwaves. This inherent radiation is, however, so weak that it is hardly perceptible. Only the infrared radiation is noticeable when a stone lying in the sun feels warm after a while. Fluorescence (visible light energy) is a property of some minerals but will only become visible to the naked eye in darkened rooms under UV light. Microwaves are completely invisible to us. The only visible effect is that a portion of the white light falling upon an object 'disappears', the remaining reflected part gives a stone its colour.

Colour centres created by electrically charging mineral-forming elements

This is the most common source of colour. Many metals, particularly chromium, iron, copper, cobalt, manganese and nickel, are able to absorb certain wavelengths of light. For this reason they are also called 'colour carriers' or 'chromophores' (Greek *chroma*, 'colour' and *phoros*, 'carrying'). If any of these metals represent the largest component of a mineral, that is, if they also appear in its chemical formula, we speak of its 'self colour' in mineralogy or 'idiochromatic colouring' (Greek *idio*, 'own, self'). The colour is created by the mineral-forming elements characteristic of this mineral. If the colour is caused by fractional components or trace components, it is called a foreign colour (or xenochrome, from the Greek *xenos*, 'strange'), caused by foreign substances.

Idiochrome and xenochrome can be distinguished by the so-called streak test. This requires rubbing the mineral against a rough tablet of porcelain, or scratching the specimen with the tablet. Very hard minerals will be pulverized. The resulting fine dust of scratching will only leave a coloured mark if the colour of the mineral is its own. Only then will the scratched off dust contain enough colour centres to make the colour visible. In the case of a xenochrome, insufficient colouring substance will be contained and the scratch will appear white.

The streak test is, therefore, a reliable method for identifying minerals. Idiochromes are rarer: hematite, for example, displays a red scratch, malachite a green one, azurite a blue one and pyrite a black one. The multi-coloured fluorite, also the coloured quartzes, all display a white scratch as, in all these cases, we are dealing with xenochromes. Particularly colour variations in the same mineral usually arise through xenochromes.

Colour centres created by free electrons in the crystal lattice

The effect of ionizing (or radioactive) radiation, in particular during the formation of a mineral, can cause electrons to be precipitated out of an atom and then re-deposited in another part of the lattice. The completed, compact crystal lattice then prevents the electron from returning to its original position. These free electrons find it particularly easy to absorb light energy and become colour centres in this manner. In some cases, the entire light spectrum is absorbed which allows the stone to appear dark brown to black. The best example for this is smoky quartz.

Minerals coloured through free electrons logically also display a white streak line. The colour will be destroyed again, as a rule, if the mineral is heated, because heating makes the crystal lattice resonate, making it possible for the electron to return to its original position.

Colours based on structural characteristics

Microscopically fine structures inside minerals also cause light to be bent and colours to be created. The 'Tyndall effect', named after its discoverer, the Irish physicist John Tyndall, is well known: light is scattered or bent on very small particles (for example microscopically small droplets or fibres) and is broken up into rays of different colours, with the red portion usually being absorbed and the blue portion being reflected. This is how the blue colour of chalcedony is created along its fine, fibrous crystals.

Internal cracks, splits, lamella or irregular surfaces may also lead to colourful light reflections. The best example for this is the opal, which consists of minute SiO_2 globules. The light reflected by these globules is broken up into all the colours of the rainbow and gives the opal its unique play of colours. A similar phenomenon occurs along the fine lamellar structure of moonstone and labradorite. Here, too, the light is scattered and reflected, leading to the appearance of a blue and coloured play of lights.

Colours based on inclusions

Inclusions are deposits of a solid, liquid or gaseous nature in minerals. Inclusions, too, can have an effect on the light falling upon them. In this way, the tiny, fine rutile needles contained in many minerals provide a light-scattering effect that is displayed as asterism (star formation), for example, in star rubies, star sapphires or star rose quartz. In blue quartz, for example, this leads to the Tyndall effect and a blue colouring. Finely distributed gas and water inclusions will make obsidian shine with a golden or silver sheen (gas), or even in all colours of the rainbow.

The interesting thing about this is that colour is not a phenomenon denoting purity or perfection, but actually occurs precisely through these deposits of foreign substances or faults in the lattice structure. Apparently incomplete absorption or reflection of light corresponds with the imperfection of the mineral. This brings us back to the original, Old High German meaning of the word *farawa*. Colour actually does demonstrate the property of a being or thing, the only question being which property or quality is owned by the individual mineral colour?

The effects of mineral colours

We experience colours in a deep way: whether we 'see red', 'go green with envy' or are 'yellow' (cowardice), our use of language shows that colours have been endowed with more properties than physics books allow. The healing properties of colours are no longer news these days. Colour therapy can be successfully employed for allergies, chronic problems and psychic illnesses, and shows results that orthodox medicine can only dream of. The reasons for these comprehensive, positive results are very simple.

Colour balancing

All of our inner processes are linked with each other and create energy phenomena. Our mental activities influence our spiritual experiences and vice versa. The latter definitely cause certain emotions that, in turn, create interactions with physical perceptions, the functioning of the nerves and the endocrine system (hormone metabolism). In this way, every thought and every feeling go hand in hand with certain metabolic processes and chemical reactions in our body.

Also during these processes, energy is created or used up – depending on the situation. To sum up: our entire experience leads to a kind of 'colour formation' (colour = light = energy) in our bodies that seeks a balance in order to attain the neutral 'white' state (or black). This balance simply occurs through externally adding another colour, namely the complementary colour!

This is the reason our taste in colour changes: an article of clothing that we absolutely have to have today can appear as 'impossible' on another day. A different colour would muddle us completely today, even though it appeared calming and harmonious a few days ago. Usually, we unconsciously follow these impulses by dressing in a certain way or, without noticing it, tend to linger in places with certain colours, or prefer to gaze at certain colours.

It is never the eyes alone that perceive colour. As already mentioned above, feelings about temperatures depend on the colour. Our skin is the largest sensory organ and can absorb colour and conduct it inside the body. If we 'perceive' colour in this manner, and it helps balance our inner state, we will attain a comprehensive feeling of well-being. Tensions disappear, disharmony evaporates, and we are able to cope with psychological problems and physical disorders.

Seen another way, colours that appeal to us and create a feeling of well-being will help us identify and understand our inner state of mind: just as fresh spring green balances the red that accumulated through a heightened energy requirement in winter, gazing at a complementary colour will always indicate how a particular colour deficiency came about. The colour wheel will be helpful with this: if we are drawn towards two colours, we can first of all determine the mixture of these colours that is located exactly between them on the wheel. Their complementary colour to this corresponds to our inner state.

Wearing or having coloured minerals or precious stones next to the skin can be used in healing with stones to attain this colour balance. If we wear a certain mineral for a lengthy period of time directly on our skin, the colour radiation will gradually percolate throughout the whole organism. If we place the stone only briefly on a particular spot, the effect will remain localized. In this way, the colour effect can be targeted exactly as desired. In the following, I should like to summarize the effect of the mineral colours as I have experienced them myself over the years. The list will not encompass all the healing effects known in colour therapy, and in some points it may even contradict some statements from colour therapy. However, conversations with colour therapists have shown that different uses of colour will also produce different results. And if there is a difference between using coloured pieces of cloth, coloured foil and colour rays, then we may also assume that the colours of minerals, some of them very specific, will have their own special effects too.

■ *Black minerals*

Black minerals absorb all the light and are, therefore, suitable for 'stripping off' excess energies. This effect is particularly noticeable with pain: pain arises – looked at from the point of view of energy –

wherever there is a blockage, and therefore, an energy back-up or bottleneck. Black minerals, for example smoky obsidian, smoky quartz or black tourmaline, will absorb this excess energy, causing pain to disappear and relaxation to set in. This does not always mean that the cause is also eliminated; however, freedom from pain is the best prerequisite for further treatment.

Black, therefore, does not apply to any organ in particular, but works for relaxation in the entire organism. The mental state is similarly affected: here too, tensions are eliminated and this makes us more resistant, resilient and more able to cope with stress. Black minerals give us security and stability.

Psychologically, black keeps away distractions and helps us concentrate on what is important and essential. Black helps bring hidden matters out into the open, pleasant as well as unpleasant ones, and through the absence of outer light, leads us to discover our own inner source of light.

▮ Red minerals

Red minerals have a strongly stimulating effect, produce heat and speed up things. They stimulate the circulation, the blood vessels and the blood itself. Dark red stimulates the activity of the heart, while light red (pink) helps create harmony in the heart. Red and reddish brown minerals stimulate the small intestine and improve the absorption of nutrients, vitamins and mineral-forming elements. This, too, is good for the blood and improves its quality.

In a similar manner, our psychological experiences also become more intense. Our inner world of images is fortified and feelings are expressed more clearly; in particular the elementary emotions such as love or hate are enhanced. Red minerals make us more impulsive and extrovert. They strengthen the willpower and the ability to persevere. Pink is a little different in this respect: the large proportion of white makes its effect more peaceful, more sensitive to others and sometimes slightly oversensitive.

Red stimulates the inner fire. It encourages all processes of learning, and the processing of experiences in the mind, and, in this way, accelerates our spiritual growth. Red encourages willingness to help others as a basic prerequisite for living together with all other beings. Pink minerals encourage sympathy.

▪ Orange minerals

Orange minerals have a vitalizing effect. They strongly stimulate the circulation, fortify the blood vessels and encourage an even distribution of energy throughout the body. The function and sensitivity of the sexual organs is improved. Dark orange and brown stimulate the body's sensitivity and regulate the metabolism and growth of tissues. The entire organism is strengthened and protected in this way.

On a mental level, orange enhances the quality of life and puts us in a cheerful, happy frame of mind. There is room for sensuality and spontaneity. Orange minerals help us to move out of apathetic states and they encourage creativity. Dark orange and brown help us to collect ourselves on an inner level, providing a feeling of security, peace, relief and down-to-earth realism.

Orange lends joy to life and a certainty of existing in harmony with a higher order and being on the right course in our life. Orange minerals help us find harmony and balance and encourage a sense of justice.

▪ Yellow minerals

Yellow and gold-coloured minerals have a cheering effect and help produce a positive attitude towards life. They stimulate the digestion and the activity of the stomach, spleen and pancreas. Yellow improves the digestion of food and the supply of energy to the body. The vegetative nervous system (the nerves that control the inner organs) is supported in its work, likewise the immune system.

Yellow lends happiness, a carefree attitude and energy to do things. It makes us aware of our needs and desires and helps fight off harm. Yellow and gold-coloured minerals help us overcome depression and lend self-confidence, trust and belief in our own success.

On a mental level, yellow encourages an understanding of our daily experiences (mental digestion). From this arises a certainty of being able to shape our own life, that is, the ability to take on responsibility. Yellow minerals help us discover the meaning in our own existence and in this way lead us to spiritual maturity.

■ Green minerals

Green minerals have a harmonizing, neutralizing effect. They stimulate the liver and gallbladder and thus encourage detoxification and regeneration of the body. The liver here has a central function, as the organ of building up (synthesis of proteins, blood formation, formation of enzymes, etc.), storing (energy and nutrient storage) and cleansing, and it regulates the most important metabolic processes.

Green releases emotions and makes emotions more intense, in particular anger and fury, although by discharging the latter, in the long term it leads to an inner peace. Green minerals enhance speed and the ability to react and awaken interest and enthusiasm. They stimulate the inner world of pictures, clarify our dream experiences and encourage the imagination.

Green brings initiative and the will to live. It encourages the senses and perceptions and draws our attention to the material world. Green minerals help us to deal with 'spiritual toxins' and encourage a healthy optimism. Green is indeed the colour of hope.

■ Blue minerals

Blue minerals have a cooling, calming effect. They regulate the activities of the kidneys and the bladder and thereby the balance of liquids, hormones, acid/alkali and mineral-forming elements. Blue activates elimination and the movement of body fluids.

On the mental plane, blue encourages relaxation, openness and honesty, accelerates instinctive reactions and keeps things in motion. Blue minerals help us to overcome fear and take courage. They promote the ability to form partnerships.

Blue encourages a balanced flow by helping us to recognize and overcome barriers and external influences. Blue minerals help us develop strength and an inner equilibrium. They encourage striving for knowledge and a search for truth.

■ Violet minerals

Violet minerals have a cleansing, freeing effect. They encourage brain activity, the sensory and motor nervous systems, the skin and the lungs and respiratory tract. In this way, they regulate breathing (including the breathing of the cells) and absorption of oxygen, and they help overcome acidity by releasing carbon dioxide. In the large intestine, the colour violet stimulates the absorption and elimination of water.

Violet lends relief in sorrow and helps dissolving traumas. It encourages memory, a wealth of ideas and consciousness, as well as communication and interactions with others. Violet minerals encourage an understanding of the problems of others, even if they are foreign to our personality. Violet protects us from foreign influences of an energetic and psychological nature.

Violet lends spiritual freedom. It awakens our deep innate knowledge, encourages the absorption of information and helps us distinguish between what is useful and what is harmful. Violet minerals promote inner calm and composure and help us recognize who we are.

☐ Clear, white and silver minerals

All of these are characterized by the fact that they do not absorb light or colours but reflect everything. This means they are neutral and guide the light to us that contains all possibilities. In this way they support and enhance what is already present. Clear, white and silver minerals are suitable for conducting energy in cases of deficiency (feelings of coldness, lack of feelings, weakness, paralysis) and for promoting the effect of other minerals.

On a psychological level, these minerals promote the very properties we see in them: clear minerals encourage clarity and purity, white minerals promote neutrality, silver minerals work like a mirror: they promote self-recognition.

Spiritually, clear, white and silver represent purity and the creative power that contains all possibilities and can realize all things. Clear, white and silver minerals bring abundance and wholeness (if they were not whole, they would be a colour.

■■■ Coloured and colourfully scintillating minerals

These minerals reveal the playful side of nature. Minerals like opals, labradorite or rainbow obsidian reveal plays of colour that are more than just the sum of the colours involved. They stimulate activity in the entire organism and accelerate the healing process.

Psychologically, coloured and scintillating minerals have an enlivening effect. They provide joy, desire and enjoyment, may awaken old memories or offer relief and relaxation through pleasant pastimes. Colourful and scintillating minerals are 'holiday' stones.

On a spiritual plane, coloured and scintillating minerals lend us the ability to play. This means that we voluntarily devote all our attention to a certain idea, undertaking or task and are completely absorbed in it. In such a 'playful' life, we are the source of our own fate; this will, in turn, bring unimaginable possibilities.

Colour healing with minerals

According to the descriptions given above, the suitable mineral colour can be found in two ways:

1. If one of the descriptions exactly fits the state you would like to experience, it will be sufficient to choose a stone of the right colour and to wear it, close to the skin if possible. You should be very careful when choosing among the many different nuances of colour – make the choice that gives you the best feeling. According to the laws of colour balance, you should be guaranteed to pick exactly the right shade. The correctness of your choice will soon be proven to you through an improvement in your feeling of well-being.

2. If you recognize your own state in one or two of the descriptions given here and wish to change your life but do not know how, then choose a colour complementary to that of your present state. If two descriptions fit you, work out the colour that results from a mixture of the two, then choose the relevant complementary colour. The crystal, stone or gem chosen in this manner should, as far as possible, be worn next to the skin.

In the second case, it may be that you do not like the complementary colour at all. This means you have an inner aversion to this colour and, unfortunately, also towards the qualities and properties associated with it. This aversion, however it may have arisen, is hindering you from changing the circumstances that you do not like.

By confronting the complementary colour with the help of the respective crystal or stone, you will be able to overcome this aversion in time and change your life in the desired way. In the second case, it may well be that you will not feel at all well to begin with, but speaking bluntly – you need to go through with it! It is very important simply to observe what is happening: what do you want, feel, think and do, what do you remember and what do you encounter? On no account judge or evaluate, accept yourself during this period just as you experience yourself. Then a change will come about much more quickly.

With this last aspect of colour, the world of crystals and stones has now been described fairly comprehensively. From their formation to their structure, minerals and colours, you have now become acquainted with the most important basic concepts from both the field of mineralogy as well as from the field of healing. Provided you immerse yourself and absorb the contents of this first part to the point where you have understood and can apply them, you will be in a position to work out the inherent healing effects of practically any mineral. I emphasize – these are the basic principles!

Every stone is an individual. What has been described so far has demonstrated the mutual features of a particular type of stone, the individual stones themselves can still be very different. Let me illustrate this with an analogy.

When studying embryonic development in humans, we study anatomy, physiology and biochemistry. Even when we have some knowledge of the individual environment, all we know is that a human is, in principle, an upright two-legged creature who uses tools, shapes his or her own environment and is able to speak. These are important basic principles, but they do not, however, give us much information on what the very next person we happen to come across will have to say to us!

This is how we will end Part 1. We have dealt with the most important things that can be described about minerals and healing crystals and stones. The remaining part of the story, which is even more important, will have to be told by the stones themselves, when you carry or wear them, surround yourself with them or use them for healing purposes. What you encounter then is the truly lived experience of the world of crystals. The second part of this book is intended to introduce you to this aspect.

PART 2

The art of healing with crystals

The phenomenon of light

The source of the healing properties of minerals

As you may have already experienced, through being stimulated by the information in the first part of this volume, minerals and precious gems do indeed have healing effects, the mineralogical connections of which have been researched and are known. The question remains unanswered, however, as to how and through what devices minerals are actually able to unfold their healing effects. What does this communication between stone and human being consist of? How can a piece of matter exert an influence on our organism? If one were able to ingest a mineral or stone, inhale it or absorb it into the body in some other way, one could perhaps imagine an effect taking place, but how can just placing it on our skin or wearing it as an ornament work – how does the effect take place?

The healing effect of a crystal becomes more easily understandable if we put aside the notion that the limits of our being are identical with the limits of our physical bodies. This notion is definitely a fallacy. Even in physics, it has been known for well over a hundred years that every body, every organism, every 'material object', be it a stone, a plant or a plastic bucket, possesses what is referred to variously as an 'emanation' or aura. Many physical and all chemical processes involve the absorption and emanation of radiation, which means that, whatever takes place, heat, light or another form of electromagnetic radiation is either absorbed or heat, light or another form of electromagnetic radiation is released.

This means we ourselves, and everything around us, are constantly surrounded by energy fields. This also means we are involved in a constant energy exchange with our environment. It all begins with the sunlight that we absorb and radiate out again in the form of heat, and ranges right through to the influences of energy from electrical currents, radio transmitters and microwaves. Maybe you have seen something similar with an internal aerial on a portable television set. You may have had those annoying evenings when a perfectly adjusted picture appeared to suffer permanent interference merely through your presence. Not always, but on some days, it is difficult to find the right position in the room where you will not disturb the reception. The problem is not solely due to physical shielding of the signal, as sometimes another person can sit down in the very same armchair from which you have managed to ruin the entire reception without causing any effect at all! It appears from this that it is your very own 'radiation' that interacts with the box.

As this example makes clear, all of us are constant receivers and transmitters of radiation. In recent years evidence has emerged from various tests that 'electrosmog', caused by electrical currents and radio transmitters, can affect people's health, as can the influences of currents of water and fault lines in the ground.

Radiation from stones

Stones, minerals and crystals also possess this kind of radiating property, as has already been discussed in Chapter 1.4, *The colours of minerals*. Their radiation results from the transformation of absorbed light, lying mainly in the infrared region and only to a very small degree in the visible and microwave regions of the spectrum. But despite their lesser quantity , the latter are of great importance. Infrared radiation is absorbed by the outermost layers of skin into the body, which is why we feel it as heat. Microwaves, however, penetrate the entire organism so, in principle, reach all tissues and organs.

The fact that we cannot normally perceive the visible portion of radiation of precious gems and minerals with the naked eye is simply due to the low intensity (Latin *intensus*, 'violent') of this radiation. Radiation from our bodies, for example, is comparable to the glimmer of light from a candle about 20 kilometres (12.5 miles) away. During the daytime it cannot, of course, be seen. However, in total darkness, we would gradually become aware of this light. This radiation is a real effect; the difficulties experienced in science with measuring this subtle radiation has little to do with the radiation itself but rather more with the limitations of the measuring equipment available.

Light in the organism

Nowadays, even children know that the stars are still in the sky in the daytime, even though they are not visible because the intensity of the sunlight blots them out. The same goes for us: in principle we, too, are all sources of light. Our organisms glow: every cell, every tissue and every organ has its own specific radiation and also produces its own specific magnetic field. These are now made use of in medicine for the diagnosis of illnesses. The technique of magnetic resonance imaging is used to measure the magnetic fields in our bodies and can produce three-dimensional images of all our inner organs that are considerably more accurate and precise than X-ray images.

There is more: results of biochemical research published in 1993 have proven that this radiation is actually used for communication. Every cell nucleus emits photons (the tiniest light particles or packages) with a high intensity and in this way communicates with neighbouring cells. This is how metabolic processes, growth, development and the differentiation of cells, tissues and organs are coordinated in the body. The nervous system and hormones only intervene in a guiding capacity in processes that are normally regulated automatically. This 'conversation' from cell to cell, this 'chatting over the garden fence', actually occurs via the medium of light

Radiation as an information carrier

What can light really do? What we refer to as 'light' is only a small part of all existing electromagnetic radiation – merely the portion that is visible to our eyes. This portion is also called the 'visible spectrum' (Latin *spectrum*, 'appearance'). In addition to the visible spectrum, there are other types of electromagnetic radiation: radio waves, infrared rays (heat radiation), ultraviolet light (UV light), microwaves and radiation given off by some radioactive materials (gamma rays). All of these have something in common: every type of radiation is an information carrier!

We make use of these properties in everyday life: whether it is for information sent via radio and television transmitters or mobile phones, or for remote control devices of every kind, the relevant information is always transmitted via a particular type of radiation, so that it passes from the transmitter to the receiver completely invisibly.

Healing with crystals as a form of information therapy

This is exactly what is taking place between stones and humans! Stones, too, emit radiation and, being extremely durable and permanent (at least, as a rule), they emit the same information in a very constant way. They could be compared to radio transmitters that constantly broadcast the same programme. Every stone or crystal has its own specific light, or put another way, its specific radiation that naturally influences our organisms. If contact is made between a crystal and our bodies, the absorbed light will inevitably have an influence on the 'light communication' between the cells and cause certain reactions.

An effect therefore definitely exists. Whether this influence becomes a healing influence will depend upon two factors: (1) what we require at the moment, and (2) what the stone, or rather the information radiated by the stone, can offer us. If a need is fulfilled, healing will take place. This means that healing with crystals, just like homeopathy, Bach flower remedies or aromatherapy, belongs with the information therapies. It is not the chemical substance that is effective, but the information emitted by it.

What information exactly the crystals are able to supply us with in each individual case was discussed in detail in Part 1. Based on the mineralogical data on the crystal system, manner of formation, mineral class, content of mineral-forming elements and colour, we will know what basic programme is involved in each case. In this way, we have exact instructions at our disposal as to how to identify exactly the right information transmitter (the right mineral) for us from our personal lifestyle, the given situation, the desired change, and so on. The systematic structure needed to do this will be found in the next chapter, *The analytical art of healing with crystals*.

The analytical art of healing with crystals

The basic principles of healing with crystals discussed in Part 1 of this volume – manner of formation/life situation, crystal system/lifestyle, mineral-forming element effect and colour effects – make it possible for us to analyse and choose precisely the right mineral for any project, any problem or illness. This means that the analytical art of healing with crystals differs considerably from the usual symptomatic correspondences used in other therapeutic literature. A thorough examination of the nature and the given situation makes it possible to understand why a certain problem or a particular illness has arisen and can thus help to heal the root cause.

A mineral identified in this manner will activate your own inherent powers of self-healing and can, therefore, help with situations for which the literature – and even this volume – will not yield any suggestions. Providing the analysis is carried out thoroughly, the mineral will, in all probability, help as it will deliver the appropriate information. So, trust in your choice, even if you should pick out a seemingly unusual or atypical mineral. Also, remember that the modern art of healing with crystals is in its infancy and that we can almost certainly say that only a fraction of all possibilities have, so far, been investigated.

It is for this very reason that the following table includes not only the healing crystals described in this volume, but also all crystals and minerals currently obtainable which are known to have been used for therapeutic purposes. Short descriptions of all these minerals can be found in my book *Heilsteine von A – Z (Healing crystals from A – Z)*, which was published by Osterholz Verlag in 1997. In the present volume, I shall only be describing those minerals whose healing effects have already been investigated very thoroughly and have been confirmed several times over. It is very important to me to pass on strictly authentic information in this volume; this means only describing the healing effects of minerals that I can vouch for personally or have observed myself. This is the reason why some of the lesser known healing crystals are missing in Part 3 – I hope you will bear with me over this.

In principle, there is no dividing line between healing crystals and 'ordinary minerals' in the art of healing. Every mineral, because of its inherent properties, may have an effect upon us. Whether this will turn into a healing effect will simply depend upon what we require at that moment. You could, therefore, extend all the principles described in Part 1 and apply them to all known minerals. The most important thing is to work out very thoroughly and exactly each principle in turn. The more precisely the chosen mineral suits the individual person in a given situation, the greater the success.

The following table is intended to serve initially as a concise, easy-to-scan analysis of crystal systems, formation principles and mineral classes, to help you to choose a suitable mineral for each case. Where the choice is between several minerals, the indication of the mineral-forming substance and the colours will provide further means of differentiating. Some minerals are formed in different ways, so certain ones may be referred to several times; however, only the most common and frequent types of formation are presented here, being those of the minerals that are obtainable in the trade. Descriptions in the mineralogical literature may, therefore, differ somewhat from those given in the table.

Chemical formulas have been presented according to current nomenclature. Mineral-forming substances that are present in a given mineral in small quantities have been indicated by '+ X', while traces are indicated as '+ (X)'. The table also includes healing rocks (granite, marble, porphyrite, obsidian, oolite, rhyolite), which are assigned to the system of the main component of the healing crystal in question.

The analytical approach to the art of healing with crystals: systems of known healing crystals

(current status: June 1995; CS, crystal system, MF, manner of formation)

CS	MF	Mineral class	Mineral / Chemical formula and mineral-forming substance	Colour
CUBIC	I	Natural element	meteoritic iron	grey metallic
			$Fe + Ni,Co + (C,Cu,P,S)$	
			gold	gold metallic
			$Au + Ag + (Cu)$	
			copper	coppery red to brown
			$Cu + Fe + (Ag,Bi,Sb)$	
			pallasite (meteoritic)	silvery grey + olive green
			$Fe + $ approx. 5% $(Mg,Fe)_2[SiO_4]$ (olivine)	
			silver	silvery, yellowish, black
			$Ag + Au,Bi,Cu + (Sb)$	
		Sulphide	galena	lead grey metallic
			$PbS + Ag,Cu,Fe,Sb,Zn,Bi$	
			pyrite (various)	golden metallic
			$FeS_2 + Co,Ni,Sb + (Cu,Au,Ag,Zn)$	
			schalenblende	silvery/yellow brown striped
			$ZnS + Mn + (Cu,Sb,Sn,Pb)$	
		Halide	fluorite	transparent, yellow, green, blue, violet
			$CaF_2 + (C,Cl,Fe,Ce,Y)$	
		Oxide	magnetite	black, grey, metallic
			$Fe_3O_4 + Al,Co,Cr,Ni,Ti,V$	
			spinel	red, pink, orange, red-violet
			$MgAl_2O_4 + Fe,Cu,Cr,Mn,Zn$	
		Lattice silicate	analcite	grey, reddish, green
			$Na[AlSi_2O_6] \cdot H_2O + K,Ca,Mg + (OH,P)$	
			hauyne	dark blue, green-blue, yellow
			$(Na,Ca)_{8-4}[(SO_4)_{2-1}/(AlSiO_4)_6]$	
			sodalite	dark blue
			$Na_8[Cl_2/(AlSiO_4)_6] + Be,K,Mg$	
	II	Sulphide	galenite	lead grey, metallic
			$PbS + Ag,Cu,Fe,Sb,Zn,Bi$	
			pyrite (cubes)	golden metallic
			$FeS_2 + Co,Ni,Sb + (Cu,Au,Ag,Zn)$	
			boji stones	grey through brown
			$FeS_2 + FeOOH \cdot n\,H_2O$	
		Oxide	cuprite	red through grey
			$Cu_2O + Fe$	
		Halide	halite (salt)	white, pink, brown, blue
			$NaCl + K,Mg + (Mn)$	
		Lattice silicate	analcite	grey, reddish, green
			$Na[AlSi_2O_6] \cdot H_2O + K,Ca,Mg + (OH,P)$	
	III	Natural element	diamond	transparent, pink, yellow, green, blue
			$C_n + (Al,Ca,Cr,Fe,Mg,Mn,Si,Sr,Ti)$	

Sulphide	pyrite (sun)	golden metallic
	$FeS_2 + Co,Ni,Sb + (Cu,Au,Ag,Zn)$	
Oxide	magnetite	black, grey, metallic
	$Fe_3O_4 + Al,Co,Cr,Ni,Ti,V$	
	spinel	red, pink, orange, red-violet
	$MgAl_2O_4 + Fe,Cu,Cr + (Mn,Zn)$	
Island silicate	almandine garnet	red, brown to black
	$Fe_3Al_2(SiO_4)_3 + Ca,Mg,Mn,Ti$	
	andradite garnet	khaki, brown, blackish
	$Ca_3Fe_2(SiO_4)_3 + Al$	
	grossularite garnet	grey, green to pink
	$Ca_3Al_2(SiO_4)_3 + Fe,Mn$	
	hessonite garnet	red, yellow, orange, brown
	$Ca_3(Al,Fe)_2(SiO_4)_3$	
	melanite garnet	black
	$(Ca,Na)_3(Fe,Ti)_2(SiO_4)_3$	
	pyrope garnet	dark red
	$Mg_3Al_2(SiO_4)_3 + Fe,Ti$	
	rhodolite garnet	dark red to red violet
	$(Mg,Fe)_3Al_2(SiO_4)_3 + Ti$	
	spessartite garnet	yellow, reddish brown, brown
	$Mn_3Al_2(SiO_4)_3 + Fe$	
	uvarovite garnet	emerald green
	$Ca_3Cr_2(SiO_4)_3$	
Lattice silicate	lapis lazuli	blue
	$(Na,Ca)_8[(SO_4/S/Cl)_2/(AlSiO_4)_6] + Fe$	

CS	MF	Mineral class	Mineral	Colour
CS	MF		Chemical formula and mineral-forming substance	
TETRAGONAL	I	Phosphate	apatite	grey, yellow, green, blue
			$Ca_5[(F,Cl,OH)/(PO_4)_3]$ + Mg,Mn,Si,Sr	
		Ph./arsenate	nickeline (niccolite)	coppery red, brown, greenish
			NiAs + Co,Fe,Sb,S	
		Ring silicate	aquamarine	green through light blue
			$Be_3Al_2(Si_6O_{18})$ + K,Li,Na + (Fe)	
			beryl	transparent through yellow
			$Be_3Al_2(Si_6O_{18})$ + K,Li,Na	
			bixbite	dark red
			$Be_3Al_2(Si_6O_{18})$ + K,Li,Mn,Na	
			golden beryl	golden yellow
			$Be_3Al_2(Si_6O_{18})$ + K,Li,Na + (Fe,U)	
			heliodor	yellow, green to blue-green
			$Be_3Al_2(Si_6O_{18})$ + K,Li,Na,Fe	
			morganite	pink
			$Be_3Al_2(Si_6O_{18})$ + K,Li,Na + (Cu,Mn,Ni)	
			emerald	emerald green
			$Be_3Al_2(Si_6O_{18})$ + K,Li,Na + (Cr)	
			sugilite	violet
			$(K,Na)_2/(Fe,Ti)_2(Li,Al)_3[Si_{12}O_{30}]$	
	II	Sulphide	covellite	blackish blue
			CuS + Fe + (Ag,Pb,Se)	
		Phosphate	apatite	green, blue
			$Ca_5[(F,Cl,OH)/(PO_4)_3]$ + Mg,Mn,Si,Sr	
			pyromorphite	white, red, brown, orange, green
			$Pb_5[Cl/(PO_4)_3]$ + Ca,As + (Cr,V)	
		Ph./vanadate	vanadinite	brown, orange, yellow
			$Pb_5[Cl/(VO_4)_3]$ + P + (Zn)	
	III	Ring silicate	emerald	emerald green
			$Be_3Al_2(Si_6O_{18})$ + K,Li,Na + (Cr)	

CF	MF	Mineral class	Mineral	Colour
			Chemical formula and mineral-forming substance	
	I	Natural elements	bismuth	silvery white, yellowish, coloured
			$Bi + (Fe,S,Sb)$	
		Sulphide	proustite	dark red, cinnabar red
			$Ag3AsS_3 + Sb + (Co,Ni,Pb,Zn)$	
		Oxide	hematite	grey metallic, powder: red
			$Fe_2O_3 + Mg,Ti + (Al,Cr,Mn,Si,H_2O)$	
			oolite	brown with red speckles
			$Fe_2O_3 + FeOOH$	
			ruby	red
			$Al_2O_3 + Cr,Ti$	
			sapphire	transparent, yellow, blue, black
			$Al_2O_3 + Fe,Ti$	
		Oxide, quartz	agate	grey blue, brown, red, yellow
			$SiO_2 + Al,Ca,Fe,Mn$	
			amethyst	violet
			$SiO_2 + (Al,Fe,Ca,Mg,Li,Na)$	
			ametrine	violet and yellow zones
			$SiO_2 + (Al,Fe,Ca,Mg,Li,Na)$	
			aventurine	green iridescent
			$SiO_2 + KAl_2[(OH,F)_2/AlSi_3O_{10}] + (Cr)$	
			dendritic quartz	white with moss-like inclusions
			$SiO_2 + Fe,Mn,Si$	
			rock crystal	transparent
			SiO_2	
			blue quartz	light to dark blue
			$SiO_2 + TiO_2$	
			cacoxenite	violet with golden yellow inclusions
			$SiO_2 + FeOOH + (Al,Fe,Ca,Mg,Li,Na)$	
			chalcedony, blue	light blue
			SiO_2	
			chalcedony, dendritic	light blue, black inclusions
			$SiO_2 + Mn,O$	
			citrine	yellow
			$SiO_2 + (Al,Fe,Ca,Mg,Li,Na)$	
			falcon's eye	blue black
			$SiO_2 + Na_2(Mg,Fe,Al)_5(OH/Si_4O_{11})_2$	
			agate, fire	brown, coloured iridescent
			$SiO_2 + SiO_2 (opal) + Fe$	
			hematite quartz	transparent with red speckles
			$SiO_2 + Fe_2O_3$	
			carnelian	brown, red, orange, yellow
			$SiO_2 + (Fe,O,OH)$	
			onyx	black
			$SiO_2 + C,Fe$	
			prase, crystalline	leek green
			$SiO_2 + Ca_2(Mg,Fe)_5[(OH,F)/Si_4O_{11}]_2$	
			smoky quartz	light to dark brown
			$SiO_2 + (Al,Li,Na)$	

TRIGONAL

	Oxide, quartz (continued)	rose quartz	pink
		SiO_2 + Na,Al,Fe,Ti + (Ca,Mg,Mn)	
		rutile	transparent with yellow/red inclusions
		SiO_2 + TiO_2	
		sard	brown
		SiO_2 + (Fe,O,OH)	
		sardonyx	black-white-reddish brown
		SiO_2 + C + (Fe,O,OH)	
		snow quartz	white
		SiO_2	
		tourmaline quartz	transparent with black inclusions
		SiO_2 + $NaFe_3(Al,Fe)_6[(OH)_4(BO_3)_2Si_6O_{18}]$	
	Oxide/silicate	granite (rock)	speckles of combinations of colours with white, red, brown, black
		SiO_2 + (Ca,K,Na)$[AlSi_3O_8]$ + $(K,Mg,Fe,Mn)_{2-3}[(OH,F)_2/(Al,Fe)Si_3O_{10}]$	
		rhyolite (rock) (leopard skin and orbicular jasper)	white, grey, greenish, reddish with clearly visible inclusions
		SiO_2 + (Ca,K,Na)$[AlSi_3O_8]$ + $Ca_2NaK(Mg,Fe)_3(Fe,Al)_2[(O,OH,F)_2/Al_2Si_6O_{22}]$	
	Carbonate	calcite	white, pink, yellow, green, blue
		$CaCO_3$ + Fe,Mn + (Cu,Pb,Sr)	
		dolomite	brown, red, white
		$CaMg(CO_3)_2$ + Fe,Mn + (Pb,Zn,S)	
	Island silicate	phenacite	white, pink, yellow, green
		Be_2SiO_4 + (Al)	
	Ring silicate	benitoite	blue
		$BaTi[Si_3O_9]$ + Na,Fe	
		tourmaline (general)	all colours
		$(Na,K,Li,Ca)(Li,Mg,Fe,Mn,Al)_3$ $(Al,Fe,Cr,Ti,V)_6[(OH,O,F)_4(BO_3)_2Si_6O_{18}]$	
		tourmaline, dravite	brown, yellow, green, grey
		$NaMg_3(Al,Fe,Cr)_6[(OH,O,F)_4(BO_3)_2Si_6O_{18}]$	
		tourmaline, elbaite	all colours, incl. transparent
		$Na(Li,Al)_3Al_6[(OH,O,F)_4(BO_3)_2Si_6O_{18}]$	
		tourmaline, indicolite	blue
		$Na(Fe,Li,Al)_3(Fe,Al)_6[(OH,O,F)_4(BO_3)_2Si_6O_{18}]$	
		tourmaline, rubellite	red, pink
		$Na(Li,Mn,Al)_3Al_6[(OH,O,F)_4(BO_3)_2Si_6O_{18}]$	
		tourmaline, verdelite	green
		$Na(Li,Al)_3(Al,Cr,V)_6[(OH,O,F)_4(BO_3)_2Si_6O_{18}]$	
		tourmaline, schorl	black
		$NaFe_3(Al,Fe)_6[(OH,O,F)_4(BO_3)_2Si_6O_{18}]$	
		tourmaline, uvite	light to dark brown
		$CaMg_3(Al_5Mg)[(OH,O,F)_4(BO_3)_2Si_6O_{18}]$	
II	Oxide	hematite	grey metallic, powder: red
		Fe_2O_3 + Mg,Ti + (Al,Cr,Mn,Si,H_2O)	
	Oxide, quartz	aventurine	green iridescent
		SiO_2 + $KAl_2[(OH,F)_2/AlSi_3O_{10}]$ + (Cr)	

157

Oxide, quartz (continued)	chalcedony, blue	light blue rosettes
	SiO_2	
	chalcedony, copper	blue-green, copper inclusions
	$SiO_2 + Cu + (Cu)$	
	chalcedony, pink	pink, pinkish violet
	$SiO_2 + (Mn)$	
	chalcedony, red	dark red
	$SiO_2 + Fe$	
	chrysoprase	apple green
	$SiO_2 + (Ni)$	
	heliotrope	green with red/yellow inclusions
	$SiO_2 + Al,Fe,Mg,OH,Si$	
	jasper, yellow	yellow, sandy, brown
	$SiO_2 + Fe,O,OH$	
	jasper, green	light to dark green
	$SiO_2 + Fe,Si$	
	jasper, red	brick red
	$SiO_2 + Fe,O$	
	mookaite	red-yellow-beige marbled
	$SiO_2 + Fe,O,OH$	
	moss agate	light blue with green inclusions
	$SiO_2 + Al,Ca,F,Fe,K,Mg,Na,OH,Si$	
	pietersite	blue-black/brown speckles
	$SiO_2 + Na_2(Mg,Fe,Al)_5(OH/Si_4O11)_2$	
	agate, pyrite	grey with yellow inclusions
	$SiO_2 + FeS_2 + Co,Ni,Sb + (Cu,Au,Ag,Zn)$	
	fossilized wood	brown, reddish, yellow
	$SiO_2 + C,Fe,O,OH$	
Carbonate	calcite	white, pink, yellow, green, blue
	$CaCO_3 + Fe,Mn + (Co,Pb,Sr)$	
	dolomite	brown, red, white
	$CaMg(CO_3)_2 + Fe,Mn + (Pb,Zn,S)$	
	coral	white, red, brown, black
	$CaCO_3 + Fe$	
	magnesite	white, grey, yellow, brown
	$MgCO_3 + Ca,Fe,Mn$	
	nickel magnesite	light green
	$MgCO_3 + Ni,Ca,Fe,Mn$	
	Paua shell, mother-of-pearl	white, coloured iridescent
	$CaCO_3$	
	pearl	silvery white
	$CaCO_3$	
	rhodochrosite	raspberry red to pink
	$MnCO_3 + Ca,Fe,Zn$	
	septaria	yellow in grey
	$CaCO_3$ (calcite cysts in clay-bearing rock)	
	siderite	yellow, brown, black
	$FeCO_3 + Al,C,Ca,Mg,Mn,Zn$	
	smithsonite	white, yellow, green, blue
	$ZnCO_3 + Ca,Cu,Fe,Mg,Mn,Pb$	

		Ring silicate	dioptase $Cu_6(Si_6O_{18}) \cdot 6\,H_2O$	dark green
△	III	Oxide	hematite $Fe_2O_3 + Mg,Ti + (Al,Cr,Mn,Si,H_2O)$	grey metallic; powder: red
			ruby $Al_2O_3 + Cr,Ti$	red
			sapphire $Al_2O_3 + Fe,Ti$	transparent, yellow, blue, black
			tiger iron $Fe_2O_3 + SiO_2 + Al,Na,Fe,Mg$	grey/red/yellow striped
		Oxide, quartz	aventurine $SiO_2 + KAl_2[(OH,F)_2/AlSi_3O_{10}] + (Cr)$	green iridescent
			golden quartz $SiO_2 + FeOOH$	yellow-brown
			prase, rough $SiO_2 + Ca_2(Mg,Fe)_5[(OH,F)/Si_4O_{11}]_2$	leek green
			tiger's eye $SiO_2 + FeOOH$	golden brown
		Carbonate	marble (rock) $CaCo_3 + Fe,M$	white, yellowish, brown, black

CS	MF	Mineral class	Mineral Chemical formula and mineral-forming substances	Colour
TETRAGONAL	I	Sulphide	bornite Cu_5FeS_4 + Ag	red-brown, coloured swirled
			chalcopyrite $CuFeS_2$ + (Ag,Au)	brown, yellow, black metallic
		Oxide	cassiterite SnO_2 + Fe,Mn,Ti,Zr	brown to black
			pyrolusite MnO_2 + Fe,Si	iron grey
			rutile TiO_2 + Cr,Fe,Sn	red, yellow, brown, black
		Sulphide/ wolframate	scheelite $Ca(WO_4)$ + Cu,Pb	grey, yellow, greenish
		Island silicate	zircon $ZrSiO_4$ + Al,Ca,Fe,P,Y,Ce,Hf,Th,U	red, orange, brown, yellow
		Phyllo or sheet silicate	apophyllite $KCa_4[F/(Si_4O_{10})_2] \cdot 8\,H_2O$	white, yellowish, blue-green
		Lattice silicate	scapolite (mineral group) $(Na,Ca)_8[(Cl_2,SO_4,CO_3)_{1-2}/Al_{1-2}(Si_{2-3}O_8)_6]$ + F,OH	colourless, grey, rarely red, straw yellow, green, grey-blue
	II	Sulphide/ molybdate	wulfenite $Pb(MoO_4)$ + Ca + (Cu,Cr,Mg,V)	yellow to orange
	III	Sulphide	chalcopyrite $CuFeS_2$ + (Ag,Au)	brown, yellow, black metallic
		Group silicate	vesuvianite (idocrase) $Ca_{10}(Mg,Fe)_2Al_4[(OH)_4/(SiO_4)_5/(Si_2O_7)_2]$ + B,Be,Co,Cr,Cu,F,Li,K,Na,Ni,Mn,Sr,Ti,Z	grey, brown, green, yellow, rarely blue, red, pink

CS	MF	Mineral class	Mineral	Colour
			Chemical formula and mineral-forming substance	
	I	Natural element	sulphur	yellow, greenish, brownish
			S_8 + Al,C,Se,Te,Tl	
		Sulphide	antimonite	grey
			Sb_2S_3 + Fe,Cu,Pb,Zn + (Co,Ag,Au)	
			marcasite	grey, yellow with green tinge
			FeS_2 + Co,Ni,Sb + (Cu,Au,Ag,Zn)	
		Halide	atacamite	light green, blackish green
			$Cu_2(OH)_3Cl$	
		Oxide	chrysoberyl	brown, yellow, greenish
			Al_2BeO_4 + Ti	
		Carbonate	aragonite, crystalline white, brown	
			$CaCO_3$ + Fe,Mn,Pb,Sr,Zn	
		Phosphate	wavellite	greenish white
			$Al_3[(OH)_3/(PO_4)_2] \cdot 5\ H_2O$ + Fe,V,Zn	
		Sulphate	barite	transparent, red, brown, blueish
			$BaSO_4$ + Ca,Pb,Sr + (Fe)	
		Island silicate	andalusite	red, pink, yellow, green, brown
			$Al_2[O/SiO_4]$ + Ca,Cr,Fe,K,Mg,Mn,Ti	
			chiastolite	brown, grey with black cross
			$Al_2[O/SiO_4]$ + C,Ca,Cr,Fe,K,Mg,Mn,Ti	
			dumortierite	blue, violet-blue, brown
			$(AlFe)_7[O_3/BO_3/(SiO_4)_3]$ + Mn	
			peridot, olivine,	colourless, bottle green,
			chrysolite	olive green, yellow-green
			$(Mg,Fe)_2[SiO_4]$ + Al,Ca,Mn,Ni,Co,Cr,Ti	
			topaz	transparent, brownish, light blue
			$Al_2[F_2/SiO_4]$ + OH + (Cr,Mn)	
			topaz, Imperial	golden yellow
			$Al_2[F_2/SiO_4]$ + P	
		Group silicate	prehnite	colourless, greenish
			$Ca_2Al[(OH)_2/AlSi_3O_{10}]$	
		Chain silicate	bronzite	bronze colour
			$(Mg,Fe)_2[Si_2O_6]$ + Al,Ca,Mn,Ni	
			enstatite	colourless, greyish white, greenish
			$Mg_4[Si_2O_6]_2$ + Al,Ca,Fe,Mn,Ni	
		Ring silicate	cordierite, iolite	blue/yellow interchanging
			$(Mg,Fe)_2Al_3[AlSi_5O_{18}]$ + Mn,Na,Zr	
		Lattice silicate	danburite	colourless, beige
			$Ca[B_2Si_2O_8]$	
			natrolite	white, reddish, yellow, green
			$Na_2[Al_2Si_3O_{10}] \cdot 2\ H_2O$ + Ca,K,Fe	
			stellerite	white, grey, yellowish, brown
			$Ca[Al_2Si_7O_{18}] \cdot 7\ H_2O$ + Fe,Na	
	II	Natural element	sulphur	yellow, greenish, brownish
			S_8 + Al,C,Se,Te,Tl	
		Sulphide	marcasite	grey, yellow with green tinge
			FeS_2 + Co,Ni,Sb + (Cu,Au,Ag,Zn)	
		Oxide	psilomelane	black, silver
			$(Ba,Mn)_3(O,OH)_6Mn_8O_{16}$ + K,Ca,Sr,Pb	

RHOMBIC

	Carbonate	aragonite, banded	pink, yellow, green, brown
		$CaCO_3$ + Fe,Mn,Pb,Sr,Zn	
		cerussite	white, grey, black
		$PbCO_3$ + S,Sr,Zn	
	Carbonate/borate	sinhalite	yellow brown, greenish brown
		$Mg(Al,Fe)[BO_4]$ + Mn	
	Phosphate	variscite	colourless, grey, green
		$AlPO_4 \cdot 2 H_2O$ + Cu,Fe,Mg	
	Phosphate/ arsenate	adamite	yellow, green, pink to violet
		$Zn_2[OH/AsO_4]$ + Co,Cu	
	Sulphate	angelite/anhydrite	white, grey, light blue
		$CaSO_4$ + (Sr)	
		celestine	white, light blue
		$SrSO_4$ + (Ca)	
	Group silicate	hemimorphite	grey, yellow, brown, green, blue
		$Zn_4[(OH)_2/Si_2O_7] \cdot H_2O$ + Al,Ca,Fe,Mg,Ti	
	Phyllo or sheet silicate	sepiolite	white, beige
		$Mg [(OH)_2Si_6O_{15}] \cdot 2 H_2O$ + 4 H_2O + Fe,Na	
III	Oxide	alexandrite	green, red in artificial light
		Al_2BeO_4 + Cr,Ti	
		chrysoberyl	brown, yellow, greenish
		Al_2BeO_4 + Ti	
	Phosphate	purpurite	pink, purple, violet
		$(Mn,Fe)PO_4$ + Li,Be,Al	
	Island silicate	sillimanite	grey, light brown, pale green
		$Al[AlSiO_5]$ + Ca,Cr,Fe,K,Mg,Mn,Ti	
		staurolite	brown
		$FeAl_4[O/OH/SiO_4]_2$ + Fe,Mg,Mn,Ti	
	Group silicate	tanzanite	blue, brown
		$Ca_2(Al,Fe)_3[O/OH/SiO_4/Si_2O_7]$ + Mg,Sr	
		thulite	reddish, pink
		$(Ca,Mn)_2Al_3[O/OH/SiO_4/Si_2O_7]$ + Mg,Cr	
		zoisite	green
		$Ca_2Al_3[O/OH/SiO_4/Si_2O_7]$ + Mg,Cr,Sr,V	
	Ring silicate	cordierite, iolite	blue/yellow interchanging
		$(Mg,Fe)_2Al_3[AlSi_5O_{18}]$ + Mn,Na,Zr	

CS	MF	Mineral class	Mineral	Colour
			Chemical formula and mineral-forming substance	
	I	Sulphide	jamesonite	grey
			$Pb_4FeSb_6S_{14}$ + Cu,Ag	
		Phosphate	brasilianite	yellow-green
			$NaAl_3[(OH)_2/PO_4]_2$	
			lazulite	blue
			$(Mg,Fe)Al_2[(OH)_2/PO_4]_2$ + Ca	
		Sulphate	creedite	colourless
			$Ca_3Al_2[(F,OH)_{10}/SO_4] \cdot 2\ H_2O$	
		Island silicate	sphene, titanite	brown, red, pink, yellow, green
			$CaTi[O/SiO_4]$ + Al,Cr,Fe,Mg,Mn,Sn,Ti,Zr	
		Group silicate	epidote	pistachio green, black, grey, rarely yellow
			$Ca_2(Fe,Al)Al_2[O/OH/SiO_4/Si_2O_7]$ + K,Mg,Mn,Sr,Ti	
		Chain silicate	augite	black, brown, green
			$(Ca,Mg,Fe^{2+},Fe^{3+},Ti,Al)_2[(Si,Al)_2O_6]$	
			hiddenite	yellow-green
			$LiAl[Si_2O_6]$ + Ca,Cr,Mg,Na	
			hornblende	black, brown, dark green
			$Ca_2(Na,K)(Mg,Fe)_3(Fe,Al)_2[(O,OH,F)_2/$ $Al_2Si_6O_{22}]$ + Mn,Ti	
			kunzite	pink to pink violet
			$LiAl[Si_2O_6]$ + Ca,Mg,Mn,Na	
			actinolite	green
			$Ca_2(Mg,Fe)_5(Si_8O_{22})(OH,F)_4$+ OH,F	
		Ring silicate	chrysocolla	green to turquoise
			$CuSiO_3 \cdot 2\ H_2O$ + Al,Fe,P	
		Phyllo or sheet silicate	biotite	black, grey, brown
			$K(Mg,Fe)_3[(OH,F)_2/AlSi_3O_{10}]$ + Mn,Na	
			euclase	colourless
			$AlBe[OH/SiO_4]$	
			fuchsite	light green
			$KAl_2[(OH,F)_2/AlSi_3O_{10}]$ + Ca,Cr,Fe,Na,Ti	
			lepidolite	pink to pink violet
			$KLi_2Al[(OH,F)_2/Si_4O_{10}]$ + Ca,Fe,Mg,Mn	
			muscovite	white, colourless
			$KAl_2[(OH,F)_2/AlSi_3O_{10}]$ + Ca,Fe,Na,Ti	
		Lattice silicate	adularia	transparent, white
			$K[AlSi_3O_8]$ + Na	
			golden orthoclase	golden yellow
			$K[AlSi_3O_8]$ + Na,Fe,Ba	
			heulandite	white, yellow, brick red (Fe)
			$Ca[Al_2Si_7O_{18}] \cdot 6\ H_2O$ + Fe,Na,Sr	
			moonstone	white, brownish, blueish
			$K[AlSi_3O_8]$ + Na,Fe,Ba	
			petalite	colourless, pink
			$Li[AlSi_4O_{10}]$ + Na,Ca	
			scolecite	colourless
			$Ca[Al_2Si_3O_{10}] \cdot 3\ H_2O$ + K,Na	
			stilbite	white, yellowish, reddish
			$Ca[Al_2Si_7O_{18}] \cdot 7\ H_2O$ + Fe,Na	

163

	Carbonate	azurite	azure blue
		$Cu_3[(OH)_2/(CO_3)_2]$	
		azurite-malachite	blue/green marbled
		$Cu_3[(OH)_2/(CO_3)_2] + Cu_2[(OH)_2/CO_3]$	
		malachite	light to dark green
		$Cu_2[(OH)_2/CO_3] + H_2O + (Ca,Fe)$	
II	Phosphate	vivianite	green, blue, brown
		$Fe_3(PO_4)_2 \cdot 8\,H_2O + Ca,Mg,Mn$	
	Phosphate/	erythrine	peach blossom red
	arsenate	$Co_3[AsO_4]_2 \cdot 8\,H_2O + Bi,Ni$	
	Sulphate	gypsum	transparent, grey, yellowish
		$CaSO_4 \cdot 2\,H_2O + (Al,C)$	
		sand rose	brown rosettes
		$CaSO_4 \cdot 2\,H_2O + BaSO_4 + SiO_2$	
	Sulphates/	crocoite	red, yellow
	chromate	$Pb[CrO_4] + S,Zn$	
	Island silicate	howlite	white, ivory
		$Ca_2[(BOOH)_5/SiO_4]$	
III	Group silicate	epidote (unakite)	pistachio green, black, grey, rarely yellow
		$Ca_2(Fe,Al)Al_2[O/OH/SiO_4/Si_2O_7] + K,Mg,Mn,Sr,Ti$	
	Chain silicate	actinolite	green
		$Ca_2(Mg,Fe)_5(Si_8O_{22})(OH,F)_4 + OH,F$	
		augite	black, brown, green
		$(Ca,Mg,Fe^{2+},Fe^{3+},Ti,Al)_2[(SiAl)_2O_6]$	
		diopside	black, grey, green
		$CaMg[Si_2O_6] + Fe,Mn,Ti,V$	
		chromium diopside	dark green
		$CaMg[Si_2O_6] + Cr,Fe,Mn,Ti,V$	
		chloromelanite	dark green
		$Na_2CaMgFeAl[(Si_2O_6)_3]$	
		hornblende	black, brown, dark green
		$Ca_2(Na,K)(Mg,Fe)_3(Fe,Al)_2[(O,OH,F)_2/Al_2Si_6O_{22}] + Mn,Ti$	
		jadeite	whitish, green
		$NaAl[Si_2O_6] + Ca,Mg,Fe$	
		lavender jade	lilac, violet
		$NaAl[Si_2O_6] + Ca,Fe,Mg,Mn$	
		nephrite	green
		$Ca_2(Mg,Fe)_5(Si_8O_{22})(OH,F)_4 + OH,F$	
	Phyllo or	biotite lenses	black, grey, brown
	sheet silicate	$K(Mg,Fe,Mn)_3[(OH,F)_2/(Al,Fe)Si_3O_{10}]$	
		charoite	grey, violet, pink
		$(Ca,Na)_4(K,Sr,Ba)_2[(OH,F)_2Si_9O_{22}] \cdot H_2O$	
		lepidolite	pink to red violet
		$KLi_2Al[(OH,F)_2/Si_4O_{10}] + Ca,Fe,Mg,Mn$	
		serpentine	green, yellow green, silvery
		$Mg_6[(OH)_8/Si_4O_{10}] + Al,Cr,Fe,Mn,Ni$	
		verdelite	green
		$Mg_6[(OH)_8/Si_4O_{10}] + Al,Cr,Fe,Na,Ti$	

CS	MF	Mineral class	Mineral	Colour
			Chemical formula and mineral-forming substance	
TRICLINIC	I	Chain silicate	larimar, pectolite	white, light blue
			$NaCa_2[OH/Si_3O_8]$ + Fe,Mn	
		Lattice silicate	albite	white, reddish, greenish, blueish
			$Na[AlSi_3O_8]$ + Ca,Ba,K,Fe,Sr	
			amazonite	blue-green, green
			$K[AlSi_3O_8]$ + Cu	
			labradorite	grey-green, iridescent colours
			$Na[AlSi_3O_8]Ca[Al_2Si_2O_8]$ + Fe,K,Ba,Sr	
			spectrolite	black, iridescent colours
			$Na[AlSi_3O_8]Ca[Al_2Si_2O_8]$ + Fe,K,Ba,Sr	
			sunstone	orange brown iridescent
			$Na[AlSi_8O_8]Ca[Al_2Si_2O_8]$ + Fe	
		Silicate (diverse)	porphyrite	black, grey, reddish, brown, with green or light coloured speckles
			$Na[AlSi_3O_8]Ca[Al_2Si_2O_8]$ + SiO_2 + $Ca_2NaK(Mg,Fe)_3(Fe,Al)_2[(O,OH,F)_2/Al_2Si_6O_{22}]$	
	II	Carbonate/ borate	ulexite	white
			$NaCaB_5O_9$ + K,Mg	
		Phosphate	turquoise	green through turquoise colour
			$CuAl_6[(OH)_2/PO_4]_4 \cdot 4\,H_2O$ + Fe	
		Sulphate	chalcanthite	blue
			$CuSO_4 \cdot 5\,H_2O$ + Co,Fe,Mg,V,Zn	
		Lattice silicate	amazonite	blue-green, green
			$K[AlSi_3O_8]$ + Cu	
	III	Island silicate	disthene, kyanite	blue, blue-grey
			$Al_2[O/SiO_4]$ + Ca,Cr,Fe,K,Mg,Ti	
		Chain silicate	rhodonite	pink
			$CaMn_4[Si_5O_{15}]$ + Al,Ca,Fe,Li,K,Na	
			sunstone	orange-brown iridescent
			$Na[AlSi_3O_8]Ca[Al_2Si_2O_8]$ + Fe	
		Lattice silicate	amazonite	blue-green, green
			$K[AlSi_3O_{81}$	

CS	MF	Mineral class	Mineral	Colour
			Chemical formula and mineral-forming substance	
AMORPHOUS	I	Oxide	natural glass	light blue, greenish
			$SiO_2 + Al,Ca,K,Na,Fe$	
			obsidian	black, grey, brown, silvery or coloured iridescent
			$SiO_2 + Fe_2O_3 + H_2O + Al,C,Ca,K,Na,Fe$	
			opal, fire opal	red, orange, yellow
			$SiO_2 + H_2O + Fe$	
			opal, hyalite	transparent
			$SiO_2 + H_2O$	
	II	Oxide	flint	black, grey, red, brown
			SiO_2 (opal) $+ SiO_2$ (chalcedony) $+ Fe$	
			girasol	transparent
			SiO_2 (opal) $+ SiO_2$ (chalcedony) $+ Ti$	
			opal, boulder	blue, coloured iridescent
			$SiO_2 + H_2O + Ca,Fe$	
			opal, chrysopal	green, blue-green
			$SiO_2 + H_2O + Cu$	
			opal, jasper opal	red, brown
			$SiO_2 + H_2O + Fe$	
			opal, milk opal	white, coloured iridescent
			$SiO_2 + H_2O + Ca,Mg$	
			opal, prase opal	green
			$SiO_2 + H_2O + Ni$	
			opal, pink opal	pink
			$SiO_2 + H_2O + Mn$	
			opal, black	black, coloured iridescent
			$SiO_2 + H_2O + C,Fe$	
			opalized wood	red, yellow, brown
			$SiO_2 + H_2O + C,Ca,Fe,Mg$	
			opalite	brown, yellow, green
			$SiO_2 + H_2O + Fe,Ni$	
		Organic stones	amber	white, golden yellow, brown, red
			$C_{10}H_{16}O + S$ (simplified!)	
			jet	black
			C (Hydrocarbons)	
	III	Oxide	moldavite	bottle green
			$SiO_2 + Al,Ca,Fe,K,Na$	
			tektite	black
			$SiO_2 + Al,Ca,Fe,K,Na$	

To identify the right mineral, I recommend working through the tables from left to right. First, identify the individual lifestyle (column 1) and the present general situation (column 2) independently of the problems that currently exist. This will immediately and clearly show you the choice of possible healing minerals and crystals. The fundamental characteristic feature of the present problem will then lead you to the right mineral class (column 3). Does something need dissolving, transforming, fortifying or stabilizing? The minerals that are then left to choose from can be further differentiated by looking at the mineral-forming substances from which they are formed (column 4). Then, by considering the colour (column 5), you will be able to home in on the right choice of mineral.

The mineral chosen in this way should then be used, if possible, with direct skin contact (see Chapter 2.4, *Practical applications*) and worn for as long as it takes to notice a clear change in the general situation, the lifestyle, a solution to the existing problem, or an improvement in the case of illness. There may be some 'initial aggravation' or 'worsening', but this will usually last for no more than one to three days, rarely a week.

If there is no improvement or initial worsening goes beyond an acceptable degree or beyond the specified time limit, the analysis should be rechecked and corrected, if necessary. Here we recommend the basic principle 'success through minimal change', which means working through the tables 'backwards', from right to left. Will the same mineral, but of a different colour, result in the desired success (column 5)? Are there varieties or related minerals with a different content of mineral-forming substances (column 4)? Does the solution of the problem require a basically different characteristic (column 3, mineral class)? Was the life situation analysed properly (column 1)? If you are basically satisfied with your analysis, then, as a rule, only minor details will need altering. In extreme cases success can be achieved with the same mineral with a slightly different appearance or from a different location.

This is where we meet the boundaries of the analytical art of healing with crystals and minerals. The basic principles described here should lead to the right mineral, but choosing exactly the right stone is often a matter that is not accessible to rational thought or logic.

Trust in your own 'instinct', or the feeling you have for the person for whom the stone is intended. Choose exactly the one that 'appeals' to you, independently of its shape, beauty or quality. And please note that a strong antipathy for a particular crystal or stone registers a 'response' to it just as much as a strong attraction does. A 'neutral stone', one that leaves you completely cold, should be ignored, as should those that do not interest you or that you might even overlook. In cases of uncertainty, simply choose the right one with your eyes closed – or use a dowsing procedure or kinesiology if you are familiar with these techniques.

In healing, intuition is just as important as rational thinking and logic. You can only use logic to analyse something on which you already have information and of which you are aware. Intuition will often take you that final step on the way. This is the reason why the next chapter is dedicated to 'intuitive' healing with crystals.

The intuitive art of healing with crystals

Choosing your healing crystals

Before you start to read this chapter, I should like to invite you to do a little test. All you will need for this is a handful of minerals (about 15–20) and a helper. Once you have both, proceed as follows.

Spread out the minerals in front of you on a table top or on the floor. Now, spontaneously pick one that you like. Do not evaluate, do not think about what you are doing or about its name, simply look and take one.

You have just intuitively chosen your first healing crystal: you chose it with your eyes.

Next, close your eyes and ask your helper to rearrange the stones so that you no longer know where each one is. Now pass your left hand, eyes closed, across the stones spread out before you. Do this for as long as it takes for you to feel an impulse to pick one up. Do not hesitate, just do it!

Now you have chosen your second healing crystal intuitively: you chose it with your hand.

Now ask your helper to call out individual keywords that match any of the stones lying in front of you, words that refer to the properties and healing powers of the stones. There should never be any indication which keyword goes with which stone. If a keyword is called out that spontaneously means something to you, or stirs something within (whether pleasant or unpleasant), say so immediately and let your helper give you the stone to which the keyword fits.

In this way, you will have intuitively chosen your third healing crystal. It was chosen by means of a word.

Next, ask your helper to lay out the stones in a row but invisible to you (for example, behind a screen of some kind). Then let your helper tell you how many stones have been laid in the row, and you then spontaneously name a number between one and the total number of stones. Your helper should then pass you the stone that is lying in the row in the position you have chosen.

In this way, you will have intuitively chosen the fourth crystal: it was chosen 'at random'.

These four crystals will now represent your personal healing crystals at this moment in time. Each of these crystals will, of course, represent a different quality, another facet of yourself as each method of choosing includes or excludes certain areas.

Choosing with your eyes: the soul stone

When we look at things, we also immediately make comparisons. Our subconscious will always compare a visual impression with old memories and experiences. This is done with lightning speed, much faster than you would be able to do consciously. Just think what is happening when you walk along a path. You are constantly taking in impressions, and you are recognizing things you see: trees, stones, flowers, grasses, birds, and so on. Now imagine you had to walk along the same path and call out by name everything you met. Everything! You would only manage a few metres an hour!

This demonstrates the incredible faculties of our subconscious or our soul. The soul is our inner world of images (our 'inner world') that has stored all impressions and experiences. The soul perceives everything, nothing is lost – something we are made conscious of through unexpected memories of things we had thought we had forgotten long ago. During this process, every new impression is not just simply stored away but is compared, similarities are recorded and assigned. The new impression will be carefully sorted and stored.

This process will also automatically stir up old memories: the feelings and images connected with past experiences will emerge. This is the reason why we feel attractions or antipathies to certain things, people or situations. If there exists an early, similar experience that we felt was positive, this will automatically create sympathy (attraction, affection). Conversely, if the present experience reminds us of something that was negative, we will experience antipathy (revulsion, disgust). Our subconscious will always compare and find similarities! It will string similar experiences together and then conclude that the outcome of what is happening now will be similar to something that happened in the past.

All of this happens almost exclusively in the subconscious. As already described above, we do not think about all this, merely respond accordingly: we trust the one situation and mistrust the other. We avoid certain people and are attracted by others, sometimes we feel quite safe while at other times our 'inner alarm bells' go off! The meaning and purpose of this soul quality is simply – survival. We all learn from experience or we are meant to. The collected experiences of the past and that rapid 'intelligence' (or grasp) of the soul increase our chances of survival. We recognize dangers more quickly, make some mistakes only once and, based on our facility for remembering, we have some bearings by which to steer our lives.

Just imagine that you were only able to remember things that happened within the last 24 hours, and everything previous to that time was forgotten. How would you be able to conduct your life at present? There would be no real opportunity for learning anything at all; no social life; you would not possess a real identity. In addition, the soul controls our unconscious bodily functions and actions. Just think what it would be like to have to drive your car in a fully conscious manner all the time, as you did in your first driving lesson: steering, changing gears, clutch, accelerating, braking, indicating, looking about. You would be continuously occupied and driving would be extremely exhausting. If, however, all these actions are safely 'stored' for further use, you are able to drive 'unconsciously' and your attention is free to concentrate on the traffic.

This means that automatic or instinctive reactions that are not under our conscious control belong to the soul also. The soul is our inner treasure, the sum total of our capabilities that we need to lead our lives. In the soul, all has been collected together that we have brought with us from the past: experiences, events, stories and images that have impressed themselves upon us in one way or another.

This does mean, however, that we have one weak point: some of the images and explanations we have absorbed from others will be wrong, that is, they will not be appropriate to our own experience. As long as we hang on to these, they will keep leading us to wrong conclusions. This is also true for some of the experiences from our childhood, which may no longer be appropriate for our adult lives. Some of our other inner images will weigh heavily on us. They may represent unpleasant experiences and cause negative manifestations in our lives the moment we are (consciously or unconsciously) reminded of them.

Among these are, in particular, all memories connected with pain – traumas (Greek *trauma*, 'wound'). Because everything in our inner soul life is treated in the same way, in situations of extreme stress, serious illness, violent pain, shock, unconsciousness (also under anaesthetic!), under the influence of alcohol, drugs, strong medication or during sleep, the same thing happens: the ability of our reasoning side to differentiate and discriminate is greatly diminished or is switched off altogether. This is not, however, the case for the soul's willingness to perceive and absorb; that will always (!) be retained. This means that all sensory perceptions we are subject to in such moments are treated in the same way.

This can lead to tragic consequences: for example, suppose you fall off your bicycle on a wet road and hit your head so that you are unconscious for a few moments (a 'black-out'). Your subconscious will connect all sensory perception during those moments with pain. The accident is stored away in a kind of formula that reads: pain = wet road (touch) = pedestrians in raincoats (visual) = screeching car brakes (hearing) = traffic fumes (smell) = blood in your mouth (taste). This, in turn, means that all those different perceptions you had during those moments are now connected and perceived as painful. Precisely because you no longer remember all this later on, the 'false' storage process is retained and determines your future life. From now on, wet roads, pedestrians in raincoats, screeching car brakes, traffic fumes and the taste of blood will trigger off the most unpleasant sensations that may even result in spontaneous black-outs – depending on how painful the experience was.

It also means that, in future, you will do everything you can to avoid any of these sensory perceptions: avoiding walking on wet streets, refusing to buy a raincoat, and so on. There may be a useful point in the message 'take care on wet roads', but all the other negatively loaded impressions represent an unnecessary limitation of your actions, and furthermore can produce the risk of making you respond with total panic to similar situations in the future. The reactive responses are quasi-mechanical, being triggered by something from outside (without will or attention). It is precisely this type of response that can often lead us to repeat negative experiences over and over again.

Our souls are our inner treasure and Pandora's box in one. The soul contains dormant experiences that help and support us when we think of them and others that limit us or stop us from using our capabilities and opportunities; some experiences may even be like 'time bombs' that are dangerous to 'touch'. The soul is both a source of power and a battlefield, depending on what images it is fed with.

The crystal you have chosen for your soul with your eyes (it must have triggered a response to some memory, or you would not have chosen it) may tell you different things:

1. It may awaken a memory in you that is supportive and strengthening and is, therefore, like recovery or leisure for you. You will soon feel this by its beneficial effect. Images and memories may increasingly pop up in your dreams. Many (but not all) dreams are first and foremost the soul's image-processing faculty (sorting process), out of which may come revelations, realizations and creative ideas.

2. The stone may endow you with trust in your own inherent capabilities and bring to light again qualities that have been dormant for a long time. In such a case, simply follow those spontaneously appearing inclinations and interests, especially if you know that you used to carry them out successfully in the past.

3. The stone may respond to an unpleasant memory that you have suppressed and may, therefore, churn things up inside you. Again, you will notice this very quickly and the important thing is to accept what is happening and face the emerging feelings and images without blocking them. In this way, the stone may help you to dissolve a 'falsely' stored event or an old misunderstanding. I should like to give you a little help here: in my own experience, only those things that are 'ripe' will come up, or in other words, we are only confronted with things that we are ready and able to handle.

4. The stone may represent something that would be a beneficial experience for you. It may remind you of that holiday you have been meaning to take for ages, or prompt you to remember something that urgently needs seeing to. Allow your soul to experience new images – the stone will show you which ones.

Whichever one of these four possibilities applies, the crystal or stone will help you find out, or you will find out yourself by simply trying it out. Having chosen it visually, it will be sufficient to lay it somewhere where you will look at it often. Or meditate daily with the stone by quietly contemplating it. Just looking at the stone will have an effect...

Choosing with the hand: the stone for your body

The second stone was chosen by you without your being able to see it. The impulse to pick it up came from your own body. Our bodies possess a very finely tuned sensitivity that is always present, even if we are not consciously aware of it. We are very capable of sensing what is good for us and what is not. Depending on our general state at a given moment we will automatically choose things that will help us balance ourselves – in this case a stone that represents a balancing factor for an inner deficiency or excess.

Our entire body works on a range of systems in equilibrium. We absorb nourishment and fluids when we require them and eliminate excess substances or fluids when there is too much of them. Every breath is calculated to take in the necessary oxygen and exhale excess carbon dioxide. If we require warmth, we release it from stored energy (fuels). If we require cooling, we obtain relief by the evaporation of perspiration.

The characteristic feature of a living system is that it is able to keep what it needs for life in a constant state of balance. This means we possess a large number of regulatory mechanisms that keep energy and substances in equilibrium. The metabolism of nutrients, vitamins, mineral substances, hormones, acids and alkaline levels are all regulated with these mechanisms. You could define physical good health as having an organism in a position to maintain an inner equilibrium of all systems at all times.

The harmful habits in our lives – unbalanced diet, stress, overwork, toxins, negative images and thoughts, or spiritual developments that we push at such a rate that our being is not able to adjust to them at the right pace – all these will often upset our inner equilibrium. This will result in a partial failure of our regulatory mechanisms, leading to deficiencies or excesses in the relevant areas of life.

A more balanced lifestyle can help these imbalances to rectify by themselves during the course of time, except that we do not always have that much time. Sometimes, when we refuse to give ourselves this time, perhaps it is because we have already ended up in a life-threatening situation that requires quick action or because we no longer know how to get back to that balanced way of life.

In those cases, it is a good idea to reach for suitable outside sources of help. However, the precise meaning of the expression 'sources of help' is important here. The source should be something that will help us regain our inner equilibrium and not just represent an outer substitute for what is lacking inside. Only by seeing it in this manner will you be able to distinguish between different medications and therapies and decide whether they make sense or are dubious.

In emergencies – I should like to emphasize this here – any form of help that ensures survival is right! The difference between this and a long-term, proper healing of a problem, however, is great. Therapies that provide information, like homeopathy, the Bach flower remedies, aromatherapy or the art we are dealing with here, offer immense advantages. They do not introduce any substances into the body, but instead provide the information needed to give us the means of finding our own inner equilibrium again, thus activating our own self-healing processes.

For this to happen, the information needs to fit the situation exactly. It has to be exactly the right key to open the locked door. The method of finding the right key with an analytical process by reasoning alone has been provided by the previous chapter, *The art of analytical healing with crystals*. Here, we shall be encountering a second, equally valid way that is based on simple laws:

> *We will always look for something 'outside'*
> *that is missing 'inside'!*

This is why, when your eyes are closed, your hand will find you exactly the right stone that will give your body the information it needs. At the precise moment when your hand is close to the stone, the information radiated by the stone will already begin to have an effect. Your body will already be registering the first indications for regaining that inner equilibrium and will receive the impulse 'Grab this!' You can trust it. There is no finer instrument than your body, a fact proven by the numerous methods such as radiaesthesia (dowsing) (Latin *radius*, 'ray', Greek *aisthesis*, 'perception') and kinesiology (the knowledge of movement; Greek *kinesis*, 'movement', *logos*, 'knowledge, teaching'), with the help of which we can repeatedly measure or identify qualities for which no physical measuring instruments exist!

Your body has two fundamental functions: it is your instrument of perception and also the means by which you act in this material world. It is perfectly adapted for these two tasks (remember, it has been evolving for millions of years). Just how perfect it is can be appreciated by noting the feeble attempts of modern science at duplicating its capabilities. Most of what we desire and wish to experience is carried out with this body, so the body stone you have chosen will demonstrate the following possibilities:

1. The stone will encourage your body to heal itself as it helps to regulate a disturbed inner equilibrium. In this case, it may initially cause temporary worsening, but will, in the long term, create a sense of well-being. This means that, to begin with, you will be more conscious of the existing imbalance. By continuing to use the stone (perhaps with short breaks) these temporary worsenings will dissolve by themselves.

2. The stone will help you improve the capabilities of your body. Depending on what is involved, this will occur through an improvement in your ability to perceive or by extending the scope of your actions. Your body will be able to accomplish more than you believe at the moment. With this attitude you will support the influence of the stone most effectively.

3. The stone will put you in touch properly with your own body. This alone will have pain-relieving and healing results but will also lead to your being able to gauge your physical needs better and to understand them. Every instrument, including your body, needs looking after but, unfortunately, we are often inclined to spend more effort on the care of our cars than on our bodies. At least you take your car regularly for servicing, and do not drive it into the ground.

To allow your body stone to unfold its full potential, if possible wear it next to your skin. You may lie down in a quiet moment and allow yourself to feel it working inside. Place it wherever it appears to produce the feeling of greatest well-being. Try out two or three positions if you are not sure, until you have found the right place, and then simply enjoy it!

Choosing via the word : the stone for the intellect

During this process of choosing, you were neither able to see the stone nor touch it, the only connection to it being through the spoken word that stimulated you to choose it. This is not an unusual way of choosing. It happens, for example, if you acquire a stone through reading the information in a book. This is your reasoning making the choice, as it is your reasoning that assigns a certain image to a sequence of sounds. Naturally, your reasoning is not entirely free of inner (spiritual) influences as they will automatically emerge whenever an image conjured up by a specific word appears before our mind's eye.

Still, this choice is a conscious one, compared with choosing visually. Whenever we choose a stone with our eyes, we are not in a position to know which feature or characteristic it was that 'spoke' to us. Perhaps the colour, the shape or was it a finer perception, its aura or similar, something that is just below the threshold of conscious perception? Perhaps we believe we know what it was but it remains a belief, a typical function of the soul.

When choosing via a word, we know what qualities of the stone are addressing us, that is the very ones named, and here we touch on the fundamental quality of reason: the urge for knowledge. While the soul believes that a momentary situation represents a previous one, your reason wants to know for sure. For this, it requires a further instrument the soul does not possess: the ability to discriminate.

The soul always draws parallels and sees things as being the same; your reason is able to do that but also discriminates. It is in a position to define what exactly about a situation is similar to another previous one and what is different. Your reason is the instrument for avoiding 'faulty storage of memories' (as discussed in the section *Choosing with your eyes: the soul stone*) or undoing such a process later by remembering a past experience consciously and analysing it (dissolving, analysing, Greek *ana-lyein*, 'to dissolve'). Your reasoning power is in a position to dissolve equalizing procedures that were incorrectly carried out.

Your reasoning corresponds to your waking state or consciousness. It is able to communicate via language and works with words, thoughts and images. It is important to emphasize this as we use many words for which we have no real inner images! Do you know what the words 'transformer', 'politics', 'index', 'studio', 'assistant' or 'therapist' really mean? Have a look in your dictionary! It is really quite interesting to see what we are jabbering about daily: for example, the word just used – 'interesting' – is from the Latin *interesse*, 'being between things', which means that if you find something interesting, something exists between you and the object you are observing. Did you know that?

With the help of our reasoning powers, we think, which means that we understand and interpret whatever is happening. Your reasoning will not simply recreate past experiences, but instead is able to develop something new out of completely different sources, coming partly from your own experiences and partly from external information. Your reasoning serves to solve problems (Greek *problema*, 'the task, the matter at hand'). Your reason will proceed logically (correct sequence), associatively (spontaneously connecting up different thoughts) or inspirationally (following inspiration). Its thought processes are always perceived, that is, we are conscious of them. It serves as a conscious control over our bodies and our lives.

The problem of reasoning lies in the fact that it has a far lesser capacity to absorb than has our soul and also works much more slowly (think of the example above with the walk along a path). Obviously, the ability to discriminate takes up more time. This makes sense, as different things really do need to be understood first (all the details and connections) before they can be compared with each other. Identifying and sorting by similarities is a much faster process.

If our reasoning does not understand a particular thing it becomes 'hung up'. This means it will focus all its attention on this thing it does not understand, until we either consciously leave it be or define the thing we do not understand for ourselves (Latin *definire*, 'to delimit'), in this way finding an explanation that helps us to distinguish this 'thing' from other things. The more we collect things we have not understood, the more our attention becomes distracted and the more the ability of our reasoning to assimilate is reduced. The best example for this state is that of the 'absent-minded professor'.

This problem can get so out of hand that our reasoning is almost totally switched off, as it is constantly occupied with puzzles it has not solved and is, therefore, unable to pay attention to the present. We also start to become 'reactive', which means we act according to the dictates of our subconscious. Then we have no other option but to deal with these unresolved problems one after the other. Every problem solved, even if it is only the clear definition of a word, helps us regain a piece of consciousness.

Unanswered questions also tend to lead to doubts. As long as two contradictory pieces of information are present, our reasoning will not find peace until it is able to distinguish which piece is correct and which is not. Doubt, therefore, stimulates decision making: either through a logical process of balancing arguments or by trying out. This is the only way to free our reasoning again.

Our reasoning is the instrument for further development of our being. It is, therefore, very important to keep it free for present experiences and also for expanding our consciousness as well as we can. Every form of learning belongs in this category, as learning increases our ability to think and understand. Bearing all this in mind, the reasoning stone you chose by means of a word can have the following meanings.

1. It can serve to increase your consciousness and guide your attention to present matters. The type of stone will show what you need to pay particular attention to. The stone will help you to control your life or your body more consciously. You will find that certain mechanisms and routines can now be changed if you so wish.

2. The stone reflects the way you think and communicate. It also represents your world view, your ideals and your ideas. Often, we are inclined to turn something into an ideal that is particularly distanced from our own reality. The stone you chose will help you to turn your ideal into reality but will, initially, confront you with reality. All this follows the motto: 'Knowing yourself is the first step towards improvement'.

3. The stone can represent a current problem and can help you develop a creative solution. In this case, depending on the stone involved, logical conclusions, chains of ideas or sudden impulsive actions may emerge. In all cases, it will serve to help you understand your situation or it may simply show you which project or possible course of action to embark on consciously.

The reasoning stone serves the flow of information. The best way to encourage its effect is by interacting with it: carry it around with you, gaze at it, meditate with it and – very important – obtain information on its mythological, mineralogical and healing nature. Always approach any information you gather with the following question: 'What do these statements (whether symbolic or real) have to do with my situation, the current problem, my task or my imminent projects?' Use Part 1 of this book, in particular, for this process. You will be inundated with ideas!

Choosing at random: the stone for the spirit

The question is, of course, whether it really is at random, or rather, how does the stone become chosen? To begin with, it is certain that neither the soul (you were unable to see it), nor your body (you did not touch it), nor your reasoning (you were given no clues) interfered with the choosing of this stone. So, it had to be a higher authority that dealt you this stone. This higher authority could be nobody other than yourself!

As you may have already noticed when reading the explanations for the soul, body and reasoning, you are neither your soul (that merely represents your memory store, your world of images), nor are you your body (which is your tool in the material world), nor your reasoning (representing your manner of thinking). So, who are you then?

Like all of us you are a free spirit being, which means that you have a soul, a body and reasoning facilities, but you are in actual fact spirit! You are a creative, non-material being that uses an earthly body in order to be able to act in a material world and have experiences in it. However, your perception and your circle of action and effectiveness go far beyond the framework of your physical body.

Just think about how often you knew things in advance: for example, you knew at the first shrill ring of the telephone who would be at the other end, or you suddenly drove more slowly just before you reached a dangerous spot in heavy traffic, or you suddenly thought intensely of a certain person and did not find out until later what was happening to that person at that precise moment. How often did you ignore a feeling or inner warning and then later said, 'I just knew it!' We do, in fact, perceive a great deal more than would be possible merely through our physical senses. We have many small experiences that confirm again and again that, as spiritual beings, we are not tied to space and time. When I was about sixteen years old, my mother had the embarrassing knack of catching me out whenever I tried to sneak into the house late at night. No matter what time it was, she always woke up when I got home, and this in spite of the fact that I was a master at opening doors silently, and negotiating creaking stairs...

Further proof of our creative faculties as spiritual beings are those statements, or postulates, we are in the habit of making that inevitably come true. A postulate is a firm decision that we sometimes just 'happen' to voice in a certain situation: 'That is bound to work/not work!', 'That's unlucky/lucky!' and so on. Among these are counted all the statements we make about ourselves: 'I'm going to do it!', 'I'm far too clumsy to do that!', 'I'll always be poor!', 'I am a lucky devil!', and many others. If you check these events carefully, you will find you always made a relevant postulate just before any kind of success or supposed failure. A 'supposed' failure, because even a negative postulate is successful in the sense that it does happen (so success or failure is that which follows a postulate).

Further indications of our spiritual nature are the many recorded 'out of body experiences' in which the people who experienced them report unanimously that they found themselves outside their bodies and were even able to see their own bodies from a detached viewpoint. I have twice had such an experience in my life, the first occasion being when I had my tonsils removed as a child of two. I found myself slightly to one side, just above my body, and was able to follow the entire operation in all its details. Of course, nobody believed what a small child had to say after waking up from the anaesthetic but, although I was only two at the time, I can still remember all of it clearly to this day.

The second incident was when I was climbing in the mountains, aged seventeen. During a school trip, I was climbing rather precariously on rocks with a friend. Suddenly I slipped off with both feet simultaneously – at the same moment I found myself outside my own body. I can still remember exactly how I calmly considered what to do to control my body hanging there on the rock face, while I was no longer 'in' my body. I was positioned about 3 metres (3 yards) behind myself, and from this position my 'detached' self was able to see where there were firm footholds for my feet. At the moment that I made the decision where to place my feet, my body carried out the thought. I was still watching this from 'outside', however. The moment I felt firm rock under my feet, I was suddenly back 'inside' again. I calmly carried on climbing and it was not until a few minutes later, when I had reached the top of the rock, that panic overcame me and I realized I could have fallen. Then I found it an effort to shake off the fear.

It need not be that dramatic. You can convince yourself of your spiritual capabilities in quite a safe way by simply crossing out the words 'coincidence' and 'chance' from your vocabulary. Belief in 'coincidences' is nothing other than a feature of our modern materialist religion, which can be truly given the term 'opiate of the people'. Reducing ourselves to mere physical existence contradicts all daily experiences of life and you would really require quite a stubborn strength of belief in the 'god of chance'. Think of how many strange experiences occur daily to help us progress further with our lives. Surely, they are too conspicuous to be chance!

Simply accept that, as a spiritual being, you are able to be effective and perceive, even over great distances, that you are not tied to space and time and that you yourself are the cause of what you experience. Perhaps you will feel some opposition to this way of viewing things, as it is often easier to make others responsible for your fate. But even if you have consciously cheated or were cheated – it always takes two to do it: one who cheats and one who allows him/herself to be cheated. What is your inner voice telling you at any given moment?

Please understand me correctly here: I am not interested in standing a sense of justice on its head. A cheat remains a cheat and should be tried. I merely wish to show that we always have the opportunity to change ourselves and our lives. Just as we may have postulated something in the past that we have to suffer from today, we are always in a position to change this postulate again and to make a new decision. We are not passively subject to fate – we create our own fate!

As spiritual beings, we have two basic capabilities: we can postulate something, that is, decide what is to happen, and we can perceive something or experience the thing (that we postulated). Once we perceive what we wished to experience, the postulate dissolves again and we are content. As long as the experience has not yet taken place, however, something is left open. Seen from this angle, life becomes a game: we can either plunge into new experiences or placidly allow things to happen to us.

This is exactly where the true fulfilment of a spiritual being lies: in play. Just observe children absorbed in their game – to them it is totally real. We grown-ups are not really doing anything different, while we are earnestly occupied with our games in our homes, at work and in our leisure time. Just think about how happy we grown-ups can be when we have been offered a new 'game' and how much enthusiasm and energy are bound up in it. If we approach a thing playfully, it works effortlessly. Playing is in our nature!

Your spirit stone that came to you through an oracle game will, therefore, reveal three things to you.

1. It represents a postulate, a decision you have made and the result of which you will experience now or in the future. You can dissolve this postulate if you no longer like it or begin happily to look forward to success. If you keep the message of the stone in your consciousness, you will experience how you actually determine your own life.

2. The stone will improve your means of perception and will make you conscious of your spiritual capabilities. Depending on which stone you have chosen, certain characteristics will be encouraged. The important thing is that you recognize the resulting phenomena as your own spiritual qualities and leave 'chance' out of the game. You will experience ever more clearly who you really are.

3. Your stone will simply show you what game you are playing at the moment or what game you want to play. Depending on where you stand now, your stone will make it clear to you how you begin your game, how you carry it on, or how you can bring it to a successful conclusion.

How you use your spirit stone is up to you. There are no rules, anything is possible. Make it into your own game!

Please read the next chapter with that last thought in mind. Chapter 2.4 deals with the 'practical application' of the art of healing with crystals. All possibilities described there are just that: possibilities. You can use them, you can change them, or you can invent new ones. Play the game according to your own rules!

Practical applications

Real skill at healing (the art of healing) requires no rules or laws but will always, and at every moment, do what is right and necessary. However, the fear of doing something wrong is apparently very great because the teaching of the art of healing is studded with advice and recipes that purport to give it an aura of general applicability. The more competent this advice appears, the more gratefully it is received by the student. Yet the danger here is that advice or rules are blindly followed without the student really seeing the sense or meaning of them.

The literature on gem therapy, for example, abounds with rules and dogmas (most of which are not clearly described or explained) about what one can and cannot do. If you took all these rules together seriously, you would end up doing nothing at all!

One 'expert' recommends using uncut stones, the other prefers spherical gems. In one volume you are forbidden to drill holes in anything, while in another you are advised to do so in all cases, and in yet another you are told that no metal should be attached to or surround a gem. For cleansing purposes, you are advised to bury your gems for weeks on end and bathe and anoint them thrice daily....

All your own valuable intuition is disregarded along with sound common sense, both of which are really our most valuable assets for healing. Yet, all the time, there is one very simple basic principle that is helpful not only in healing but also for one's entire life: 'Everyone would act the right way in a given situation if he/she knew how!'

For this reason, in all the following suggestions for use I will concentrate on explaining how certain methods work, as this understanding will leave you free to decide what you will use and when. You are then also free to vary things and invent your own new uses – which is exactly what the art of healing is! Remembering what was said in the previous chapter, take a playful approach towards the art of healing with crystals. In this way, you will benefit from a great expansion of innovation and creative energy as well as ultimately achieving success in healing.

The 'right' crystal

I am very tempted to reduce this section to a single sentence: 'Follow your own feelings!' But perhaps that would be a little too simple.

It is a fact that not every individual stone of the same type will have exactly the same effect. You can use three different criteria in order to assess the effect and healing power of a particular stone: its quality, its size and the manner in which it has been shaped.

Quality A stone is defined as qualitatively better if it displays the typical characteristics and qualities of the mineral in the most obvious and clear manner. For example, a dark green emerald is qualitatively better than a light green-grey one, a clear rock crystal is better than a milky, cloudy one, and a transparent ruby is better than an opaque one. As the healing effect of a mineral can be traced back to the mineralogical facts, as described in Part 1, it seems obvious that a qualitatively better stone has a more intense effect than a qualitatively mediocre one.

Size Large stones have a stronger effect than small ones. This is obviously connected with the fact that the power of its radiation increases with its mass. Its effectiveness at a distance also increases. A small amethyst crystal has a radius of effectiveness of a few centimetres (a few inches), a large druse, on the other hand, may 'irradiate' an entire hall.

Form The effect of form can also be traced back to one basic principle: crystals emit their greatest effective radiation along their edges. A crystal will, therefore, radiate its greatest effect from its tip. An irregular splinter will cast its rays in all directions and a sphere will emit a weaker, more regular radiation in all directions. Stones with facets are seen as more powerful, while round, polished stones, as for example tumbled stones, are felt to be gentler and more harmonious.

The effect of a crystal can, therefore, be based roughly on these three criteria. Yet the three criteria do not make any statement about which stone might objectively be more suitable because such a generally applicable criterion (good/bad) does not exist!

The stone that is suitable for the purpose is exactly the right stone! Depending on the application or the person, it might be a precious stone one time, a larger one another time, or a faceted stone or a round, polished one. For example, if you use a deep violet coloured amethyst to illuminate dreams, you may well find yourself bouncing about wide awake in bed at night! In this case, a lighter coloured, clearer one would be better. For cleansing the skin, however, an amethyst cannot be deep violet enough. Again, it is really only your own 'feeling' or instinct that will help. If you have understood the three criteria discussed above, you should know or sense, in any situation, which is the right stone.

And please, just forget those standard dogmas! In principle, you can use any stone for healing purposes. Only if the stone is so minute that you can hardly see it, or if it is of such bad quality that it can barely be identified as a specific mineral, will it be unlikely to have any healing effect.

Variations and possibilities

Healing crystals are available nowadays in many different forms, either as a rough stone or polished, as a 'comforter' (to fondle in one's hand) or as jewellery. The forms and colours of minerals are very often both beautiful and unique and, in addition to their healing powers, they also have an aesthetic value. This means that the art of healing and decoration or the art of healing and use as jewellery can be combined quite easily. In the following, I will briefly elaborate on the most important ways of effectively employing your healing crystal.

Rough stones A rough stone left in its natural state will, in many cases, display the real character of the mineral most clearly and will, therefore, also most clearly demonstrate its qualities and healing effects. Depending on their size, rough stones can be used to change the 'climate' of a room (for example, rose quartz), as a 'comforter' (for example amber, boji stones, garnet), for laying on certain parts of the body (for example biotite lenses, chalcedony rosettes, lepidolites, zoisites), or as meditation stones (for example azurite, moldavite, pyrite).

Crystals Naturally grown crystals possess the ability to channel energy from the base to the tip of the crystal and are, therefore, used for energy treatments (rock crystal, smoky quartz, tourmaline), for gem acupuncture (rock crystal, tourmaline), or can be used like other rough stones for laying on the body (hyacinth, kunzite, topaz, tourmaline).

Groups, geodes and druses Several crystals that have grown together are referred to as 'groups'. If such a group of crystals fills a small hollow or cyst in rock it is called a geode, in the case of a large hollow we speak of a druse (examples are groups of rock crystal, an agate geode, an amethyst druse). Where small crystals completely fill up a cyst (for example, agate) we speak of an 'almond'.

Groups and druses radiate very powerfully and can, therefore, also be used to alter the 'climate' in a room (for example amethyst, rock crystal, fluorite, smoky quartz). Very small groups and geodes are very suitable for treatment by laying on, particularly if an intense, powerful effect is desired (for example agate, apophyllite, rock crystal).

Slices and sections Almonds and crystals that often hide the most beautiful or characteristic part of the stone inside (agate, tourmaline) are often cut into slices. The representation obtained in this way, the 'signature' (Latin *signum*, 'sign') will enable one to 'read off' the healing effects (see *Agate*, Part 3). These slices or sections are also very good for laying on, or they can be worked into pendants.

Tumbled or polished stones To obtain polished stones, the rough stones are polished by tumbling them in large rotating drums full of water. Gradually ever-finer sand is added for finer grinding. This process, which takes several weeks, imitates the formation process of natural pebbles in rivers and other waters. The inner structure of the stones will then determine their outer shape; irregular, 'baroque' shapes are created that have given these stones their name.

Polishing all the rough edges makes the stone radiate more evenly and with a more limited spatial distribution. This means they are excellent for laying on certain parts of the body as well as for fondling in your hand. The most popular place, in your trouser pocket, is particularly advantageous as you will then (unconsciously) touch the stone whenever you need it. The effect on your entire body is also ensured because your hand, like your feet, possesses reflexology zones.

Thumb stones 'Thumb stones' represent a special form of 'comforter'. They possess a shallow, polished depression which will automatically tend to encourage you to rub your thumb in it. The unconscious desire to pick up the stone in your hand and play with it is thus encouraged.

Pendants and pierced stones This is probably one of the simplest ways to utilize a crystal for healing as the object can be worn directly on the skin. Whether you prefer a pendant with a metal ringlet or pierced stones is merely a matter of taste.

In spite of any assertions to the contrary, the stone is in no way interfered with in its effect by the presence of the metal, providing skin contact is maintained. Personally, I would recommend using only pure sterling silver (925.000), gilded sterling silver or high-quality gold alloys of at least 14 carat (585.000). Non-precious metals and alloys may irritate the skin and react with perspiration from the skin. Even silver can tarnish and irritate certain sensitive humans.

Many different shapes can now be found among the pierced stones: the classical 'caboche' and medallion shapes, baroque or free shapes, or geometrical and symbolic shapes of all kinds. Here, again, the first approach should be to make a decision based on your own feeling. The important thing is that you like the stone and enjoy wearing it. A healing crystal can quite easily be a decorative stone or piece of jewellery.

Doughnuts Doughnuts are flat, round stone discs with a central hole, a name derived from the pastry of the same name, widely distributed in the USA and Asia. The name is modern but the shape is extremely ancient: turquoise, in particular, has been worked into this shape for centuries in India, Nepal and China and amber doughnuts have been found in Palaeolithic graves. The shape may well have been created after the model of natural 'holed stones' that were looked upon as lucky in almost all cultures. Doughnuts can be used in the same way as the pendants described above.

Pyramids, spheres and healing wands The effect of their special shape has long been considered in the case of these specially polished stones. Pyramids are used as 'storage' objects or for concentrating energy, spheres are used for meditation and healing, while wands are used for acupuncture or acupressure massage. The preferred types of mineral for healing wands are amethyst, rock crystal, citrine, fluorite, obsidian, smoky quartz and rutile quartz.

Necklaces Necklaces are really the classic way to wear healing crystals. The healing effect of the stone will be very strong and the closed 'stone circle' around the head has a stronger radiative effect than a single pendant or 'comforter'. Among necklaces, those with round beads are considered to be 'mild' in their effect, whereas necklaces made of random, rough pieces are seen as 'strong'; faceted stone beads are seen as the most intense.

Jewellery Rings, bracelets, necklaces – here, too, the stones that have been incorporated unfold their full effect if direct contact with the skin is established.

If you are just as interested in the healing properties as in the decorative effect, make sure that the ring is worked with an open setting underneath the stone. The ideal is found in a piece of jewellery in which the minerals have been combined according to principles of healing or alchemy. Such pieces do indeed unfold the magic of a classic talisman. Unfortunately, nowadays only very few goldsmiths and jewellers are familiar with this ancient side of their craft.

Precious gem essences By laying a healing crystal in clear water, the information of the stone is transferred to the water. This process can be encouraged by standing a glass with the water and the stone in direct sunlight at sunrise and sunset – and only at sunrise and sunset. At these times, sunlight has a charging quality, while it has more of a discharging effect during the daytime. An essence prepared in this way can be taken internally, applied externally, or used for poultices, infusions and baths. Water treated in this way has basically the same healing effect as the stone itself and, taken internally, may often work even more rapidly and intensely as the effect is immediately distributed throughout the whole body.

Unfortunately, the information stored in water soon disperses. Adding alcohol can fix it for longer. Ready prepared precious gem essences can be obtained in the trade. These essences have been prepared according to the principle of alcoholic extracts where the relevant healing crystals are left lying in spirit or medicinal alcohol for months or years. The essences fashioned in this way are extremely intense and will keep for years.

The shape of stone you use will, therefore, depend on the desired purpose or on your personal preference. In principle, however, stones can be used in all sorts of ways. Perhaps a present or heirloom may acquire a new value when viewed from this angle.

Practical applications

In Part 3 you will find short suggestions for application among the descriptions of the individual healing crystals. Once the right stone has been chosen through the analytical or intuitive path, basically, only two more questions need to be asked:

1. In what manner is the stone to be used: wearing it, laying on, in a circle, in meditation, as an essence, positioned in a room?

2. Over what amount of time should it be used: starting time, duration, rhythm, end of treatment?

As a rule, there are several possibilities of which you can choose whichever you prefer: if you have a choice between sticking the crystal to your forehead or drinking an essence, and you would find it embarrassing to appear in your workplace with a stone stuck to your head, then it would be better to opt for the essence.

Wearing or carrying healing crystals

By 'wearing' and 'carrying' I mean all manners of application that include the stone being close to your body for a longish period. This can mean carrying a pendant, pierced stones, wearing a chain of stones, or even carrying a 'comforter' or 'thumb stone' in your trouser pocket. If you have been given exact instructions for carrying the stone, you may not get around sticking it to a part of your body with a piece of plaster. In any case, when wearing or carrying a stone it should, if possible, come into direct contact with your skin. Clothes, even if made of natural fibres, tend to have a screening effect.

Basically, healing crystals should be carried or worn until a clear improvement of the situation or symptoms has occurred or until the desired result has been obtained. In many cases, there may be an initial 'worsening' of the symptoms that merely shows that the situation or illness has been addressed ; this should be seen as a symptom of healing. These initial 'worsenings' can last from a few hours to about three days, in rare cases up to a week. If still no improvement has occurred after that, the choice of stone should be checked.

Also, if an initial 'worsening' seems unbearable, it may be better to wear the crystal intermittently rather than constantly, perhaps wearing it only two or three times for about half an hour each time. The effect will be more bearable at the beginning, but during the course of time it will be just as intense as if you were to wear it permanently. A general statement is difficult to make about the right time sequence to adopt for wearing the crystal, as every human being will react differently. When in doubt, it is always better to increase the number of occasions gradually: begin with once daily, then twice, three times, etc. At the same time, the duration should be increased: start with half an hour at a time, then increase to an hour, one and a half hours, and so on. In this way, you will gradually reach a state of permanent application

Laying on healing crystals

'Laying on' includes all temporary applications in which the stone is brought into direct contact with the body. As a rule, clear indications for the position on the body will be given in terms of where the afflicted organ, the pain or the area with an energy deficiency is located. When laying the stone on, you will notice that the crystal is almost 'sucked' to your skin if it is laid on the correct spot. When applying the stone, hold it to your body, applying light pressure for about a minute, and then carefully let go: even in spots where gravity would dictate it ought to drop off, it will usually remain stationary.

Treatment by laying on a stone can end as soon as a definite improvement is noticed. Here, it is particularly important not to extend the period unnecessarily. Rejoice in the relief you have gained, even if it is not complete, end the treatment at this point and enjoy the result. You can always resume the treatment again at a later time. Impatience is a trait that generally has an unfavourable effect in healing! You cannot force anything, even healing has to 'grow', just as the illness gradually 'grew'.

Another point to be considered, regarding the right time of treatment, is that the organs in our bodies are not active to the same degree at all times of the day or night. This is particularly noticeable with respect to activity in the brain which controls at what times of day we go to sleep and wake up again. Phases of activity and phases of rest, phases of high output and phases of regeneration are quite familiar to us.

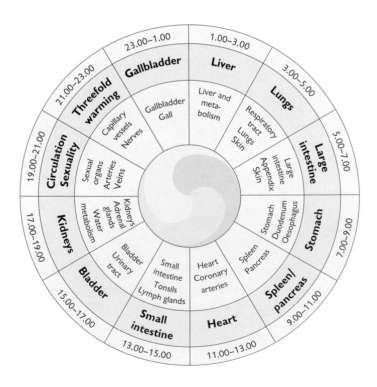

Fig. 33　*The organ clock.*

The same goes for all the other organs, each of which has its own individual 'morning', a time when its activity increases, its 'midday' when it reaches a peak, its 'evening' when activity begins to decrease and its 'night-time' when it has a rest phase.

In most cases, the organs are influenced more positively whenever their activity is just on the increase or is almost at its peak. This means that the best point in time to lay on a stone is, as a rule, before or during the phase of greatest activity. These points of time have been shown on the previous page in the form of an 'organ clock' so you can see at a glance at which time a certain treatment might promise to be most successful. Please note here that our bodies are not interested in 'political time': it will always be the real local time that counts, disregarding any displacements through 'summer time' and so on.

The stone circle

Stones radiate, so spending time in a stone circle will have a noticeable effect. 'Stone circle' is defined generously here and you will not have to travel to Stonehenge as, in this volume, stone circles are simply stones or crystals laid in a circle. Whereas laying crystals on the body means the entire organism is being influenced, spending time in a stone circle works on the most subtle planes of your being and its effects will be noticed first in spiritual, emotional and mental changes.

You can sit or lie down in a stone circle, but in all cases it is important to find the correct radius. Should you experience feelings of restriction or claustrophobia while in the circle, you will need to increase the area of the circle; if you feel distracted or uncomfortable in some way, the circle may well be too large. You will experience the optimal sense of well-being in a circle with the correct radius. Frequently repeating treatments with a stone circle will lead to your experiencing a variation in your own 'personal' radius, depending on the situation and your mood. During the course of time, your feeling for the circle will improve, so you will be able to determine the right radius from the start.

Remain sitting or lying in your stone circle as long as it takes to feel distinctly better or until you receive a strong impulse to leave the circle. Follow this impulse, whether it occurs after ten minutes or three hours. You can leave the stone circle where it is in order to continue on another occasion. It has been proved to be advantageous to use it when you are well rested, particularly if you are going to lie down in the circle, otherwise you may well sleep though all the most beautiful experiences.

Provided you have chosen your four personal healing crystals described in Chapter 2.3, *The intuitive art of healing with crystals*, you may lay these four stones in their own circle. Seen from the centre of the circle, lay your soul stone towards the south, the body stone in the west, the reasoning stone in the north, and the spirit stone in the east. Now sit down in the circle, first facing south, then after 10-15 minutes change to facing west, then north, and finally east. In this way, you will be able to experience the meanings of the soul, body, intellect and spirit very thoroughly and you will also clearly feel the effects of the healing crystals in these areas.

You can use this circle as a recovery island in your daily life. Even after a few minutes in the circle, either lying down with your head to the north, or sitting facing north, you will find it relaxing and regenerating.

Meditating with healing crystals

It is difficult to write about meditation as the phenomenon can really only be understood through actually doing it. If our eyes were only able to see black and white we would find it impossible to conceive of colour. For this reason, I can only think of two ways you might experience meditation with the help of stones. You will have to see for yourself what happens.

Contemplation Give yourself enough time, unplug the telephone, explain to everyone living with you that you do not wish to be disturbed for a while and sit down in a quiet spot. You can sit on the floor or equally well on a chair. The important thing is to be absolutely upright with a straight spine. A bent back will lead to tiredness and prevent meditation. Now lay the stone in front of you, if possible, at the same level as your eyes and at the right distance. The 'right level' and the 'right distance' are attained if you are able to direct your gaze at the stone in a fully relaxed manner for a long time.

It will be advantageous not to have a source of light in your range of vision: no candle, no lamp, no window, no sun. Sources of light

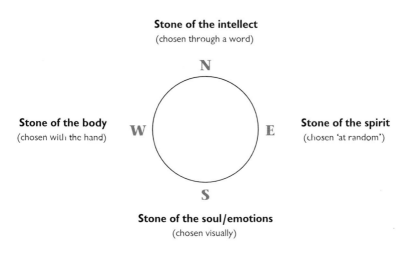

Stone of the intellect
(chosen through a word)

N

Stone of the body
(chosen with the hand)

W

E

Stone of the spirit
(chosen 'at random')

S

Stone of the soul/emotions
(chosen visually)

Fig. 34   The circle of personal healing crystals.

would simply distract your attention. The same goes for the background, which should be as neutral as possible so the stone can really stand out. Your entire attention should now be directed towards the stone lying in front of you. However, do not fixate on it, just let your gaze come to rest a little above it, into infinity.

Remain sitting in this manner quietly without moving. Every movement represents a new start and prevents meditation. If you become as slow as the stone in front of you, you will suddenly *see* it, understand it and experience it as a living being. Allow yourself to be surprised.

Meditating with laid-on stones Equipped with enough time and a calm atmosphere and, above all, having slept well (!), you will be able to experience the effect of healing crystals by lying down and placing the stone on your body. Here, again, skin contact is particularly advantageous. Favoured positions on the body for laying on the stone are the forehead (between the eyebrows), the heart, the solar plexus or the lower edge of the pubic bone. Then, consciously relax, by 'thinking' your way through from head to toe, that is, consciously relaxing each part of your body in turn and letting go of all tension. Observe your own breathing as it becomes calmer and slower until you are just as 'slow' as the stone resting on you. Now, allow yourself to be filled right up with the stone; identify with it, which means becoming like the stone, or better, become the stone itself as then the memory of the stone will open itself to you and you will see the world with its 'eyes'.

'Meditation' means complete spiritual awareness at one moment in time and space. You will recognize the state instantly and understand it once you have experienced meditation. You will also immediately know what aim meditation can have in your life. Again, allow yourself to be surprised...

Precious gem essences

Precious gem essences are able to unfold almost the same effects and reactions on our personalities and our bodies as the appropriate precious gem. Their advantages, however, lie in their application – taking them internally. Where precious gems have been laid on the body and only have a limited, localized effect, the effect of an essence taken internally will be distributed through all body fluids in the entire organism. You are 'filling' yourself with the gem. In this way, better results are achieved, particularly with generalized complaints (affecting the whole body). Where a gem may only help a blockage caused by stress locally, an essence is able to help with inner tension and stress (both physical and psychological) and will thereby improve all existing tensions and stress as well as any tendency towards being tense.

Sometimes, for practical reasons, it will not be possible to wear or carry a gem or to lay it on externall; for example, if your joints would become hampered in their movements, or – as already said – you might not exactly wish to appear in your office with a gem or crystal strapped to your forehead! In all these cases, taking an essence will be preferable. The essence will have an automatic effect on the organism in exactly the place where it is needed. Treatment with an essence also constitutes information therapy and the information will only be effective where your body 'understands' it, that is where the information is missing (principle of resonance).

Precious gem essences are very powerful in their effect. In order to achieve a comparable effect, a precious gem would have to be very large and very precious. Even leaving aside the problem of obtaining such a gem (often very difficult) and using it (how would you wear a gem weighing 2 kilograms (4.5 lb)?), there would still be the problem of price, which would be many times more than that of the essence (diamond, emerald). An essence is, therefore, also good for your wallet.

With an essence the cleansing that has to be undertaken when treating someone with precious gems is eliminated. Also, the amount of essence taken internally can be dosed very exactly.

Of course, the wearing and laying on of precious gems also has advantages over the use of an essence. In particular, experiments with gems are less binding as the gem can quickly be removed again and its effect will fade comparatively more quickly. Even if, for certain reasons, a targeted local treatment of a particular point, for example, an acupuncture point, is desired, precious gems are preferable to an essence. However, in most cases, the gem and the essence will complement each other well because, used simultaneously, they strengthen each other. Using a precious gem essence is just as simple as wearing a gem.

Taking internally Place on the tongue, about one hour before meals, or at least two hours after a meal. Essences you have prepared yourself by laying a gem in water should be taken in mouthfuls, while on the other hand a few drops will suffice of those in alcoholic extracts. It is impossible to give directions for dosage : sensitive natures should tend to take less (1–2 drops), more robust people more (5–10 drops). Also, an essence is absorbed faster, the more it is needed by the body. The daily cycle of doses can be accelerated; it is therefore better to take lots of small doses than a few larger ones. Essences can be taken over a period of several weeks and a cyclic taking of the essence (with occasional breaks – now and then, leave it for two or three days) will prevent the body becoming used to it.

External application Diluted precious gem essences can also be applied directly to the skin, in the case of skin complaints, inflammations, wounds and so on. Mixing them into ointments is also possible. A further possibility is adding them to your bath, although the water should not be too warm as this will cause the effect to disperse too quickly.

Dilutions Diluting precious gem essences (3–5 drops in up to 30 millilitres (2 tablespoons) of water) will shift the effect onto the spiritual–soul plane. Homeopathic potencies can also be prepared.

The precious gem essence will then correspond to the original tincture.

Combinations In principle, precious gem essences should be taken unmixed with anything else. A number of gems like rock crystal, diamond, white topaz etc. will, however, enhance the effect of others and can, therefore, be added if necessary (elixir fortifiers). Certain mixtures for particular applications can be obtained in the specialist trade. Compared with the old herb tea recipes, these are the result of years of research, have been carefully measured and are in tune with each other, both with respect to the combination of gems as well as the quantitative composition.

Storage Precious gem essences should be stored in cool, dark places in order to prevent mutual influencing. The elixir fortifiers in particular, for example rock crystal, will easily absorb the qualities of other essences. They should not be kept near sources of energy, such as electric power lines or cables, sockets, television or computer screens or neon lights.

Positioning healing crystals in a room

The atmosphere in which we live and work will have a lasting effect on our health and on the results of what we do. This means that we can even use healing crystals in our daily environment to obtain fast, positive results. The important thing here is that the stones we place in certain positions are effective across a sufficient radius. Rough stones, crystals and druses are, therefore, preferable.

Whenever you are within the radius of influence of the crystal or stone, you will always feel physically better. If you also want enrichment on the level of the soul, the crystal should be placed in such a way that you can see it, even if only out of the corner of your eye. Aesthetics play a great part here too, so choose a crystal or stone that you love unconditionally!

The exchange between the crystal and the human being occurs in both directions. This means that the crystals also receive information from us, especially if we lay them directly on our bodies or against our skin. This is the reason why, after using a crystal for a while, it may suddenly feel unpleasant. This happens at the moment when the information received becomes so powerful that the crystal begins to reflect it back at us. At that moment, the point has been reached when the crystal should be cleansed.

Cleansing and care

There is a great deal of confusion in the existing literature with respect to energy cleansing of crystals, and this is obviously based on the fact that the meaning of the different processes has not been understood properly. Very often three different procedures have been combined under the heading 'cleansing': discharging, cleansing and charging of healing crystals, gems and stones.

Discharging Particularly when crystals come into direct contact with the body, they will become statically charged. The most extreme example is amber, which may become quite hot in a few minutes. This static charge can be discharged again under running water.

Cleansing The information received will, however, remain stored even after the stone has been discharged and it will recharge again. In order to wipe this information, a more intense action is required. Complete wiping of stored information can be achieved with two simple procedures, by laying the crystal on an amethyst druse or by laying it in salt.

The amethyst druse represents the gentler procedure. The finely distributed iron atoms and the energy concentration of quartz give amethyst a powerful, fiery radiation. Healing crystals 'irradiated' in this way are stripped of the information they have stored. The time required is generally one day, or if the stone was only used briefly, an hour will be sufficient. You can, however, allow the crystal to lie in the druse for longer; it will not come to any harm.

Salt needs more careful handling. In particular, direct contact with salt may produce chemical reactions with some crystals, making the stone lose its polished finish or change colour. Laying an opal in dry salt would mean its death as the salt will extract water from the opal and it will be transformed into chalcedony. Chalcedony is also a healing stone, but is usually worth a great deal less!

We recommend, therefore, laying the crystal in a small glass dish that is embedded in a larger glass dish full of salt. The energy cleansing process is still maintained, but the stone itself is not affected. You can add mineral-poor water to the crystal where there are chains or necklaces attached to it whose threads might be damaged. This procedure will extract information even more quickly. The water should be changed each time you do this, but the salt can be used for months. The cleansing power of salt is very quick. If the stone has been worn for weeks, four to six hours of cleansing will be enough; if the crystal was only briefly laid on, ten minutes of cleansing will be sufficient. Carrying out cleansing for too long may 'leach' out the energy of the stone and its effectiveness will be decreased!

Other methods that have been recommended, such as laying the stone in salt water, burying it in soil or cleansing it in fire, are definitely to be avoided, as many crystals will be severely damaged by this: salt water will penetrate pores and cracks and make the stone cloudy, some secondary minerals will be attacked by acids in the soil and transformed, and fire will obviously tend to disperse too efficiently!

Charging The intensity of radiation from a crystal is connected with the absorbed energy, so its healing effect can be increased and fortified through targeted charging. The most gentle method consists of laying the stone in sunlight at sunrise and sunset. The period of time during which we can dare to look almost into the sun without damage to our eyes is when the sun possesses a charging quality. Never at midday, however! At this time the sun's energy tends to be discharging rather than charging. Immediately before using a crystal for treatment, the stones used can be warmed up in your hand or near a radiator. This, too, will intensify its effect. In many cases, charging is not necessary as the stone will be warmed up and stimulated by body contact.

Care Physical cleansing should be restricted to eliminating dust from mineral groups and mineral druses. Use a fine paintbrush for the purpose. If you are cleaning a druse, for example with water, only use mineral-poor water in order to avoid obtaining ugly calcium deposits on the crystals. Please never use any strong, abrasive household cleaning agents on your crystals. Some of them are almost impervious to such substances, while others extremely sensitive. By the time you have noticed the difference, it will already be too late!

Storage It is, of course, very natural to want to display beautiful stones so you can see them most of the time. However, if you do not want regular dusting to become your main hobby, I definitely recommend keeping them in a lockable display cabinet. I would also like to recommend you do not use a windowsill, with the exception of agate sections (which actually look rather good hanging in a window) and light-insensitive crystals (such as rock crystal, hematite, jasper, lapis lazuli, tiger's eye, black tourmaline), as many of them will lose their colour in direct sunlight (amethyst, kunzite, rose quartz).

Please do not stand any rock crystal spheres in sunlight. They will work like extremely good lenses, as I have experienced to my cost through burn holes in boxes and car seats!

Healing crystals as aids

To end this section of 'practical applications', here are a few thoughts that are important to me personally: there *is* life without healing crystals! These objects should never become a substitute for your own creativity and ability to solve problems. Healing crystals are aids. Every aid also has the possibility of becoming superfluous at some time. This is why I would like to point out here again something that should be considered along with the treatment with crystals.

The overall effect of healing crystals is enhanced and supported by consciously dealing with the particular problem: asking yourself 'why?' and 'wherefore?' the problem or illness exists and working out possible solutions. Every illness conceals a potential gain, so the question that has to be asked is, how can I rid myself of the problem or illness without losing the gain? Healing crystals will encourage this conscious effort but will not do it for you.

The effect of healing stones will only remain stable after you have stopped using them, if the insight gained is then transformed into action. We ourselves are the causes of our problems and we our-selves can change them. Crystals, precious gems and essences are merely aids in the process – nothing more.

The listing of qualities and symptoms in Part 3 of this volume, therefore, serves mainly to provide information, to give a brief characterization of the healing crystals, gems and stones, and specifically to stimulate the intuitive side of using the art. Whenever an illness is present, or for the solution of soul–spiritual problems, you should always pay attention to the entire situation, your character, the whole range of symptoms and your ideas, desires and goals in the art of healing with crystals. This holistic approach may lead you to an entirely different healing crystal than perhaps one isolated symptom would lead you to suppose.

For this reason, I would like to point out again that this volume serves to provide information about the art of healing with crystals and will not replace a doctor, complementary medical practitioner or therapist. In cases of severe illness or serious problems, please seek expert advice.

PART 3

Healing crystals

The healing properties of precious stones

It is important to establish that in the descriptions that follow of the healing powers and effects of precious gems, only those effects that have been tested and confirmed for many years have been recorded. Suppositions and phenomena that have been observed only in isolated cases have been left out or are clearly stated to be such. This has been done in order to offer security and certainty, something that is greatly needed in view of the contradictory and confusing information currently being offered in various publications.

However, this also means that none of the crystals or stones has been exhaustively and comprehensively described. At present nobody can offer this information, simply because the entire subject has only been rediscovered and developed for about a decade. Ten years is a very short time short compared with the time other healing methods have been practised, some based on traditions centuries or millennia old. The main work with healing crystals and stones is still in fundamental research, with every year bringing new insights.

When choosing a particular healing crystal, please rely mainly on the analytical or intuitive paths described in Part 2. The descriptions in Part 3 are primarily meant to confirm the choice you have made. Still, trust your own choice, even if the information that follows in the book does not appear to offer a connection between your desire and the stone you have chosen. Perhaps you are on the brink of discovering something completely new and unknown. If this is the case, I would be very glad to hear about it.

Such an exchange of information is also possible through the various crystal healing associations, the addresses of which can be found at the end of the book. The work of these associations consists, among other things, in collecting and evaluating reports on the healing effects of minerals and precious stones and in publishing the results after checking them. All contributions will be much appreciated.

Descriptions of the healing crystals

In order to make the connection between the crystals and the first part of the book clear, the descriptions that follow of the healing effects of each particular mineral include the most important mineralogical facts. The **crystal system**, the **manner of formation**, the **mineral class**, the **colour** and the **mineral-forming substances** contained are listed first, followed by the (extended) chemical formula. This information allows you to take into account the descriptions of Part 1 when studying the healing crystal, thus providing a considerably deeper and more comprehensive understanding of its healing effects. Refer back to the table on p. 89 if you need help in identifying the chemical abbreviations of the mineral-forming substances.

The important elements of the formation of the mineralogical qualities of the healing crystals are emphasized in the section headed 'mineralogy'.

Wherever traditions and mythological anecdotes about a certain stone exist, these have been briefly sketched under the heading **'mythology'**. Frequently, this will include the name of the crystal and – very importantly – an indication that, during the Middle Ages, often quite different minerals were designated by a name that is used nowadays! This is why many old traditions cannot be transferred to present-day minerals. A definite identification of modern minerals in ancient texts is often very difficult, but I hope to have eliminated 'translation errors' for the main part.

Under the heading **'healing'** are listed the currently known and tested healing effects of the mineral. They are divided up into the **spiritual** effect, which describes how the crystal can affect the transient state of the spirit, or what motivations and stimulation it will offer. Then follows the **emotional** effect, which comprises the influence on the subconscious, the inner images, feelings and moods. The **mental** effect describes changes in understanding, thoughts and conscious action, and finally the **physical** effect refers to the organism and the energy system of our bodies.

This structuring makes clear the interplay on all four levels and the special effects of the crystal with regard to the intuitive side of the art. The final notes on **'application'** of the crystal offer uses that have been shown to lead to good results (based on experience). Here too, the underlying principles suggest that much more may be possible! Make it your own game...

Finding your chosen crystal

The photographs that accompany the descriptions of the healing crystals have been taken directly from the original German edition of this book. As a result, the order is not strictly alphabetical by the English names of the crystals. The list opposite gives the relevant page numbers for the crystals.

Contents

(in alphabetical order)

Agate

CRYSTAL SYSTEM: trigonal
TYPE BY MANNER OF FORMATION: primary
MINERAL CLASS: oxide, quartz group
COLOUR: grey blue, brown, red, yellow
CHEMICAL FORMULA, MINERAL-FORMING SUBSTANCES: SiO_2 + Al,Ca,Fe,Mn

Mineralogy

Agate is formed hydrothermally in silicic acid-poor volcanic rock. Hot silicic acid solutions accumulate in hollow spaces formed by gas bubbles in the cooling lava. On cooling, the solutions solidify into quartz, which is deposited layer by layer on the walls of the hollow spaces. The agate obtains its typical banded appearance through the deposition of other substances in the layers, and the bands may consist of the most varied representatives of the quartz group: crystal quartzes (rock crystal, amethyst), members of the chalcedony family (chalcedony, carnelian, onyx) and jasper. Wherever the resulting agate fills up the entire hollow space, it is called an agate almond, and if a hollow remains in the centre, it is called an agate geode.

Mythology

Agate enjoyed a high reputation as a protective and good luck stone in the ancient world, as well as in India, Nepal and Tibet. Amulets were carved out of agates with straight, parallel bands and the continuation of this art has resulted in the present-day gem cutting art. Agates whose central hollow was filled with water ('water agates', 'enhydros' or 'eagle stones') were particularly popular and were considered to be charms for pregnancy.

Healing

Spiritually Agate supports retreat and spiritualization. It encourages a calm and contemplative view of life and helps with a concentrated, positive regulation of our affairs. Agate encourages the conscious 'digesting' of our life's experiences and leads to spiritual maturity and growth, inner stability and a sense of reality.

Emotionally Agate gives protection, security and safety by dissolving internal tensions, andalso makes us better able to resist external influences. Examples that consist of regularly shaped, concentric banding are particularly effective for this. Agates that contain rock

Agate, Brazil.

crystal at their core stimulate the ability to remember things, even as far back as prenatal memories (past lives).

Mentally Agate strengthens logical/rational thought that we use to help ourselves analyse problems back to their causes. Agate helps find simple, pragmatic solutions that are put into action, calmly but without delay. Agate also enhances concentration on that which is essential and avoids distractions.

Physically Agate balances our auras and the energy body. On this level, it has, therefore, a protective effect, is harmonizing and stabilizes health. Agate encourages regeneration and growth and is the pregnancy stone for both mother and child. Because of its layered structure made of different quartzes, agate works on those organs that are built up of different layers of skin and tissue. It helps with diseases of the eyes (conjunctivitis), gastritis and stomach ulcers, bladder and intestinal inflammation, as well as diseases of the uterus. It protects from prolapse of the uterus and encourages normal shrinkage of the uterus after childbirth. Agate stimulates the digestion and elimination, strengthens the blood vessels and helps with skin diseases.

Application

When using agate for specific physical complaints, the agate chosen should always carry the 'signature' (Latin *signum*, 'sign') of the respective organ. When in doubt, I recommend consulting a book on anatomy. This mineral should be worn with direct skin contact and laid on the respective part of the body shortly before or during the 'organ peak' (see the organ clock, Chapter 2.4). It will be sufficient to place the agate somewhere where it can be seen for much of the time, in order to obtain an effect on the emotional/spiritual level; for example hang it up in the window. Meditating in a circle of agate pieces is particularly powerful.

Actinolite

CRYSTAL SYSTEM: monoclinic
TYPE BY MANNER OF FORMATION: primary or tertiary
MINERAL CLASS: chain silicate
COLOUR: green
CHEMICAL FORMULA, MINERAL-FORMING SUBSTANCES:

$Ca_2(Mg,Fe)_5(Si_8O_{22})(OH,F)_4 + OH,F$

Mineralogy

Actinolite is an alkaline calcium magnesium iron silicate that forms crystals that radiate outwards or broad stalk-like, fibrous aggregates. It is formed metamorphically in actinolite, green, talc, and serpentine slates, more rarely magmatically in hydrothermal processes.

Mythology

Actinolite has been known as a 'ray stone' for centuries but there are no extant traditions on its healing powers.

Healing

Spiritually Actinolite is supportive when taking new directions. It helps with setting new goals and will help initiate the requisite action. Actinolite encourages straightforwardness.

Emotionally Actinolite helps us to recognize our own capabilities. It strengthens our sense of self-worth and encourages inner balance, patience and a sense of timing.

Mentally Actinolite helps us to obtain an awareness of when and where we have diverged from our original, real goals. This will help us to correct our course.

Physically Actinolite stimulates the functioning of the liver and kidneys, as well as all building and growth processes. In the form of actinolite quartz (actinolite in rock crystal) it stimulates all elimination of toxins, etc.

Application

Actinolite is slow to unfold its effects, so it should be used over a longer period of time as a hand 'comforter' or as a pendant worn against the skin.

Amazonite

CRYSTAL SYSTEM: triclinic
TYPE BY MANNER OF FORMATION: primary, secondary and tertiary
MINERAL CLASS: lattice silicate, feldspar family
COLOUR: blue-green, green
CHEMICAL FORMULA, MINERAL-FORMING SUBSTANCES: $K[AlSi_3O_8]$ + Cu

Mineralogy

Amazonite is a microclinic mineral (feldspar family) coloured green through copper. It can be formed in magmatic (hydrothermally or in pegmatites), sedimentary (in sediments) or metamorphic (during the formation of crystalline slate) processes.

Mythology

By declaring it to be the same as a nephrite that the South American Indians along the Rio Negro said came from a 'land of women without men', it was called 'amazon stone'. Amazonite was defined first in the eighteenth century, then renamed green feldspar, so no older traditions are known.

Healing

Spiritually Amazonite encourages self-determination. It helps us discard the notion of being the victim of all-powerful fate and encourages us to take charge of our own life.

Emotionally Amazonite balances extremes of moods and has a calming effect. It dissolves sadness and feelings of apprehension and encourages a healthy trust in God.

Mentally Amazonite helps solve problems through encouraging a proper interaction between rational thought and intuition.

Physically Amazonite regulates metabolic disturbances (liver) and has a relaxing, cramp-dissolving effect. It is also helpful during childbirth by helping the birth canal to expand naturally. It strengthens the nerves and helps with brain disorders. It harmonizes the pituitary gland and thymus gland as well as the autonomic nervous system and the inner organs. Amazonite also helps with heart complaints due to grief.

Application

The best ways are by wearing it, laying it on the body or taking it internally as an essence.

Actinolite, Corsica;
amazonite, Namibia.

Amethyst

CRYSTAL SYSTEM: trigonal
TYPE BY MANNER OF FORMATION: primary
MINERAL CLASS: oxide, quartz group
COLOUR: violet
CHEMICAL FORMULA, MINERAL-FORMING SUBSTANCES:
SiO_2 + (Al,Fe,Ca,Mg,Li,Na)

Mineralogy

Amethyst belongs to the group of crystal quartzes, those representatives of the quartz group that form large, visible crystals. Its colour is largely due to the traces of iron it contains that are lodged in the crystal lattice in two valencies (Fe^{2+}, Fe^{4+}). It is formed hydrothermally from weak, iron-containing silicic acid solutions, mainly in hollows formed by gas bubbles in volcanic rock, more rarely also in rock clefts and rocks with cracks and passages running through them. A hollow that is lined on the inside with amethyst crystals is called an amethyst druse (large) or an amethyst geode (small).

Mythology

The name of the amethyst is derived from Greece and means 'non-inebriated' (*amethustos*). Its sobre, clearing effect was already known in antiquity and the crystal itself was, therefore, highly prized. In the Middle Ages, Konrad von Megenberg quite aptly defined the amethyst as a mineral that 'makes a person better, disperses bad thoughts, brings good commonsense and makes one mild and gentle'.

Hildegard von Bingen left us information on its healing effects on skin diseases and swellings, and in Arabic countries we know that amethyst was put under the pillow to prevent nightmares.

Healing

Spiritually Amethyst encourages constant spiritual wakefulness, a sense of spirituality and insight into the reality of the spirit. It imbues a sense of justice and the ability to judge and provokes honesty and uprightness. As a meditation stone it helps quieten the mind and is an aid to finding deep inner peace and discovering the wisdom residing in ourselves.

Emotionally Amethyst will help in sadness and grief and lend support in coming to terms with loss. It clarifies the inner world of images and also our dream lives. If you put amethyst under your

Amethyst on chalcedony, Uruguay; amethyst, Brazil.

pillow, you will find that, initially, it will strongly stimulate dreaming until all undigested impressions have been clarified. After a few days, however, sleep will suddenly become calmer, deeper and more refreshing. During waking consciousness, amethyst stimulates inspiration and intuition.

Mentally Amethyst encourages sobriety and awareness. It helps us face up to all experiences, even unpleasant ones, and encourages consciously dealing with perception. This heightens concentration and effectiveness in thinking and acting and encourages the overcoming of blocks, uncontrolled mechanisms and addictive behaviour.

Physically Amethyst helps get rid of pain and release tension, especially tense headaches, and helps with injuries, bruises and swellings. The latter will go down rapidly. It helps with all illnesses of organs that have been formed out of ectodermis, that is, it helps with nervous complaints, diseases of the lungs and respiratory tract, skin blemishes such as verrucas, and intestinal complaints. It regulates the flora of the large intestine; it is also helpful in cases of intestinal parasites and encourages reabsorption of water.

Application

The amethyst should be worn, for a long period of time, either as a chain or pendant next to the body, or contemplated steadily during (regular!) meditations. A stone circle of amethyst crystal tips is extremely powerful. For helping with understanding dreams, it will be sufficient to place a light-coloured, clear (!) crystal under your pillow. For further mind and mental effects use amethyst druses, or pieces of these that can be stood up around the room. Their radiation will be so strong that it will transform the entire (spiritual) climate of the room. Finally, for use on the body, I recommend laying the crystal either directly in the general area of the relevant organ or taking a gem elixir (for example, for nervous disorders and intestinal problems), or applying it diluted externally (for skin diseases).

Amethyst, Vera Cruz, Mexico.

Ametrine

CRYSTAL SYSTEM: trigonal
TYPE BY MANNER OF FORMATION: primary
MINERAL CLASS: oxide, quartz group
COLOUR: yellow and violet in clearly delimited colour zones
CHEMICAL FORMULA, MINERAL-FORMING SUBSTANCES:
SiO_2 + (Al,Fe,Ca,Mg,Li,Na)

Mineralogy

Ametrine is an unusual crystalline quartz that unites amethyst and citrine colour zones, clearly defined and separated within the crystal. It arises through hydrothermal formations out of iron-containing silicic acid solutions.

Mythology

Ametrine has only been known for a few years so there are no ancient traditions on its effects.

Healing

Spiritually Ametrine makes a connection between the wakefulness of amethyst and the dynamic energy of citrine and thus provides a crystal of well-thought out, sure action. It helps connect apparent contradictions and helps give the wearer luck, that intuitive means of success on all levels.

Emotionally Ametrine encourages optimism and *joie de vivre*. It brings harmony and an inner feeling of well-being that will not disperse even when there is great stress from outside.

Mentally Ametrine harmonizes perceptions and conscious action. It stimulates the extraordinary creativity that goes hand in hand with great energy. Ametrine improves our control over our own lives.

Physically Ametrine has a strong cleansing effect on the metabolism and in the tissues. It enhances the activity of the autonomic nervous system and harmonizes the interplay between the inner organs.

Application

In all applications, ametrine should be worn directly on the body for long periods of time. Spiritual and mental aspects are also fortified in meditation, and the mind strengthened through laying a crystal on the solar plexus.

Ametrine, Bolivia.

Antimonite

CRYSTAL SYSTEM: rhombic
TYPE BY MANNER OF FORMATION: primary
MINERAL CLASS: sulphide
COLOUR: grey
CHEMICAL FORMULA, MINERAL-FORMING SUBSTANCES:
Sb_2S_3 + Fe,Cu,Pb,Zn + (Co,Ag,Au)

Mineralogy

Antimony is formed in quartz and ore passages, where in hollows and cysts it forms beautiful, grey silvery crystals that radiate from one point.

Mythology

In antiquity, antimonite was used as a healing medium for the sexual organs, the throat and eyes, and was also applied in a pulverized form as eye shadow. The ray form of the crystal caused it to be seen as a symbol of the Sun.

Healing

Spiritually Antimonite encourages creative energy, general creativity and the aesthetics of form. It helps bring our personal interests and higher ideals into harmony so that our lives become joyful and full of meaning.

Emotionally Antimonite helps us to control our feelings as well as give up habits, replace gratification (for example, eating out of frustration) and reduce excessive sexual desire.

Mentally Antimonite enhances objective, sobre thought and helps us to overcome limiting views ('I can't ...') and oppressive feelings. It makes it easier to follow our inner voice.

Physically Antimonite regulates digestive processes and helps with stomach problems, particularly acid indigestion, nausea and vomiting. It helps with skin diseases, dry, cracked skin, skin eruptions of all kinds, eczema and constant itching.

Application

Antimonite is a very fragile mineral, so for personal use, only very careful laying on of individual crystals can be undertaken. Otherwise, I recommend use with meditation.

Antimonite, Rumania.

Apatite

CRYSTAL SYSTEM: hexagonal
TYPE BY MANNER OF FORMATION: primary and secondary
MINERAL CLASS: phosphate
COLOUR: grey, yellow, green, blue
CHEMICAL FORMULA, MINERAL-FORMING SUBSTANCES:
$Ca_5[(F,Cl,OH)/(PO_4)_3] + Mg,Mn,Si,Sr$

Mineralogy
Apatite is a usually fairly opaque, rarely transparent, crystalline phosphate mineral with magmatic, or rarely sedimentary, origin.

Mythology
Apatite was often confused with other minerals (beryl, calcite) in the past, which is why it did not receive the name apatite (Greek *apatao*, 'to delude') until 1786. This is also the reason why nothing is known about any earlier healing uses.

Healing

Spiritually Apatite provides openness and social ease. It makes the wearer extroverted and instils motivation and drive, helping us to live a life full of variety.

Emotionally Apatite helps with apathy. It encourages liveliness, helps with exhaustion, particularly if periods of extreme activity are followed by complete lack of activity, and also reduces irritability and aggression.

Mentally Apatite eases apathy, sorrow, anger and lack of incentive and helps to turn our attention to happier circumstances.

Physically Apatite stimulates healthy eating habits. It mobilizes energy reserves, encourages the formation of new cells, as well as the growth of cartilage, bone and teeth. It ameliorates damage to posture, rickets, arthritis and joint problems, and promotes the healing of broken bones.

Application
For all applications, apatite should be worn next to the skin. Lay it directly on the relevant part of the body for alleviating pain and healing bones.

Apatite, Mexico

Apophyllite

CRYSTAL SYSTEM: tetragonal
TYPE BY MANNER OF FORMATION: primary
MINERAL CLASS: phyllo or sheet silicate
COLOUR: white, yellowish, blue-green
CHEMICAL FORMULA, MINERAL-FORMING SUBSTANCES:
$KCa_4[F/(Si_4O_{10})_2] \cdot 8\ H_2O$

Mineralogy

Apophyllite is a phyllo or sheet silicate containing water that is formed hydrothermally. Because of its water content, it is much more conductive of energy than sheet silicates normally are.

Mythology

Apophyllite has only been known since the beginning of the nineteenth century. There are no known traditions about its effectiveness. Any broken surfaces shine like mother-of-pearl.

Healing

Spiritually Apophyllite encourages a calm attitude, tranquillity and honesty. It helps us to be open, as we really are, without hiding things; it gets rid of pretence, reserve or a bad conscience.

Emotionally Apophyllite helps reduce fears, inner pressure and feelings of apprehension and helps overcome anxieties, worry and uncertainty. It helps us to be in control and to release suppressed emotions.

Mentally Apophyllite provides that saving light in times of great pressure and stress. It helps us get rid of blocks and negative thought patterns and, above all, helps us get rid of the thought habit of 'wanting' things.

Physically Apophyllite heals respiratory problems, particularly asthma. It stimulates regeneration of the skin and mucous membranes, the activity of the nerves and helps with allergies.

Application

The spiritual effect of apophyllite is fully unfolded during meditative contemplation of small groups of crystals that often look like plants or flowers. When using it on the body, I recommend carrying crystals with you and, in cases of asthma attacks holding them directly against your chest.

Apophyllite, India.

Aquamarine

CRYSTAL SYSTEM: hexagonal
TYPE BY MANNER OF FORMATION: primary
MINERAL CLASS: ring silicate
COLOUR: green to light blue
CHEMICAL FORMULA, MINERAL-FORMING SUBSTANCES:
  $Be_3Al_2(Si_6O_{18})$ + K,Li,Na + (Fe)

Mineralogy

Aquamarine is a member of the beryl family. It is formed in pegmatites, provided the magmatic solution is sufficiently enriched with beryllium. Traces of iron give it its blue-green to blue colour.

Mythology

The name aquamarine (Latin/Italian *aqua marina*, 'seawater') was coined in the Renaissance period, but the blue-green beryl has been known for a long time. Old legends tell of how it changes colour to reveal true and false, friend and foe. According to tradition, it brings well-being, a good memory and clairvoyance.

Healing

Spiritually Aquamarine encourages spiritual growth, foresight, far-sightedness, mediumistic qualities and clairvoyance. It makes us upright and honest, goal-oriented, dynamic, persistent and successful.

Emotionally Aquamarine bestows light-heartedness and a happy, relaxed disposition that is due to all things undertaken developing quickly and smoothly.

Mentally Aquamarine clears up confusion and stimulates orderliness, bringing unfinished business to a conclusion.

Physically Aquamarine harmonizes the pituitary gland and the thyroid gland, thereby regulating growth and the hormone balance. It improves the sight in cases of short- or long-sightedness and calms overreactions of the immune system, autoimmune diseases and allergies, in particular hayfever.

Application

Aquamarine can be worn constantly on the body. In cases of eye infections, it can also be laid directly on the eyelids in the evening.

Aragonite

CRYSTAL SYSTEM: rhombic
TYPE BY MANNER OF FORMATION: primary or secondary
MINERAL CLASS: carbonate
COLOUR: white, pink, yellow, light green, brown
CHEMICAL FORMULA, MINERAL-FORMING SUBSTANCES:
$CaCO_3$ + Fe,Mn,Pb,Sr,Zn,H_2O

Mineralogy

Formed hydrothermally or in a sedimentary process, aragonite can be found in clefts and cysts in rock. It can also be formed as a sinter in hot springs, as well as through the inorganic deposition of calcium in shallow waters. Aragonite will often transform into calcite over a long period of time.

Mythology

Aragonite received its name in 1788 after a source on the Rio Aragon in Spain. No traditions about its effects are known.

Healing

Spiritually Aragonite stabilizes spiritual developments that are moving too fast, that lead to excessive demands or to a decrease in interest.

Emotionally Aragonite is calming in cases of oversensitivity, inner restlessness and nervous twitching. Aragonite makes us feel physically well in our own body.

Mentally: Aragonite brings flexibility and tolerance; however, if our behaviour tends to be erratic, aragonite helps us to keep our concentration focused on the matter in hand.

Physically Aragonite also stabilizes developments that are proceeding too fast. It regulates the metabolism of calcium, stimulates muscle activity and encourages the build-up and elasticity of the intervertebral discs. Aragonite strengthens the immune system and helps with digestive complaints.

Application

Aragonite can be used constantly as a hand 'comforter' or worn as a pendant.

Aventurine

CRYSTAL SYSTEM: trigonal
TYPE BY MANNER OF FORMATION: primary, secondary and tertiary
MINERAL CLASS: oxide, quartz group
COLOUR: green iridescent
CHEMICAL FORMULA, MINERAL-FORMING SUBSTANCES:
$$SiO_2 + KAl_2[(OH,F)_2/AlSi_3O_{10}] + (Cr)$$

Mineralogy

Aventurine is a rough quartz that obtains its green, sparkling appearance from deposits of fuchsite (chromium mica). It is a rock-forming element in igneous rocks, sediments and crystalline slates.

Mythology

Aventurine received its name around the seventeenth century from the Italian *a ventura* ('randomly'), which refers to its randomly deposited mica platelets. No traditions on its effects are known.

Healing

Spiritually Aventurine reveals what makes us happy or unhappy. It fortifies our own self-determination and individuality and stimulates dreaming and making dreams come true.

Emotionally Aventurine enhances relaxation, regeneration and recovery. It helps with problems getting to sleep, makes us more patient and is calming to anger and annoyance.

Mentally Aventurine bestows a multitude of ideas and enthusiasm, but at the same time encourages tolerance and acceptance of others' suggestions.

Physically Aventurine encourages regeneration of the heart. It stimulates the fat metabolism and lowers the cholesterol levels. In this way, it prevents arteriosclerosis and heart attack. Aventurine also has an anti-inflammatory effect, helps with skin diseases, skin eruptions and allergies and fortifies the connective tissues. Aventurine also alleviates pain.

Application

Aventurine can be worn for long periods of time on a chain, as a pendant or as a hand 'comforter'. In acute cases, it can be laid on the relevant part of the body.

Azurite

CRYSTAL SYSTEM: monoclinic
TYPE BY MANNER OF FORMATION: secondary
MINERAL CLASS: carbonate
COLOUR: azure
CHEMICAL FORMULA, MINERAL-FORMING SUBSTANCES: $Cu_3[(OH)_2/(CO_3)_2]$

Mineralogy

Azurite is an alkaline copper carbonate and is formed by the action of rainwater containing carbonic acid in the oxidation zone of copper ore deposits. It is distinguished from the related malachite by its lower water content.

Mythology

Azurite is a very rare mineral with no traditions about its effects being known. The mythology of copper appears to fit, however, particularly the quality of a strong sense of justice.

Healing

Spiritually Azurite represents a drive towards enlightenment. It awakens a hunger for our own experiences so that we are not satisfied with explanations given to us that we are unable to prove for ourselves.

Emotionally Azurite reveals and dissolves imprints from the past, in particular, those ideas and inner images that we have taken on unconsciously and believed to be true.

Mentally Azurite makes us very critical. It reveals our own thought patterns and allows us to think through apparently obvious circumstances in depth, thereby encouraging awareness and self-knowledge.

Physically Azurite is primarily a liver stimulant and aids detoxification. It stimulates the activity of the brain and nerves. Azurite also stimulates the activity of the thyroid gland, thereby encouraging growth.

Application

Azurite unfolds its emotional and spiritual effects as a meditation crystal that can be either contemplated calmly or laid on the forehead. When used on the body, it should be laid directly on the skin of the relevant part.

Azurite-malachite

CRYSTAL SYSTEM: monoclinic
TYPE BY MANNER OF FORMATION: secondary
MINERAL CLASS: carbonate
COLOUR: blue/green marbled
CHEMICAL FORMULA, MINERAL-FORMING SUBSTANCES:
$$Cu_3[(OH)_2/(CO_3)_2] + Cu_2[(OH)_2/CO_3] + H_2O + (Ca,Fe)$$

Mineralogy

Azurite-malachite is a very rare, alkaline copper carbonate and is formed by rainwater containing carbonic acid in the oxidation zone of copper ore deposits.

Mythology

Azurite-malachite is far rarer than azurite and no traditions are known about its effects. The aspects of neutrality and harmonizing are derived from the mythology of copper.

Healing

Spiritually Azurite-malachite encourages an interest in our surroundings and fellow human beings. It makes us open, honest and helpful, and leads to well-being on all levels.

Emotionally Azurite-malachite brings harmony, particularly in conditions of inner conflict and disunity. It helps with overcoming pain and sadness as well as releasing suppressed emotions.

Mentally Azurite-malachite encourages harmony between the intellect and feelings. It helps us listen to our feelings and be able to put them into words as well as arriving at a positive view of life.

Physically Azurite-malachite stimulates the liver and detoxifies and releases cramps. It also stimulates the immune system and dissolves disharmonious cell growth (tumours, etc.).

Application

Azurite-malachite can be worn on the body either as a rough stone or hand 'comforter' or it may be taken internally in the form of a gem essence. The stone itself should be laid directly on the skin of the part of the body afflicted.

Azurite, USA;
azurite-malachite, USA.

Tree agate

Crystal system: TRIGONAL
TYPE BY MANNER OF FORMATION: primary
MINERAL CLASS: oxide, quartz group
COLOUR: white with green, 'mossy' inclusions
CHEMICAL FORMULA, MINERAL-FORMING SUBSTANCES: SiO_2 + Fe,Mn,Si

Mineralogy

Tree agate is a coarse, white quartz of pegmatitic formation with green iron silicates deposited in its cracks that are reminiscent of plant structures. In previous times, the term tree agate was also used for dendrite chalcedony which, however, belongs to the chalcedony family and not to the rough quartzes. For this reason, the term agate for this mineral is actually false and it should be 'dendritic quartz'. Unfortunately, this term is already in use as a synonym for 'fossilized wood'. So we have to stick with the old name.

Healing

Spiritually Tree agate encourages inner peace and certainty. It makes us aware of our own strength and thus gives security and stability.

Emotionally Tree agate strengthens endurance and constancy. It gives courage in situations in which we feel unprotected and bereft of power.

Mentally Tree agate helps see difficulties as challenges and how to deal with them. It awakens the warrior in us and the urge to strive and conquer.

Physically Tree agate ensures vitality, stable good health and a well-functioning immune system. It makes us more resistant to frequent bouts of infection.

Application

Tree agate should be worn for long periods of time in order to be effective. It is not a stone to be used for rapid effects but will work on 'building up' slowly, inconspicuously but persistently.

Tree agate, Brazil.

Rock crystal

CRYSTAL SYSTEM: trigonal
TYPE BY MANNER OF FORMATION: primary
MINERAL CLASS: oxide, quartz group
COLOUR: clear
CHEMICAL FORMULA, MINERAL-FORMING SUBSTANCES: SiO_2

Mineralogy

Rock crystal is a clear, pure crystal quartz. It is formed in passages or hydrothermally in druses and clefts out of pure, silicic acid solution with no foreign substances contained in it. Phantom quartzes are formed through further deposits on the surfaces, when the crystal has lengthy periods of dormancy in its growth (millions of years).

Mythology

The Greeks believed rock crystal to be deeply frozen ice (Greek *krystallos*). In all cultures it was thought to be a healing and magical crystal. Rock crystal was thought to be able to drive away demons and disease and was used as a strength and energy supplier. Crystal balls were used for predicting the future.

Healing

Spiritually Rock crystal encourages clarity and neutrality and thus improves perception and understanding. It strengthens our conviction in own point of view and encourages development that is appropriate to our own inner nature.

Emotionally Rock crystal recalls forgotten memories and brings them into conscious awareness. It helps with solving problems in simple ways and in revitalizing capabilities we thought we had lost.

Mentally Rock crystal brings self-knowledge and, in the form of phantom quartz, helps us to overcome what we believe are mental limits.

Physically Rock crystal revitalizes parts of the body that have lost feeling, are cold, numb or paralysed. It balances the working of both halves of the brain, fortifies the nerves and stimulates glandular activity. Rock crystal supplies energy but can still reduce fever and alleviate pain, swelling, nausea and diarrhoea.

Application

Rock crystal can be used as a crystal, a group, a cut stone, or in the form of an essence. Rock crystal also enhances the effectiveness of other crystals.

Rock crystal, Brazil;
phantom quartz, Brazil.

Amber

CRYSTAL SYSTEM: amorphous
TYPE BY MANNER OF FORMATION: secondary
MINERAL CLASS: organic stone
COLOUR: white, golden yellow, brown, red
CHEMICAL FORMULA, MINERAL-FORMING SUBSTANCES: $C_{10}H_{16}O + S$
(simplified)

Mineralogy
Amber is a tree resin that has 'aged' during the course of millions of years by losing water, and has gradually mineralized. Amber is found mainly in brown coal deposits.

Mythology
Amber was the first precious stone in human history. It has been used as a healing stone and amulet for at least 7000 years.

Healing

Spiritually Amber encourages a sunny nature, which appears gentle and pliable, but is actually very self-confident. It makes the wearer spontaneous and open but a respecter of tradition at the same time.

Emotionally Amber bestows freedom from care, good luck and happiness. It makes the wearer peace-loving and trusting and strengthens self-belief. It is the source of easily obtained success.

Mentally Amber dissolves oppositions, making us more flexible, and encourages creativity. Motivation arises from personal wish fulfilment that will often become the main drive in our lives.

Physically Amber helps with stomach, spleen and kidney complaints as well as with liver, gallbladder and metabolically based skin complaints. Amber helps joint problems (build up of cartilage), fortifies the mucous membranes, enhances healing of wounds and alleviates teething pain in small children.

Application
Amber works best if it is worn frequently and for long periods of time. Chains of amber for babies work better if they are worn by the mother for a while first (they absorb relevant information).

Amber, Eastern Prussia.

Beryl

Crystal system: hexagonal
TYPE BY MANNER OF FORMATION: primary
MINERAL CLASS: ring silicate, beryl family
COLOUR: yellow, green (beryl), gold (golden beryl), yellow to blue
   green (heliodor), red (bixbite), transparent (goshenite)
CHEMICAL FORMULA, MINERAL-FORMING SUBSTANCES:
   $Be_3Al_2(Si_6O_{18})$ + K,Li,Fe,Mn,Na + (U)

Mineralogy

Beryl is formed in pegmatites whenever the magmatic solution is sufficiently enriched with beryllium. The various different colours arise from foreign substances: iron colours it yellow and golden (beryl, golden beryl), sometimes bluish (heliodor); lithium and manganese colour it red (bixbite). Completely pure, clear beryl (not shown here) is called goshenite.

Mythology

Since antiquity, beryl has been believed to be a detoxifying crystal that strengthens the eyes. From the earliest times it was used to polish and make lenses and seeing aids. The German word *Brille* (spectacles, glasses) is believed to be derived from the word 'beryl'.

Healing

Spiritually Beryl makes us goal-oriented and effective but at the same time, versatile, far-sighted and full of *joie de vivre*. Golden beryl and heliodor both have a very harmonious effect and bixbite makes us dynamic.

Emotionally Beryl (better still golden beryl) helps nervousness and emotional eruptions caused by excessive stress. Bixbite helps with apathy and lack of drive.

Mentally All types of beryl encourage a feeling of security and self-confidence. They stimulate a thoughtful manner and a gradual but determined development in carrying out all plans.

Physically Beryl has a detoxifying, liver-stimulating effect and has a balancing effect on the autonomous nervous system. It helps with short-sightedness and long-sightedness (best with heliodor) and any symptoms typical of constant stress.

Application

The best way is to wear beryl close to the body and use it for meditation. For the eyes, it should be laid on the eyelids in the evenings.

Bixbite, USA; golden beryl, South Africa
heliodor, South Africa

Biotite lenses

CRYSTAL SYSTEM: monoclinic
TYPE BY MANNER OF FORMATION: tertiary
MINERAL CLASS: phyllo or sheet silicate, mica family
COLOUR: black, grey, brown
CHEMICAL FORMULA, MINERAL-FORMING SUBSTANCE:
  $K(Mg,Fe)_3[(OH,F)_2/AlSi_3O_{10}] + Mn,Na$

Mineralogy

Biotite lenses are metamorphic mica aggregates from Northern Portugal that were produced in the formation of mountains. In the summer, when the rocks heat up, they expand into lens shapes, shattering the rock explosively and 'jumping out' spontaneously.

Mythology

Owing to their manner of formation and their use in childbirth, biotite lenses are called 'birthing stones' in the area they come from. They are also used as protective stones in Portugal.

Healing

Spiritually Biotite lenses stimulate individual self-fulfilment. They allow flexibility and adaptation as long as the wearer does not become untrue to him/herself.

Emotionally Biotite lenses protect us from outer influences. They help us to free ourselves from other people's influences and demands whenever they contradict our innermost convictions.

Mentally Biotite lenses enhance the ability to make clear-cut decisions. They amplify creativity and intuition and help turn decisions and ideas into reality much more quickly and easily.

Physically Biotite lenses are used as aids during the birth process. They speed up the birth as they trigger labour, while simultaneously softening the neck of the womb. Furthermore, they have a detoxifying effect and are helpful with constipation, kidney problems, excess acid, sciatica, rheumatism and gout.

Application

Biotite lenses work best when carried close to the body. They can be laid on the lower abdomen (pubic area) to start labour or alleviate labour pains.

Biotite lense (birthing stone), Po▪

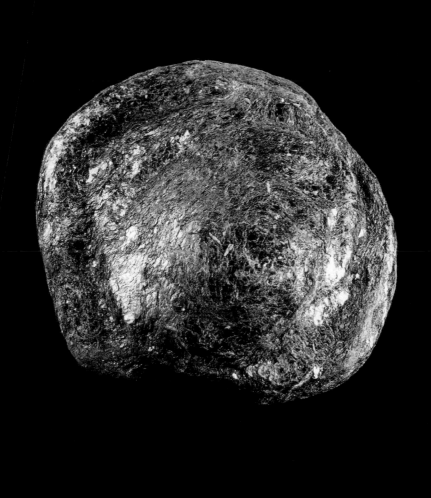

Boji stones

CRYSTAL SYSTEM: cubic
TYPE BY MANNER OF FORMATION: secondary
MINERAL CLASS: sulphide
COLOUR: grey to brown
CHEMICAL FORMULA, MINERAL-FORMING SUBSTANCES:

$FeS_2 + FeOOH \cdot n\, H_2O$

Mineralogy
Boji stones are spherical pyrites that were formed by a secondary process in the mud at the bottom of primeval oceans. They were then later weathered on the surface of the Earth where they obtained a coating of limonite. Depending on how far the weathering has progressed, the cubic crystals will still be visible (so-called 'male bojis') or absent ('female bojis').

Mythology
A number of modern myths have been spun around boji stones, none of which have any real foundation. No traditions regarding healing effects are known.

Healing
Spiritually Boji stones encourage conscious self-awareness and draw our attention to the present moment. They encourage all spiritual processes without judging them.

Emotionally Boji stones make us aware of blocked emotions, images and memories. They enhance emotions and moods and confront us with our shadow selves.

Mentally Boji stones encourage the acknowledgement of the kinds of thoughts and behaviours that hinder us and make us ill. They reveal clearly imprints and correspondences from the past.

Physically Boji stones stimulate the flow of energy in the meridians and make it easier for blockages to be dissolved in a pain-free manner. More severe blockages are brought into conscious awareness. Bojis are ideally suited to general prophylaxis in illnesses, but less for the treatment of acute illnesses.

Application
Simultaneously hold one stone each of a pair of bojis in each hand for about 10 to 30 minutes. This creates a battery-like charge that enhances the inner flow of energy.

Pair of boji stones.

Calcite

CRYSTAL SYSTEM: trigonal
TYPE BY MANNER OF FORMATION: primary or secondary
MINERAL CLASS: carbonate
COLOUR: white, pink, yellow, green, blue
CHEMICAL FORMULA, MINERAL-FORMING SUBSTANCES:
   $CaCO_3$ + Fe,Mn + (Co,Pb,Sr)

Mineralogy

Calcite is formed out of solutions containing calcium. It forms large crystals hydrothermally in clefts and druses. Far more frequently, however, calcite is formed through the sedimentation of solutions of weathered material.

Mythology

Calcite has been used for thousands of years as lime in folk medicine. It was used as a poultice mainly for skin diseases, ulcers, warts and suppurating wounds.

Healing

Spiritually Calcite has a strong effect in speeding up development. This is particularly noticeable in small children but also in adults who no longer believe in a positive turn in their lives.

Emotionally Calcite bestows stability, trust in ourselves and constancy. It is effective against laziness and fortifies the ability to overcome difficulties.

Mentally Calcite encourages the ability to transform ideas into actions. It improves the ability to discriminate and differentiate, also enhances memory and makes us more energetic, industrious and successful.

Physically Calcite stimulates the metabolism, fortifies the immune system and is growth-enhancing in small children. It alleviates skin and intestinal complaints, stimulates blood-clotting and encourages healing of tissue and bone. Calcite normalizes the rhythm of the heart and strengthens the heart.

Application

Calcite should be used as a hand 'comforter' or worn as a pendant for long periods of time or taken as an essence. The effects of the essence are stronger and more quickly noticeable.

Calcite, Brazil.

Chalcedony, blue

CRYSTAL SYSTEM: trigonal
TYPE BY MANNER OF FORMATION: primary or secondary
MINERAL CLASS: oxide, quartz group
COLOUR: white to light blue, partly banded
CHEMICAL FORMULA, MINERAL-FORMING SUBSTANCES: SiO_2

Mineralogy

Blue chalcedony is a pure, fibrous quartz formed at temperatures of below 100 degrees Celsius out of solutions rich in silicic acid, usually of magmatic origins and rarely of secondary origin,. These solutions percolate through fine cracks and veins in rock and collect in larger clefts and cysts, where they solidify and crystallize. Chalcedony obtains its light blue colour through bending light through its microscopically fine crystals (the 'Tyndall effect'), whereby the red portion of the light is absorbed and the blue portion is reflected.

Mythology

In antiquity, chalcedony was already known to represent the elements of air and water. As such, it was employed for weather magic and for healing illnesses that were connected with the weather, such as colds, sensitivity to changes in the weather or circulatory problems. It is also used for the spiritual aspect of the element air, in communication. It has always been considered to be the crystal of orators.

Healing

Spiritually Blue chalcedony represents both aspects of communication: the ability to listen and to understand, as well as the ability to communicate effectively. It encourages the pleasure of contact with other humans, with animals, plants and beings from all worlds. Just as the mineral itself is able to form itself into any given spaces during its formation, chalcedony also helps us to accept new situations and to get rid of resistance without at the same time losing our own character.

Emotionally Blue chalcedony bestows a light-heartedness, a carefree, elated feeling for life with an optimistic tenor. It enhances conscious self-awareness through improving perception of our feelings, emotions, desires and needs. This is how we learn about the true motives for our actions and are able to change them. In addition,

Banded chalcedony, Brazil;
chalcedony rosette, Brazil.

blue chalcedony improves memory, has a calming effect and dissolves stress (touchstone).

Mentally Blue chalcedony improves oratory, verbal dexterity and the ability to speak foreign languages. For this reason, chalcedony is also the crystal of diplomats. With this crystal, we remain mentally open to new ideas; it generally eases understanding and helps us to translate ideas we agree with into action. This increases creativity and openness to inspiration.

Physically Blue chalcedony alleviates problems of the respiratory tract such as colds or the effects of smoking. Banded chalcedony, in particular, encourages regeneration of the mucous membranes. Blue chalcedony also helps with complaints caused by extreme sensitivity to changes in the weather, problems with the eyes that relate to pressure (glaucoma), the ears, and our sense of balance. It has an anti-inflammatory effect, lowers the blood pressure and has a cooling effect in raised temperatures. It stimulates the flow of the lymphatic fluids and body fluids, abolishes water retention in the tissues (oedema) and enhances the immune system and the secretions of the glands. By stimulating insulin production, it can help with the early stages of diabetes.

Clear blue, white or rose coloured chalcedony, owing to its Type by manner of formation, encourages the formation of milk in nursing mothers. Mother's milk too is formed in spaces between the cells of the breast and then flows through finest channels to be collected in the gland of the breast.

Application
Chalcedony can be used as a hand 'comforter', worn on a chain or as a pendant or decorative jewellery for long periods, or laid directly on the diseased part of the body. When used for healing specific organs, chalcedony rosettes are recommended that have the 'signature' of the relevant organ. For example, rosettes with a 'signature' of female sexual organs help to encourage a healthy flora in the vagina and prevent fungal infections as blue chalcedony produces a slightly acid milieu in fluids.

Chalcedony, dendritic chalcedony

CRYSTAL SYSTEM: trigonal
TYPE BY MANNER OF FORMATION: primary or secondary
MINERAL CLASS: oxide, quartz group
COLOUR: white, light blue with black 'dendrites'
CHEMICAL FORMULA, MINERAL-FORMING SUBSTANCES: $SiO_2 + MnO_2$

Mineralogy

Dendritic chalcedony is formed from solidified silicic acid into which liquid containing manganese has penetrated without creating a mixture . This forms the black dendrites (Greek *dendron*, 'tree') that give the stone its name.

Mythology

In the Middle Ages, the manganese contained in this chalcedony was assigned to the cleansing aspect of the element fire; coloured, impure glass did indeed become clear and pure through melting it together with manganese dioxide.

Healing

Spiritually Dendritic chalcedony represents an affable, sociable nature which is, however, still able to discriminate clearly between its own goals and the opinions and influences of others.

Emotionally Dendritic chalcedony encourages clear thinking, systematic research, the art of unravelling confusion as well as the ability to identify precisely what motives and values really lie behind a piece of information.

Mentally: Dendritic chalcedony encourages precise thinking, systematic enquiry, the ability to clarify confusion, as well as the ability to comprehend the real meaning and motives behind information received.

Physically The effects of dendritic chalcedony are similar to those of blue chalcedony. Its effects are even stronger in the case of chronic illnesses and the physical problems associated with smoking.

Application

Dendritic chalcedony can be used as a hand 'comforter', a pendant or a piece of jewellery and worn for long periods of time close to the body or directly on the afflicted part of the body.

Chalcedony, copper chalcedony

CRYSTAL SYSTEM: trigonal
TYPE BY MANNER OF FORMATION: secondary
MINERAL CLASS: oxide, quartz group
COLOUR: blue green with copper inclusions
CHEMICAL FORMULA, MINERAL-FORMING SUBSTANCES: SiO_2 + Cu + (Cu)

Mineralogy

Copper chalcedony is formed in the cementation zone of rock that contains copper. The copper, which is initially dissolved by the silicic acid, is then partially reduced and is, therefore, preserved as metallic copper in the chalcedony.

Mythology

There are no known traditions for copper chalcedony itself, although copper has always been considered a metal of Venus. It represents love, beauty, sensuality and harmony, and also balance and neutrality.

Healing

Spiritually Copper chalcedony helps us live in the present in full awareness, to face unpleasant things, to communicate calmly when attacked, and to remain relaxed. It helps reveal the true meaning of life and awakens a sense for aesthetics and harmony. It helps us enjoy life.

Emotionally Copper chalcedony stimulates proper processing of inner images and memories. It eases an open, friendly attitude towards fellow human beings and the environment.

Mentally Copper chalcedony helps us preserve neutrality and see situations, other humans and experiences without judging. It encourages both a proper sense of judgement and tolerance.

Physically Copper chalcedony stimulates the metabolism of copper in the body and the detoxification of the liver. It hinders inflammations of the female sexual organs and prevents fungal infections (thrush) in the vagina. Copper chalcedony has an immunity-enhancing effect.

Application

Copper chalcedony can be worn for long periods of time on the body or laid directly on the relevant part.

*Blue chalcedony, Turkey,
dendritic chalcedony, Brazil*

Chalcedony, pink

CRYSTAL SYSTEM: trigonal
TYPE BY MANNER OF FORMATION: secondary
MINERAL CLASS: oxide, quartz group
COLOUR: pink to pink violet
CHEMICAL FORMULA, MINERAL-FORMING SUBSTANCES: SiO_2+ (Mn)

Mineralogy
Pink chalcedony is formed by sedimentary processes. It is formed from surface water containing silicic acid that penetrates the oxidation zone of rock that contains manganese.

Mythology
No traditions are known for pink chalcedony but there are some for manganese that gives this mineral its rosy colour. Here it represents sustaining warmth, inner fire and liveliness.

Healing
Spiritually Pink chalcedony represents liveliness, understanding and helpfulness. It enhances the ability to listen, to understand and to help others deal with their problems and sorrows.

Emotionally Pink chalcedony encourages goodness, kindness and warm-heartedness. It bestows a carefree attitude, inner peace and deep trust, particularly in the case of conflicts and psychosomatic illnesses, such as anxiety about the heart (heart neuroses).

Mentally Pink chalcedony teaches us to view the world with a sense of wonder. It bestows a child-like curiosity, the willingness to learn new things and encourages the gift for story telling.

Physically Pink chalcedony bestows liveliness and warmth. It fortifies the heart so it can function strongly without effort. Pink chalcedony eases breastfeeding and provides the inner tranquillity for the task. Just like blue chalcedony, it enhances the immune system and the flow of lymphatic fluids.

Application
Pink chalcedony can be worn close to the body for longer periods of time or can be laid directly on the relevant part of the body. In cases of heart problems or for easing breastfeeding, it should, if possible, be in contact with the skin.

Pink chalcedony, Turkey.

Chalcedony, red

CRYSTAL SYSTEM: trigonal
TYPE BY MANNER OF FORMATION: secondary
MINERAL CLASS: oxide, quartz group
COLOUR: dark red
CHEMICAL FORMULA, MINERAL-FORMING SUBSTANCES: SiO_2+ Fe

Mineralogy

Red chalcedony is usually formed by secondary processes. It is formed from a viscous silicic acid solution containing iron, in which iron is not dissolved in the solution but is retained in the form of a flaky iron oxide.

Mythology

No traditions about red chalcedony have been handed down. The iron that gives it its red colour has, however, been assigned to Mars, and represents willpower, activity, dynamism and the joy of undertaking tasks.

Healing

Spiritually Red chalcedony bestows strength, persistence and the energy to overcome difficulties and attain set goals. It helps with choosing the right strategy – to give in, fight or keep still – and keeps the mind flexible without at the same time forgetting our own point of view.

Emotionally Red chalcedony bestows strength and confidence. It makes us aware of our own life's dreams and helps to prove them and realize them without letting a fixation upon them arise.

Mentally Red chalcedony encourages the ability to design strategies. It encourages openness and inspiration and fortifies our intentions, which makes it easier to be heard.

Physically Red chalcedony encourages clotting of the blood and stimulates the blood circulation without allowing the blood pressure to become high. It inhibits the absorption of nutrients in the small intestine and reduces hunger pangs.

Application

Red chalcedony should only be used continuously for about two to three weeks. As it inhibits the absorption of nutrients, longer use may induce temporary nausea.

(clockwise from left to right): Blue chalcedony, pink chalcedony, copper chalcedony, Turkey; red chalcedony, Russia.

Charoite

CRYSTAL SYSTEM: monoclinic
TYPE BY MANNER OF FORMATION: tertiary
MINERAL CLASS: phyllo or sheet silicate
COLOUR: grey, violet, pink
CHEMICAL FORMULA, MINERAL-FORMING SUBSTANCES:
$(Ca,Na)_4(K,Sr,Ba)_2[(OH,F)_2Si_9O_{22}] \cdot H_2O$

Mineralogy

Charoite is formed metasomatically in the zone of contact between magmatic and metamorphic rocks from a combination of alkaline magmatic solutions with mineral-forming substances of the surrounding rocks.

Mythology

Charoite originates from Siberia and has only been available in the West for a few years. Unfortunately, no traditions on its healing effects are known.

Healing

Spiritually Charoite helps us cope with profound changes in our lives. It bestows determination, spontaneity, vigour and drive, whenever tasks that have not been dealt with threaten to grow into unmanageable proportions, and also helps overcome resistance.

Emotionally Charoite imparts a relaxed attitude towards things and makes us impervious to stress and worry. It bestows quiet, refreshing sleep with intense, creative dreams.

Mentally Charoite helps us make decisions in a thoughtful but unhesitating fashion. It encourages perceptive observation, including that of oneself, and dissolves heteronomy (feeling subjected to orders by others) and compulsions.

Physically Charoite helps relieve cramps and encourages an alkaline metabolism. It calms the nerves, alleviates pain and helps with problems of the autonomous nervous system, particularly if the heart is affected by them.

Application

Charoite should be worn about the body with skin contact. Spending time in a circle of charoite stones also has a very intense effect.

Charoite, Russia; chiastolite, Chile.

Chiastolite

CRYSTAL SYSTEM: rhombic
TYPE BY MANNER OF FORMATION: primary
MINERAL CLASS: island silicate, andalusite family
COLOUR: brown, grey with black cruciform inclusions
CHEMICAL FORMULA, MINERAL-FORMING SUBSTANCES:
$Al_2[O/SiO_4]$ + C,Ca,Cr,Fe,K,Mg,Mn,Ti

Mineralogy

Chiastolite is an andalusite formed in carbonaceous clayey slates. Carbon is deposited along the crystal edges of this mineral. Because the growth process of the crystal occurs in layers, carbonaceous diagonal cruciform shapes are formed as it grows.

Mythology

The cross with equal sized 'arms' as displayed in chiastolite is an ancient symbol for multiplication (hence the 'x' symbol for multiplying). The meaning of the symbol has, therefore, also been transferred to this mineral.

Healing

Spiritually Chiastolite gives us persistence in realizing our own identity and our life's task. It encourages a proper sense of reality, sobriety and alertness and dissolves illusions.

Emotionally Chiastolite is extremely calming in cases of nervousness, fears and feelings of guilt. It centres, stabilizes and helps us, particularly against the fear of going mad.

Mentally Chiastolite fortifies the analytical capabilities of the intellect. It enhances conscious awareness and helps us discard behavioural patterns of holding on and holding back.

Physically Chiastolite alleviates excess acidification and its consequences, for example, rheumatism and gout. It fortifies the nerves and helps in states of weakness, slowed perception and movement, even in cases of paralysis.

Application

The best idea is to meditate daily with chiastolite, in order to obtain the desired spiritual, emotional and mental effects. It can also be worn or laid on the body.

Chrysoberyl

CRYSTAL SYSTEM: rhombic
TYPE BY MANNER OF FORMATION: primary or tertiary
MINERAL CLASS: oxide
COLOUR: brown, yellow, greenish
CHEMICAL FORMULA, MINERAL-FORMING SUBSTANCES: Al_2BeO_4 + Ti

Mineralogy
Chrysoberyl is formed magmatically, mainly in pegmatites, or metamorphically during the formation of mica slates. Its crystals are, as a rule, only a few millimetres long (there are about 25 millimetres in an inch).

Mythology
In antiquity, chrysoberyl was seen as identical to golden beryl. Its name was not transferred to the present-day mineral until the eighteenth century. Present-day chrysoberyl is only known for being the stone of rulers and generals.

Healing
Spiritually Chrysoberyl bestows severity, authority and leadership qualities. It encourages (self) discipline, self-control, ambition and independence and brings to light hidden talents.

Emotionally Chrysoberyl helps with fears, feelings of apprehension and nightmares. It enables us to do what is necessary without becoming overwhelmed by feelings and moods.

Mentally Chrysoberyl encourages strategic thinking and planning, as well as becoming conscious of and recognizing thought, behavioural and social structures.

Physically Chrysoberyl enhances the self-healing properties of the body and helps with illnesses and inflammations in the area of the chest. Chrysoberyl fortifies the liver.

Application
Chrysoberyl works simply by being worn about your body. Permanent skin contact is not necessary. It will be sufficient to hold it in your hand occasionally.

Chrysoberyl, alexandrite

CRYSTAL SYSTEM: rhombic
TYPE BY MANNER OF FORMATION: tertiary
MINERAL CLASS: oxide, chrysoberyl family
COLOUR: green in sunlight, in artificial light red to violet
CHEMICAL FORMULA, MINERAL-FORMING SUBSTANCES: Al_2BeO_4 + Cr,Ti

Mineralogy

Alexandrite is a metamorphic chrysoberyl containing chromium. It is created during the formation of mica slates. The chromium contained in it causes a fascinating change of colour: alexandrite looks green in sunlight and red to violet in artificial light.

Mythology

Alexandrite was discovered in the Ural mountains of Russia in 1833 and was the favourite stone of the Russian Czar Alexander II. It rapidly became the national stone of Russia owing to the colour change from red to green, which corresponded to Russia's military colours.

Healing

Spiritually Alexandrite combines stark contrasts: intuition, clairvoyance and mediumistic tendencies are encouraged, just as are a strong will, spiritual greatness and personal magic.

Emotionally Alexandrite intensifies our experience of imagery. This helps make not only dreams and inner images but also feelings and desires clearer. It also refines our perception of imagination and visualization.

Mentally Alexandrite, like chrysoberyl, encourages strategic thinking and planning, but also enhances the willingness to take risks and to trust our inner voice more than logic.

Physically Alexandrite amplifies the power of self-healing and helps particularly with inflammations of all kinds. It has a detoxifying effect and stimulates the regenerative powers of the liver.

Application

I recommend meditating with alexandrite for spiritual and emotional effects, used alternately in sunlight and by candlelight. Otherwise, it will be sufficient to carry it about your person.

Chrysoberyl, Zimbabwe;
chrysoberyl triplet, Brazil;
alexandrite, Russia.

Chrysocolla

CRYSTAL SYSTEM: monoclinic
TYPE BY MANNER OF FORMATION: secondary
MINERAL CLASS: ring silicate
COLOUR: green to turquoise
CHEMICAL FORMULA, MINERAL-FORMING SUBSTANCES:
   $CuSiO_3 \cdot H_2O$ + Al,Fe,P

Mineralogy

Chrysocolla is formed in the oxidation zone of copper ore mines, wherever surface water containing silicic acid dissolves copper out of the rock.

Mythology

Chrysocolla was known as healing stone mainly among the native American Indian cultures, where it was used for strengthening the body's resistance and for calming upset feelings.

Healing

Spiritually Chrysocolla encourages a balanced nature and self-awareness. It helps us accept situations that are constantly changing and to pursue our own goals in spite of ups and downs.

Emotionally Chrysocolla bestows drive in cases of laziness but, at the same time, improves nervousness and irritability.

Mentally Chrysocolla helps us keep a 'cool head'. It encourages neutrality and clarity.

Physically Chrysocolla helps with infections, particularly those of the tonsils and throat area. It detoxifies and fortifies the liver functions. Chrysocolla has a cooling effect, lowers the blood pressure and speeds up healing of burns. It regulates the functioning of the thyroid gland and helps in cases of stress-related digestive disturbances. Chrysocolla also has fever-reducing properties and alleviates cramps, particularly in menstruation problems.

Application

In any cases of physical complaints, chrysocolla helps best if it is placed directly on the afflicted part of the body. Wearing chrysocolla helps the mind/soul, and laying it on the forehead (as a 'third eye') helps spiritually.

Chrysocolla, USA;
chrysocolla, Peru.

Chrysoprase

CRYSTAL SYSTEM: trigonal
TYPE BY MANNER OF FORMATION: secondary
Mineral class: oxide, quartz group
COLOUR: apple green
CHEMICAL FORMULA, MINERAL-FORMING SUBSTANCES: SiO_2 + (Ni)

Mineralogy

Chrysoprase is an apple green chalcedony that obtains its colour from nickel traces. It is formed through a secondary process from solutions of silicic acid in the oxidation zone of nickel deposits. The nickel that is dissolved out of the surrounding rock by silicic acid will only give the mineral its colour as long as there is also water contained in the crystal lattice of the mineral. During the intermediate stage, prase opal is created, which looks almost identical to chrysoprase. This, in turn, is transformed into chrysoprase through loss of water. When it dries out completely, it loses its characteristic green colour and turns pale.

Mythology

In antiquity, chrysoprase was assigned to Venus. It does not, however, represent physical sensuality or love for the other sex but the 'very divine love of truth', as later summarized by the seer Emmanuel Swedenborg. This aims at a sense of justice that is also an attribute of the goddess Venus. Hildegard von Bingen assigned a detoxifying effect to chrysoprase and mentions its healing power particularly with gout. She also recommended it for calming anger and even for preventing speaking thoughtlessly in anger. This also demonstrates its relation to chalcedony.

Healing

Spiritually Chrysoprase endows us with the experience of being part of a greater whole. It makes us alert and quick-witted and draws our attention to seemingly random coincidences in which we can perceive the activity of the spiritual realm. Chrysoprase encourages a simple, child-like world view in which guardian angels and spirit guides are not in conflict with logical or rational considerations. Chrysoprase combines a search for truth with patience so we can become happy even if we only understand a tiny fraction of the universe. It encourages an appreciation of aesthetics, art and beauty.

Chrysoprase, Australia;
citrine, Brazil.

Emotionally Chrysoprase bestows trust and a feeling of security. It helps us become independent of others and be content with ourselves. This reduces jealousy and heartache and also helps with sexual problems. Just as it physically detoxifies, chrysoprase also relieves us of oppressive images, or helps us deal with them. It puts an end to recurring nightmares, particularly in children who wake up crying at night without recognizing their surroundings.

Mentally Chrysoprase helps us recognize egotistical motives in actions and encourages us to examine whether our real actions are in harmony with our own inner ideals. It helps us to avoid compulsive actions, behaviour and thought patterns. In cases of negative attitudes, chrysoprase draws the attention to positive events and thus alters the 'perception filter' with which we normally try to confirm our own inner attitude through selective perception.

Physically Chrysoprase stimulates detoxification and elimination. Even heavy metals and other substances that are difficult to dissolve are eliminated from the body. In addition, the liver's functions are strongly stimulated. Illnesses that have occurred as a result of toxification (including through taking strong medicines) can be healed in this way. Chrysoprase also helps many skin diseases, even some forms of neurodermititis, and helps in combination with smoky quartz for fungal infections. It also stimulates fertility in women, particularly if infections have led to infertility.

Application

Chrysoprase can be used on a chain, pendant or hand 'comforter' for longer periods of time or be laid directly on the relevant part of the body. Its eliminating properties are supported by diet cures. The strongest effect in acute cases is achieved by taking an elixir of chrysoprase.

Citrine

CRYSTAL SYSTEM: trigonal
TYPE BY MANNER OF FORMATION: primary
MINERAL CLASS: oxide, quartz group
COLOUR: yellow
CHEMICAL FORMULA, MINERAL-FORMING SUBSTANCES:
  SiO_2 + (Al,Fe,Ca,Mg,Li,Na)

Mineralogy

Citrine is a yellow crystal quartz that derives its colour from minimum amounts of additional iron and from slightly ionizing radiation. By contrast to amethyst, the iron in citrine is present in its three-valent (Fe^{3+}) form. Citrine is formed in pegmatites or hydrothermally in druses and clefts.

Mythology

The term 'citrine' was used up until the sixteenth century for many different yellow coloured stones (beryl, zircon, etc.). It was not until 1546 that the term was first clearly assigned to yellow quartz. Modern citrine was then said to be able to strengthen the intellect and provoke a sunny disposition.

Healing

Spiritually Citrine encourages individuality, self-confidence and the courage to face and enjoy life. It makes us dynamic and encourages a desire for variety, new experiences and self-realization.

Emotionally Citrine bestows *joie de vivre*. It helps us overcome depression and free ourselves from oppressive influences. Citrine makes us extroverted and encourages self-expression.

Mentally Citrine helps us digest impressions we have received. It stimulates the ability to confront and help ourselves, to draw conclusions rapidly and to understand them.

Physically Citrine stimulates the digestion. It promotes the working of the stomach, spleen and pancreas and will even alleviate diabetes in its early stages. Citrine fortifies the nerves and has a warming effect.

Application

Citrine should be worn in contact with the skin or used, for example, as a sphere or crystal for meditation.

Diamond

CRYSTAL SYSTEM: cubic
TYPE BY MANNER OF FORMATION: tertiary
MINERAL CLASS: natural elements
COLOUR: clear, pink, yellow, green, blue
CHEMICAL FORMULA, MINERAL-FORMING SUBSTANCES:
C_n + (Al,Ca,Cr,Fe,Mg,Mn,Si,Sr,Ti)

Mineralogy

Diamonds are formed in peridotite and eclogite rock at depths of approximately 150–200 kilometres (90–125 miles). The pressure at these depths of around 40 000 atmospheres and temperatures of more than 2000 degrees Celsius are such that carbon that is present in the form of hexagonal graphite is transformed into diamond in a very sudden and rapid metamorphosis. The mineral is then brought to the surface from the inside of the Earth through volcanic eruptions, when rising lava rips entire pieces of rock from the deep rock and takes them up with it. This mixture of lava and rock in the volcanic chimney then forms rocks called kimberlite and lamproite, in which diamonds are later found.

Because of its material purity (pure carbon), diamonds can be absolutely clear and transparent. Its ability to bend light is very pronounced (its 'fire') and it is the hardest mineral known (by a wide margin). Trace deposits of other elements in diamond will display a great variety of colours. Nitrogen will give rise to the colours yellow and green; aluminium, oxygen, magnesium, iron and boron will produce a blue colouring; manganese will create a pink colour.

Mythology

The name 'diamond' is derived from the Greek *adamas*, 'invincible'. This is precisely the theme that runs through the entire mythology of the diamond. In many cultures, the diamond was assigned to Venus. It was seen as a liberator from demonic influences and represented justice and virtue. In the Middle Ages, it symbolized strength, courage and invulnerability. The diamond was thought to protect whoever carried it from the threat of danger and also to encourage the development of a noble character. Woe betide anyone, however, who dared to steal it or obtain it by foul or unjust means. Then it appeared to bring bad luck, as demonstrated by the history of all the great and famous diamonds. The tradition that the diamond is helpful with

mental illnesses and nervous complaints has been upheld to the present day.

Healing

Spiritually The diamond endows us with a clear insight into our own life's situation. It helps us cope with life's trials and tests and serves to ennoble the character. Diamonds bring order into our life and help us get rid of both poor compromises and unnecessary rules and restrictions. It encourages spiritual freedom and helps us to develop integrity, that is, to be true to ourselves. It fortifies our sense of ethics and inner justice. Thus, it creates objectivity, the ability to do what is right without prejudice.

Emotionally Diamond helps us overcome fear, depression and a feeling of a lack of meaning in our lives. It helps overcome crises that have arisen through the failure of plans and goals. Diamonds make us aware of the causes of problems or illnesses and also make it possible to examine them without bias. This enables us to achieve better control of our inner images, our feelings and moods, and ultimately of our entire lives.

Mentally Diamonds help us gain a complete overview of the consequences of our own actions. They encourage logical thinking and make it possible for us to observe broader connections between things. Diamond bestows the ability to learn easily, making immediate connections between new impressions and familiar things. This means that things we have learned can be applied quickly. Diamond encourages the ability to make clear decisions and solve problems.

Physically Diamond can be employed whenever insight or long overdue change in our life become necessary. In particular, it heals diseases of those organs that have a direct bearing on mental activities, for example the brain, nervous system, sensory organs and hormonal glands. Just as it is able to improve the mental control of our lives, it also fortifies control of our body.

Application

Diamond can be worn as jewellery in a proper setting, on the body, or on our forehead during meditation ('third eye'). Diamond also enhances the effects of other crystals.

Dioptase

CRYSTAL SYSTEM: trigonal
TYPE BY MANNER OF FORMATION: secondary
MINERAL CLASS: ring silicate
COLOUR: dark green
CHEMICAL FORMULA, MINERAL-FORMING SUBSTANCES: $Cu_6(Si_6O_{18}) \cdot 6\ H_2O$

Mineralogy

Dioptase is formed in the sedimentary process out of silicic acid solutions containing copper in clefts of limestone and sandstone rock, or in the oxidation zone of copper ore deposits.

Mythology

Dioptase (also called 'copper emerald' in German) was always considered to be a stone of abundance and riches. It was assigned to Venus and represents a sense of beauty.

Healing

Spiritually Dioptase makes us aware of our inner riches. It helps shed light on our own capabilities and realize our ambitions.

Emotionally Dioptase encourages self-awareness. It bestows vivid dreams, hope and depth of feeling and stimulates us to place ourselves at the centre of general interest.

Mentally Dioptase enlivens the imagination and the ability to use the imagination creatively. It stimulates creativity, engenders abundance of ideas and makes it easier for them to be translated into action.

Physically Dioptase stimulates the regenerative power of the liver. It has a pain alleviating effect, loosens cramp, and helps with chronic headaches.

Application

Dioptase forms only very tiny crystals and fragile small groups. This means it can only very rarely be worn. To help unfold its spiritual, soul and mental effects, I therefore recommend resting the gaze on it during meditation or laying it on the forehead. For healing work on the body, it should be carefully placed on the relevant afflicted area.

Disthene, kyanite

CRYSTAL SYSTEM: triclinic
TYPE BY MANNER OF FORMATION: tertiary
MINERAL CLASS: island silicate
COLOUR: blue, blue-grey
CHEMICAL FORMULA, MINERAL-FORMING SUBSTANCES:
$Al_2[O/SiO_4] + Ca,Cr,Fe,K,Mg,Ti]$

Mineralogy

Disthene, also called kyanite, is formed during the metamorphosis of crystalline slates and is numbered among their characteristic leading minerals.

Mythology

In antiquity, kyanos was a collective term for blue minerals (azurite, lapis lazuli). The present mineral did not receive its name until the eighteenth century. This is why there are no existing traditions on the effects of disthene/kyanite. The name disthene originated in the nineteenth century and neither of the two names has managed to gain a clear upper hand.

Healing

Spiritually Disthene helps us to detach ourselves from a belief in fate and to recognize when and where we have created the causes that have certain effects later on. Disthene also gives us determination.

Emotionally Disthene leads to a calming effect on the inner world of images and stirred-up emotions. It encourages a pleasant, peaceful nature and liberates us from frustrations and stress.

Mentally Disthene encourages logical, rational thought and spontaneous action whenever necessary. Disthene also encourages conscious self-awareness.

Physically Disthene fortifies the functions of the cerebellum and of the motor nervous system, thus improving mobility and dexterity.

Application

Disthene is, at present, only known in the form of crystals or as a component of metamorphic rock. The best way to use it is to carry it about.

Disthene, Brazil.

Dolomite

CRYSTAL SYSTEM: trigonal
TYPE BY MANNER OF FORMATION: primary or secondary
MINERAL CLASS: carbonate
COLOUR: brown, red, white
CHEMICAL FORMULA, MINERAL-FORMING SUBSTANCES:
$CaMg(CO_3)_2$ + Fe,Mn + (Pb,Zn,S)

Mineralogy
Dolomite is sometimes formed hydrothermally in cracks and passages where it forms small, often bent crystals. It is found much more frequently in rock-forming processes as grainy masses in sediments (for example, in the Dolomites).

Mythology
In 1791, during his journeys through the Alps, a man called Dolomieu discovered limestones that differed in their properties from the usual limestone. Following this, the composition of dolomite was investigated for the first time. This is why there are no traditions regarding dolomite as it was previously always identified with calcite.

Healing
Spiritually Dolomite encourages self-realization. It makes it easier to be ourselves without pretending otherwise. At the same time, it fortifies a sense of tradition and helps us fit into developing communities.

Emotionally Dolomite ensures stability. It has a balancing effect in cases of sudden, violent emotional outbursts and bestows contentment.

Mentally Dolomite encourages simple, pragmatic thought and helps with the easy, uncomplicated realization of goals we have set for ourselves. Dolomite also stimulates healthy commonsense.

Physically Dolomite stimulates the metabolism of calcium and magnesium and keeps the balance between these two 'opponents'. This means it stabilizes health, particularly blood, the heart and the circulation, and has a relaxing, cramp-dissolving effect.

Application
Dolomite can be worn or laid on. The strongest effect is achieved by spending time in a place with dolomite rock or in a stone circle of dolomite.

Dolomite, Brazil;
dolomite with pyrite, Switzerland.

Dumortierite

CRYSTAL SYSTEM: rhombic
TYPE BY MANNER OF FORMATION: primary or tertiary
MINERAL CLASS: island silicate
COLOUR: blue, violet blue, brown
CHEMICAL FORMULA, MINERAL-FORMING SUBSTANCES:
  $(Al,Fe)_7[O_3/BO_3/(SiO_4)_3] + Mn$

Mineralogy
Dumortierite is formed mainly magmatically in pegmatites or through pneumatolytic displacement (the influence of boric acid on aluminium silicate rock) and may also have a contact metamorphic or regional metamorphic origin.

Mythology
Dumortierite was not discovered until the end of the nineteenth century and named after the French palaeontologist Eugène Dumortier. This is why there are no existing traditions about its effects.

Healing

Spiritually Dumortierite bestows a positive attitude towards life. It provides courage and trust in difficult situations and helps us gain control over our own life or preserve it.

Emotionally Dumortierite confers an easy, cheerful outlook on life and is, therefore, often termed the 'take-it-easy' stone. Dumortierite helps us cope with panic and fear and encourages harmony and trust.

Mentally Dumortierite helps us recognize compulsive behavioural patterns and dissolve them. It is, therefore, also used as a supportive aid in addiction therapy.

Physically Dumortierite helps with nausea, vomiting, cramp, colic and diarrhoea. It alleviates skin irritation caused by toxins or radiation (UV light) and helps with nervous problems, for example with severe headaches, epilepsy or disturbances of perception.

Application
Dumortierite can be worn for long periods of time or, in acute cases, directly on the afflicted part of the body.

Epidote

CRYSTAL SYSTEM: monoclinic
TYPE BY MANNER OF FORMATION: primary or tertiary
MINERAL CLASS: group silicate
COLOUR: pistachio green, black, grey, rarely yellow
CHEMICAL FORMULA, MINERAL-FORMING SUBSTANCES:
$Ca_2(Fe,Al)Al_2[O/OH/SiO_4/Si_2O_7]$ + K,Mg,Mn,Sr,Ti

Mineralogy

Epidote is formed in many magmatic types of rock. It can be found as large, dark green to black crystals, but these are rare, as they are formed almost exclusively hydrothermally in clefts. During contact or regional metamorphoses, epidote very often orginates as a rock-forming mineral where the transformed rocks are alkaline and rich in calcium and aluminium. Mingled with red feldspar, it forms a rock that is obtainable in the mineral trade as 'unakite'.

Mythology

Epidote was not identified as a separate mineral until the beginning of the nineteenth century, by the French crystallographer Rene-Just Haüy (see also Part 1, Chapter 1.2). Before that, it was always considered to be the same mineral as actinolite. Epidote also received its name from Haüy. It means something like 'addition' (Latin) as epidote, unlike actinolite, has two 'extended' sides. Unfortunately, there are at no traditions about the healing effects of epidote.

Healing

Spiritually Epidote bestows patience. It dissolves false self-images, makes us aware of reality and highlights the weaknesses and strengths of the true self-image. This results in desires for change that are, however, realistic so they can be realized and success can then build on success. In this manner, epidote takes us back to the original positive inner images of a healthy, happy existence. This is exactly the meaning of 're-generate' (re, 'back, again, anew'; generere, 'to form').

Emotionally Epidote encourages recovery and regeneration after severe illnesses or in cases of great exhaustion caused by overwork, stress and painful experiences. It lifts the emotions and dissolves sadness, sorrow, self-pity and grief. Epidote also helps overcome frustration caused by failure and teaches us not to devalue ourselves because of mistakes we have made.

Mentally Epidote improves our capabilities. It helps us live up to our own demands on ourselves in an appropriate fashion, that is, with due consideration of our own strength and ability, and in this way saves us from failure. By gradually increasing these demands, our own capabilities can then be harmoniously expanded and developed. Epidote also helps us accept and admit to our weaknesses.

Physically Epidote strengthens the constitution and our general condition, stimulates the immune system and generally supports all healing processes. It can, therefore, be added to other minerals if their choice is appropriate but the effect is not able to unfold properly if there is a great weakness present. Along with all this, epidote also stimulates the liver in its function as our central organ of regeneration, encourages the production of gall, and improves the digestive processes in the small intestine. This means that more nutrients are absorbed into the bloodstream which, in turn, has a building up, fortifying effect.

Application

The spiritual effect of epidote is most obvious in meditation. In this case, an epidote crystal can be either laid on the forehead or on the solar plexus. A similar effect is achieved by spending time in an epidote circle (it may even be formed into a double circle) that will, at the same time, noticeably stimulate the regeneration of mind and body. Otherwise, this mineral can be worn for a long period of time as a chain, pendant or hand 'comforter', and can be laid on the afflicted part of the body in cases of acute illness.

Dumortierite, Peru;
epidote, USA.

Falcon's eye

CRYSTAL SYSTEM: trigonal
TYPE BY MANNER OF FORMATION: primary
MINERAL CLASS: oxide, quartz group
COLOUR: blue-black
CHEMICAL FORMULA, MINERAL-FORMING SUBSTANCE:
$$SiO_2 + Na_2(Mg,Fe,Al)_5(OH/Si_4O_{11})_2 + P$$

Mineralogy

Falcon's eye is formed hydrothermally/metasomatically during the silicification of crocidolite (black-blue asbestos fibres). The fibrous crystals of crocidolite are tightly enclosed in the quartz.

Mythology

The silky gleam which the asbestos fibres create in the quartz makes light play in the round polished stone in a way that resembles an eye. This is how the stone gets its name, and also explains an ancient belief that falcon's eye can cure eye complaints and give protection. In the Middle Ages, falcon's eye was worn as an amulet against witchcraft, demons and the evil eye.

Healing

Spiritually Falcon's eye helps us see the seemingly random events of everyday life in a broader context. It bestows an understanding of our own life plan.

Emotionally Falcon's eye lends a proper distance to our own feelings and emotions and, thereby, helps us be less influenced by mood fluctuations.

Mentally Falcon's eye helps us gain a better overview in complicated situations and helps with difficulties in making decisions.

Physically Falcon's eye has a pain-alleviating effect. It tones down the flow of energies in the body, so helping with nervousness and trembling, as well as with an excitability of the glands that govern hormone production.

Application

Bearing in mind that falcon's eye buffers the flow of energies in the body, it should never be worn continuously for more than a week. Meditation with the stone is preferable for achieving emotional/spiritual effects.

Falcon's eye, South Africa.

Fluorite

CRYSTAL SYSTEM: cubic
TYPE BY MANNER OF FORMATION: primary
MINERAL CLASS: halide
COLOUR: clear, yellow, green, blue, violet
CHEMICAL FORMULA, MINERAL-FORMING SUBSTANCES:
CaF_2 + (C,Cl,Fe,Ce,Y)

Mineralogy

Fluorite can be formed in primary, secondary or even tertiary processes. The largest occurrences are, however, of magmatic origin, in which fluorite arises as a component of acid magmatic rocks or in passages and in clefts. Much more rarely, it is formed in a secondary process through the action of fluoric acid released during weathering of calcium-bearing rock.

Mythology

Fluorite has been known as fluorspar since the eighteenth century. Before that, it was not recognized as a separate mineral but simply belonged among the 'spars', a general term for minerals that break in 'leaves' (related to 'cleaving', from the German *spalten*). It was also classed among substances called by the German name *Fluss* ('flow'), an equally general term denoting additives that enable ore to reach a melting point more quickly (German *fliessen*, 'to flow, melt'), or even among the German *Glasflusse* ('molten glasses'), products that arise during the production of glass. Fluorite, like glass and coloured quartzes, can be used for the production of imitation gems. This is the reason why it is not possible to establish now whether the old names 'ruby glass', 'topaz glass', etc. actually refer to fluorite or to quartz and glass. This makes it equally difficult to establish any definite traditions concerning its healing properties!

Healing

Spiritually Fluorite stimulates the 'free spirit' that wishes to determine and shape his/her own life. It makes us aware of where we are being controlled by outside influences and are 'not playing our own game', and helps us rapidly dissolve these undesirable influences. Fluorite can make us radical and uncompromising whenever we come across injustice or oppressive structures. At the same time, it helps us structure our own existence and enables us to find systems that are stable but dynamic. Generally speaking, fluorite

Fluorite, Black Forest, Germany; fluorite, USA.

makes us creative and inventive, with the dominant theme being 'free decision-making'.

Emotionally Fluorite makes us aware of suppressed feelings. It does not, however, emphasize their expression, but helps them 'happen gradually'. Fluorite opens the gateway to the subconscious, but as a rule an external event will have to trigger this until we suddenly recognize the depth of feeling we have achieved. Overall, fluorite has an emotionally stabilizing effect, gives us self-confidence, and clears up confusion.

Mentally Fluorite helps dissolve blocks, fixed ideas, 'small thinking', narrow-mindedness and constricting thought and behavioural patterns. It also helps with organization and the rapid processing of information. This makes it an excellent learning aid as it stimulates us to make cross-references to existing knowledge and become more aware of things that have not yet been understood conceptually. Fluorite stimulates rapid absorbing of information and quick thinking.

Physically Fluorite stimulates the regeneration of the skin and mucous membranes, particularly in the respiratory tract and the lungs, and helps with ulcers and suppurating wounds. It fortifies the bones and teeth, decreases adhesions and helps with posture problems. Fluorite makes us physically mobile and improves stiffness and joint problems, including cases of arthritis (inflammation of the joints). The activity of the nervous system, particularly the cerebrum, is encouraged and psychosomatic allergies are alleviated.

Application

The spiritual effect of fluorite is felt most through meditating with banded Chinese fluorite (expression of creativity) or with fluorite octahedrons (expression of order). In order to achieve more sense of order, it will be sufficient to place fluorite groups or octahedrons in your personal environment, or as a learning aid on your desk. Otherwise, fluorite can be carried or laid directly on the body.

Fluorite octahedra, USA.

Garnet

CRYSTAL SYSTEM: cubic
TYPE BY MANNER OF FORMATION: tertiary
MINERAL CLASS: island silicate
COLOUR: red, pink, orange, yellow, green brown to black
CHEMICAL FORMULA, MINERAL-FORMING SUBSTANCES:

$Me^{2+}_3Me^{3+}_2(SiO_4)$ + Al,Ca,Fe,Mg,Mn,Ti

Mineralogy

Garnet is really a mineral group that consists of a number of different representatives. They are so different in their chemical make-up that a number of mineralogists are of the opinion that the individual varieties should be looked upon as completely different minerals. This view is, however, contradicted by four facts. First, without exception all garnets possess the same structure, and they all belong in the cubic crystal system. Second, all garnets share a very similar Type by manner of formation. They are formed mainly meta-morphically during the formation of crystalline slates or other metamorphic rocks. Third, all garnets belong among the island silicates, and fourth, even the variation in the content of their mineral-forming substances follows strict laws: every garnet consists of two-valency metal ions, three-valency metal ions and island silicate molecules in a constant ratio 3 : 2 : 3 (general formula: $Me^{2+}_3Me^{3+}_2(SiO_4)$). With so many correspondences, a certain degree of kinship is guaranteed. The following garnets are known and in use for healing at present:

Variety	Formula, mineral-forming substances	Colour
Almandine:	$Fe_3Al_2(SiO_4)_3$ + Ca,Mg,Mn,Ti	red, brown through black
Andradite:	$Ca_3Fe_2(SiO_4)_3$ + Al	khaki, brown, blackish
Grossularite:	$Ca_3Al_2(SiO_4)_3$ + Fe,Mn	grey, green through pink
Hessonite:	$Ca_3(Al,Fe)_2(SiO_4)_3$	red, yellow, orange, brown
Melanite:	$(Ca,Na)_3(Fe,Ti)_2(SiO_4)_3$	black
Pyrope:	$Mg_3Al_2(SiO_4)_3$ + Fe,Ti	dark red

Almandine in slate, Austria
Aandradite, USA
rainbow andradite, Mexico

Rhodolite:	$(Mg,Fe)_3Al_2(SiO_4)_3 + Ti$	dark red to reddish violet
Spessartite:	$Mn_3Al_2(SiO_4)_3 + Fe$	yellow, red-brown, brown
Uvarovite:	$Ca_3Cr_2(SiO_4)_3$	emerald green

Mythology

Garnet is identical to the medieval carbuncle. It is the stone that was reputed to glow in the dark. Even in the Middle Ages, however, this was considered to be on a spiritual level: the carbuncle that illuminates the darkened soul and brings light and hope where the path (of life) seems to have no end. It was the stone of heroes who had to deal with difficult tasks and trials in order to prove their courage. This is demonstrated by the fact that a rough garnet often looks very inconspicuous and needs to be polished first before its hidden inner colour and fire are brought to light. Correspondingly, life's trials and difficulties were seen as a spiritual 'polishing process' that ennobled the character. Warriors in the Middle Ages often had garnets set into their shields and sword hilts to protect themselves against injury in battle and garnet amulets were thought to bring luck, wealth and blessings.

Healing

In general, garnet does the following:

Spiritually Garnet helps in situations with no way out. It is the classical stone of crises, whenever our world view collapses or general life circumstances become extremely difficult. It is a fact that it has always been in fashion in times of crisis (for example, after the First and Second World Wars). Garnet also helps us cope with and surmount everyday problems in extreme situations. It fortifies that inner flame, the desire for self-realization and encourages the basic dynamics of shared survival: mutual help. Garnet also helps us see further than our own narrow horizon and to be committed to the good of the community.

Emotionally Garnet promotes self-confidence, strength of character and *joie de vivre*. It bestows courage, hope and trust; obstacles are seen as challenges that have to be dealt with. In difficult situations, garnet displays an endurance that will surprise its wearer. Garnet eliminates unnecessary inhibitions and taboos, ensures active, balanced sexuality, and helps with potency problems.

Grossularite, Russia; grossularite, Mexico, hessonite, Italy; pyrope, Alaska.

Mentally Garnet helps us say goodbye to unusable or outworn ideas, views, agreements and correspondences and to begin a new life. It dissolves behavioural patterns and habits that hinder us from achieving a free lifestyle. Garnet bestows a wealth of new ideas and the necessary dynamic to realize them in spite of resistance, enmity or conscious sabotage.

Physically Garnet fortifies the power of regeneration in the body. It eliminates blocks, stimulates the metabolism and harmonizes the composition of body fluids, particularly of the blood. Garnet stabilizes the circulation and fortifies the immune system, encourages absorption of nutrients in the intestines and accelerates healing of inner and external wounds.

Application
Garnet can be worn as a chain (only available in a few varieties), pendants, hand 'comforters' or as a rough stone. It can also be laid directly on the afflicted part of the body. Contact with the skin is essential. Special varieties are recommended for certain applications:

Almandine: thirst for action, capacity for work, gift for imagination, absorption of iron in the intestine, wound healing.

Andradite: dynamic, flexibity, creative thoughts, stimulates liver, encourages formation of blood.

Grossularite: relaxation, fortifies the kidneys, good for skin and mucous membranes, good against rheumatism and arthritis.

Hessonite: self-respect, spiritual growth, regulates hormone production.

Melanite: honesty, resistance, strengthens the spine and bones.

Pyrope: courage, good quality of life, charisma, fortifies the circulation, improves the quality of the blood.

Rhodolite: *joie de vivre*, warmth, sincerity, trust, healthy sexuality, stimulates the metabolism.

Spessartite: willingness to help others, strengthens the heart, antidepressive, helps with nightmares and sexual problems.

Uvarovite: individuality, enthusiasm, detoxification, anti-inflammatory, helps with fever.

Melanite, USA;
spessartite, Madagascar;
uvarovite, Russia.

Hematite

CRYSTAL SYSTEM: trigonal
TYPE BY MANNER OF FORMATION: primary or tertiary
MINERAL CLASS: oxide
COLOUR: grey metallic, powder: red
CHEMICAL FORMULA, MINERAL-FORMING SUBSTANCES:
Fe_2O_3 + Mg,Ti + (Al,Cr,Mn,Si, H_2O)

Mineralogy

Hematite can be formed in a variety of ways: ignaceously it is formed hydrothermally out of solutions when it forms small crystals or the well-known 'kidney growth' (see illustration), a red glassy chunk. In the sedimentary process, it forms finely distributed red weathering crusts in the oxidation zone of iron ore deposits. In the metamorphic process, it forms massive hematite deposits through loss of water in limonite sediments. In the trade, it is mainly obtainable in the primary form as the red glassy kidney ore, much more rarely in a crystalline form, and is available in the tertiary type in the form of polished stones, chains and jewellery.

Mythology

Hematite was used in ancient Egypt and Mesopotamia as a healing stone for the formation of blood and for staunching the blood flow from wounds. In the Middle Ages it was called 'bloodstone'.

Healing

Spiritually Hematite encourages the ability to survive, in the sense of a permanent further development towards better conditions.

Emotionally Hematite strengthens the will and makes us aware of unfulfilled desires. It bestows vitality and dynamism in our life.

Mentally Hematite draws our attention to our elementary basic needs and physical well-being. It helps fight for this in emergencies.

Physically Hematite stimulates the absorption of iron in the small intestine and the formation of red blood corpuscles. This improves the oxygen supply to the body and stabilizes health.

Application

Hematite is best worn with contact with the skin or laid on. Be careful in cases of inflammation, as it has an irritating effect.

Hematite, Brazil.

Heliotrope

CRYSTAL SYSTEM: trigonal
TYPE BY MANNER OF FORMATION: secondary
MINERAL CLASS: oxide, quartz group
COLOUR: green with red and yellow inclusions
CHEMICAL FORMULA, MINERAL-FORMING SUBSTANCES:
   SiO_2 + Al,Fe,Mg,OH,Si

Mineralogy

Heliotrope forms the connecting link between the quartz families chalcedony and jasper. Chalcedony coloured green by iron silicate (related to moss agate) forms its basis, but as in jasper, small, grainy quartz crystals are found, also hematite and other iron oxides may be present, appearing as yellow and red spots.

Mythology

Heliotrope is Greek and means 'solstice', which is thought to refer to its powerful healing properties. This tradition has been documented since antiquity. In medieval texts it is referred to as green jasper or blood jasper and recommended for healing infections, inflammations and poisoning.

Healing

Spiritually Heliotrope helps us protect ourselves, limiting and fending off undesirable influences.

Emotionally Heliotrope is calming in cases of irritability, aggressiveness and impatience and it revitalizes in cases of exhaustion and tiredness. It stimulates dream activity.

Mentally Heliotrope helps us adjust quickly to unexpected occurrences, so that we keep control in any situation.

Physically Heliotrope is the best immune-boosting mineral in cases of acute infections. It stimulates the flow of lymph fluid and the metabolic processes, reduces the formation of pus, detoxifies and neutralizes over-acidification.

Application

For fortifying the immune response, as soon as an infection is noticed, place the heliotrope on the thymus gland above the heart. Otherwise, it can be worn on the body.

Heliotrope, India.

Jade

CRYSTAL SYSTEM: monoclinic
TYPE BY MANNER OF FORMATION: tertiary
MINERAL CLASS: chain silicate
COLOUR: whitish, green (jadeite); lilac, violet (lavender jade)
CHEMICAL FORMULA, MINERAL-FORMING SUBSTANCES:
$NaAl[Si_2O_6]$ + Ca,Fe,Mg,Mn

Mineralogy

Jade was originally the common term for jadeite and nephrite, two minerals that are very similar in appearance and in their properties. Nowadays, those minerals are designated as 'jade' that contain mainly jadeite, and those that are composed mainly of nephrite are called 'nephrite'. Jadeite is very rare. It is formed during the metamorphosis of alkaline rocks. The even rarer lavender jade is formed when manganese is present.

Mythology

Jade has been looked upon as a good luck charm for thousands of years, especially in the Far East. It was worked into amulets and was known as a kidney healing stone in the ancient cultures of the Americas and Asia.

Healing

Spiritually Jade encourages self-realization. It helps us recognize ourselves as spiritual beings and to handle our lives in a playfully spontaneous manner. Lavender jade bestows inner peace.

Emotionally Jade enlivens inner images and dreams and awakens hidden inner knowledge. It creates a balance: activity for laziness, calm for irritability. Lavender jade helps us to set clear boundaries.

Mentally Jade stimulates ideas and promotes a readiness for action. Physical rest periods are employed for spiritual activities, and decisions are transformed into action without hesitation.

Physically Jade stimulates the functioning of the kidneys and balances the metabolism of water, salts, and acid and alkali ratios. It stimulates the nervous system and suprarenal glands, thus improving and accelerating response and reaction times.

Application

Jade can be worn or laid on. For dreamwork, it is best placed directly on the forehead in the evenings.

Jadeite, China;
lavender jade, Turkey.

Jasper

CRYSTAL SYSTEM: trigonal
TYPE BY MANNER OF FORMATION: secondary
MINERAL CLASS: oxide, quartz group
COLOUR: brown, red, yellow, sandy coloured, green
CHEMICAL FORMULA, MINERAL-FORMING SUBSTANCES: SiO_2 + Fe,O,OH,Si

Mineralogy

Jasper is a fine-grained quartz with a host of foreign material. It is formed in the sedimentary manner when the original silicic acid solution penetrates clayey or sandy rock or is itself permeated with a multitude of suspended particles. When the silicic acid solidifies into quartz, the clayey, sandy or finely distributed particles remain enclosed within the jasper as it forms and give it its opaque colour and marking. Jasper is a mineral that can occur almost anywhere, and appears in a wide variety of forms. The different markings found on these varied representatives of jasper have led to them being traded under a plethora of imaginative names. If one actually wishes to classify jasper, the only really certain criteria are the three basic colours: red, yellow and green.

Variety	Formula, mineral-forming substances	Colour
Yellow jasper:	SiO_2 + Fe,O,OH	yellow, sandy, brown
Green jasper:	SiO_2 + Fe,Si	light to dark green
Red jasper:	SiO_2 + Fe,O	brick red to brown-red

Yellow jasper is available in the gem trade under that name, but included with it are also the sandy coloured 'landscape jasper' and the brown 'turitella jasper', which contains fossilized snail shells. Yellow jasper obtains its colour from the iron oxide it contains, the iron being present mainly in its two-valency form (Fe^{2+}). Green jasper is also available under its own name and, in some cases heliotrope (see the entry *Heliotrope*) is also included in the same group. The green colour is caused by the presence of iron silicate compounds (chlorite etc.). Red jasper is also known as 'silex'; the red brecciated jasper is also counted in this group. The colour arises from iron oxide, mainly from three-valency iron (Fe^{3+}).

Landscape jasper, South Africa;
yellow jasper, South Africa;
breccia jasper, South Africa.

Mythology

The term jasper originates from the orient, and in the Middle Ages it meant the same as our present word quartz. The clear jasper mentioned in the Bible was probably rock crystal, the transparent green 'jasper' mentioned by Pliny was probably chrysoprase, and the jasper associated with Orpheus was most likely heliotrope, also mentioned by Hildegard von Bingen. Today, things are not much different: colourful minerals that are hard to identify are often termed 'jasper': 'silver eye' serpentine is called 'zebra jasper', epidote (unakite) is sometimes called 'flower jasper'. The only thing we know today about the real jasper is that it was used for making amulets in ancient Egypt; scarab amulets were carved from it, and in the Middle Ages it was considered to be the stone of warriors. According to legend, jasper was set in the hilt of 'Balmung', Siegfried's sword.

Healing

Spiritually Jasper stimulates a war-like nature. It helps us pursue and achieve goals with determination. Red jasper is supposed to be the most dynamic for this, yellow jasper the calmest, and green jasper the most balanced.

Emotionally Jasper imbues courage, readiness for conflict, aggression (in the sense of dealing with things forthrightly), willpower (red), endurance (yellow) amd the ability to protect ourselves (green).

Mentally Jasper stimulates uprightness and honesty (also towards ourselves). It bestows courage to come to grips with even unpleasant tasks. Jasper stimulates the imagination and helps transform ideas into actions.

Physically Jasper stimulates the circulation and energy flow (red). It fortifies the immune system (yellow) and has a detoxifying and anti-inflammatory effect (green). It helps with diseases of the sexual organs, and with digestive and intestinal problems. Jasper, in particular turitella jasper, increases resistance to environmental stress (pollution, toxins, radiation).

Application

Jasper should be worn in contact with the skin or laid on it.

Red jasper, South Africa
green jasper, India
turitella jasper, Wyoming, USA

Carnelian

CRYSTAL SYSTEM: trigonal
TYPE BY MANNER OF FORMATION: primary
MINERAL CLASS: oxide, quartz group
COLOUR: red, orange, yellow, brown
CHEMICAL FORMULA, MINERAL-FORMING SUBSTANCES: SiO_2 + (Fe,O,OH)

Mineralogy

Carnelian is chalcedony that contains iron and is formed in the vicinity of alkaline and acid volcanic rock out of magmatic silicic acid solutions containing iron. Red-brown carnelian is also called sard.

Mythology

In antiquity, carnelian was known generally as sard. Hildegard von Bingen was the first person known to make a distinction between the orange coloured and brown coloured varieties. In the Middle Ages, it was assigned a blood-staunching and anger-calming effect. Hildegard von Bingen recommended it for headaches and as a birthing aid. Tomb offerings in Egypt prove its importance as a protective stone for the dead.

Healing

Spiritually Carnelian promotes steadfastness and encourages a spirit of community. It makes us willing to help, be idealistic, and stand up zealously for a good cause.

Emotionally Carnelian bestows steadfastness and courage – not the risky heroic courage but everyday courage to overcome and stand up to difficulties. It lifts the emotions.

Mentally Carnelian encourages the facility to solve problems quickly and pragmatically. It helps bring actions once begun to a proper conclusion and a sense of reality whenever one is feeling confused.

Physically Carnelian stimulates the absorption of vitamins, nutrients and minerals in the small intestine, thereby improving the quality of the blood. It ensures a good blood supply to the organs and tissues. Carnelian alleviates rheumatism and stimulates the metabolism.

Application

Carnelian should be worn in contact with the skin, laid on or taken as an essence.

Carnelian, Botswana.

Kunzite

CRYSTAL SYSTEM: monoclinic
TYPE BY MANNER OF FORMATION: primary
MINERAL CLASS: chain silicate, spodumene family
COLOUR: pink to pink violet
CHEMICAL FORMULA, MINERAL-FORMING SUBSTANCES:
  $LiAl[Si_2O_6]$ + Ca,Mg,Mn,Na

Mineralogy

Kunzite is a variety of spodumene. It is formed in pegmatites exclusively out of acid, magmatic solutions containing lithium.

Mythology

Kunzite was not discovered until 1902; it was in California, and it was described by the gemologist G.F. Kunz and named after him. Consequently, no traditions about its effects are known.

Healing

Spiritually Kunzite enourages dedication and humility, also devotion to a task that needs to be carried out with all the energy we have. It teaches us to give way without being untrue to ourselves and encourages the willingness to serve.

Emotionally Kunzite gets rid of resistances. It helps us be compromising and fit in with the needs of others. Kunzite encourages the ability to remember things, has a mood-lifting effect and helps with depression.

Mentally Kunzite helps us take constructive criticism. It encourages introspection about the self as well as tolerance towards ourselves and others. Kunzite combines logic with inspiration and intuition.

Physically Kunzite alleviates nervous complaints, for example the pain of trapped nerves, sciatica, neuralgia, and also epilepsy and disorders of the sensory organs and nerves. It dissolves tension in the area of the heart and helps with joint complaints.

Application

Kunzite should be worn in contact with the body and in acute cases, such as pain, it should be laid directly on the afflicted area.

Labradorite, spectrolite

CRYSTAL SYSTEM: triclinic
TYPE BY MANNER OF FORMATION: primary
MINERAL CLASS: lattice silicate, feldspar family
COLOUR: grey, green, black (spectrolite) with iridescent colours
CHEMICAL FORMULA, MINERAL-FORMING SUBSTANCES:

$Na[AlSi_3O_8]Ca[Al_2Si_2O_8] + Fe,K,Ba,Sr$

Mineralogy

Labradorite is a feldspar (plagioclase) formed in pegmatites and alkaline igneous rocks. It obtains its iridescent colours from a fine laminate structure which bends incoming light. Spectrolite is a black, Finnish labradorite with the most wonderful play of iridescent colours found in any labradorite.

Mythology

Labradorite was found for the first time in 1770 on the Labrador peninsula; spectrolite was not found until the twentiethth century in Finland. Neither of these minerals is associated with any traditions.

Healing

Spiritually Labradorite is an outstanding 'illusion killer'. Like its colourful display of iridescence, it clearly shows us our goals and intentions – so we suddenly see their real shape. Labradorite fortifies intuition and mediumistic abilities.

Emotionally Labradorite throws up forgotten memories and bestows depth of feeling. It stimulates the imagination, making us contemplative and introverted.

Mentally Labradorite helps us develop a child-like enthusiasm and a host of new ideas. It bestows a lively although sometimes rather erratic creativity.

Physically Labradorite alleviates feeling cold, colds, rheumatic illnesses and gout. Labradorite also has a blood pressure lowering effect and is calming.

Application

Labradorite unfolds its spiritual effect best in meditation. It is physically effective if carried around.

Lapis lazuli

CRYSTAL SYSTEM: cubic
TYPE BY MANNER OF FORMATION: tertiary
MINERAL CLASS: lattice silicate
COLOUR: deep blue
CHEMICAL FORMULA, MINERAL-FORMING SUBSTANCES:
$(Na,Ca)_8[(SO_4/S/Cl)_2/(AlSiO_4)_6]$ + Fe

Mineralogy

Lapis lazuli is formed during the metamorphosis of chalk into marble. Where iron is also present, gold-coloured pyrite inclusions will occur.

Mythology

Lapis lazuli derives its name from the Persian 'lazur' and means approximately 'blue stone'. Other blue stones were also given the same name, however. The only thing that is certain is that it was used in ancient Mesopotamia and Egypt as the 'stone of rulers' and for cult purposes

Healing

Spiritually Lapis lazuli bestows wisdom and honesty and reveals our own inner truth. It helps us be ourselves and liberates us from compromises and holding back. With lapis lazuli, you can be the 'ruler in your own (spiritual) kingdom'. It was also considered to be the stone of friendship.

Emotionally Lapis lazuli encourages selfawareness, dignity, honesty and uprightness. It makes us enjoy contact with others and helps us convey feelings and emotions, quite vehemently, if necessary.

Mentally Lapis lazuli helps us face the truth that we are confronted with and to accept it, while at the same time also expressing our own opinion. It also helps us to contain conflicts.

Physically Lapis lazuli heals problems affecting the neck, larynx and vocal chords, particularly if they originate in reserve or repressed anger. Lapis lazuli lowers the blood pressure, regulates the functioning of the thyroid gland and lengthens the menstruation cycle

Application

Lapis lazuli can be worn in meditation laid on the forehead or, if possible, worn around the neck.

Lapis lazuli crystal, Afghanistan; lapis lazuli with pyrite, Afghanistan.

Larimar

CRYSTAL SYSTEM: triclinic
TYPE BY MANNER OF FORMATION: primary
MINERAL CLASS: chain silicate
COLOUR: white, light blue
CHEMICAL FORMULA, MINERAL-FORMING SUBSTANCES:
$NaCa_2[OH/Si_3O_8]$ + Fe,Mn

Mineralogy

Larimar is a light blue pectolite. It is formed hydrothermally in clefts of alkaline volcanic rock.

Mythology

Larimar was not known until very recently (the last few years). Even in its country of origin, the Dominican Republic, no early uses as a healing crystal are known.

Healing

Spiritually Larimar stimulates us to take proper control of our lives. It dissolves sacrificial behaviour and philosophies that encourage suffering. Larimar makes us aware of the extent of effectivity of our personal spiritual spectrum and shows us that the spirit only has boundaries wherever it believes in them.

Emotionally Larimar helps dissolve fear, suffering and excessive emotions. It bestows inner peace and helps us remain calm and relaxed when dramatic changes take place.

Mentally Larimar makes constructive thinking easier and stimulates creative activity. It helps us refrain from manipulating things and events unnecessarily, instead just allowing them to happen.

Physically Larimar stimulates the self-healing properties by strengthening our certainty of being able to decide about our own health or illness. Generally, it dissolves energy blocks, particularly in the chest, neck and head areas and stimulates brain activity.

Application

Larimar can be used in meditation by laying it on the solar plexus, chest or forehead, used in a stone circle or as a stone to contemplate calmly. Physically it dissolves all blocks wherever it is laid directly on the afflicted part of the body.

Lepidolite

CRYSTAL SYSTEM: monoclinic
TYPE BY MANNER OF FORMATION: primary
MINERAL CLASS: phyllo or sheet silicate, mica group
COLOUR: pink to pink violet
CHEMICAL FORMULA, MINERAL-FORMING SUBSTANCES:
$KLi_2Al[(OH,F)_2/Si_4O_{10}] + Ca,Fe,Mg,Mn$

Mineralogy

Lepidolite is a mica containing lithium. It is formed in the primary process in pegmatites or in pneumolytically transformed granites (gneiss).

Mythology

Lepidolite was discovered in the eighteenth century and initially was given the name lilalite by Abbé Poda, who was trying to create a wordplay both on its colour and the Hindu word *lila*, 'play, game'. This appeared not to be serious enough for scientists, so later on, the mineralogist Klaproth renamed it lepidolite ('scale stone').

Healing

Spiritually Lepidolite encourages independence. It helps us to set our own goals and to realize them without outside help. Lepidolite allows developments to take their course quietly and inconspicuously.

Emotionally Lepidolite protects us from outer influences and helps us preserve our own space in crowds. Lepidolite bestows calm and inner peace and helps with sleep disturbances.

Mentally Lepidolite encourages objective evaluation and targeted decision-making. It helps us concentrate on what is essential, to stick to our intentions and neutralize distractions.

Physically Lepidolite helps with nerve pain, sciatica, neuralgia and problems with the joints. It has a detoxifying effect and stimulates purification processes in the skin and connective tissues.

Application

Lepidolite can be worn on the body and laid directly on painful parts. It is sufficient to lay it under your pillow for the spiritual effects and for sleep disturbances.

Magnesite

CRYSTAL SYSTEM: trigonal
TYPE BY MANNER OF FORMATION: secondary, rarely primary
MINERAL CLASS: carbonate
COLOUR: white, grey, yellow, brown, often marbled
CHEMICAL FORMULA, MINERAL-FORMING SUBSTANCES: $MgCO_3$ + Ca,Fe,Mn

Mineralogy

Magnesite is formed mainly in the sedimentary process from the erosion of rocks containing magnesium and forms grainy, limestone-like aggregates. More rarely, there is a formation of crystals from hydrothermal solutions.

Mythology

Magnesite was discovered in the eighteenth century and was initially called 'pure talc earth', as the magnesium contained in it was not yet chemically recognized. Once magnesium was identified, the mineral was renamed magnesite. There are no traditions on its effects.

Healing

Spiritually Magnesite encourages a positive attitude towards life. It helps us accept and love ourselves.

Emotionally Magnesite has a calming, relaxing effect, helps with nervousness, fearfulness and irritability. It increases tolerance for emotional stress and makes us more patient.

Mentally Magnesite encourages the ability to listen and to stay a little more in the background.

Physically Magnesite is the most important healing crystal for magnesium deficiency. It has a detoxifying, antispasmodic, muscle-relaxing effect and helps with migraines, headaches, vascular, stomach and intestinal cramp as well as with gallbladder colic. It slows blood-clotting, stimulates the metabolism of fat and the dispersal of cholesterol, thus preventing arteriosclerosis, and it expands the coronary blood vessels. This makes magnesite a prophylactic aid to combat heart attacks.

Application

Magnesite should be worn in contact with the skin or taken internally as a gem essence.

Malachite

CRYSTAL SYSTEM: monoclinic
TYPE BY MANNER OF FORMATION: secondary
MINERAL CLASS: carbonate
COLOUR: light to dark green, banded or marbled
CHEMICAL FORMULA, MINERAL-FORMING SUBSTANCES:
$Cu_2[(OH)_2/CO_3] + H_2O + (Ca,Fe)$

Mineralogy

Malachite is formed through a secondary process in the oxidation zone of copper ore deposits. Surface water containing carbonic acid dissolves copper out of the rock and then forms compounds with it to create alkaline,water-containing copper carbonate. Malachite is related to azurite but contains more water than the latter.

Mythology

Malachite is one of the minerals that is surrounded with myths and legends. In the Ural Mountains (central Russia), it was dedicated to the Lady of the copper mountains, a personification of Venus whose rather ambiguous favours brought either bad or good luck to the malachite miners. Nobody was quite sure whether it was right to accept the gifts of this goddess, as in many cases wealth brings nothing but unhappiness. Some of those who declined to accept her gift went away happy and contented. This is probably an indication of the balancing justice of creation. Malachite was always a women's mineral and ws always dedicated to a goddess in whatever culture: in Egypt to Hathor, in classical times to Aphrodite/Venus, in northern Europe to Freya. Malachite represented seduction, sensuality, beauty, curiosity, aesthetics and the arts of the Muses. It was considered to be the stone of Paradise, which later was represented as meaning we mortals ought to avoid it. It still has a scent of Lucifer about it to this day. Since the Middle Ages, it has been known that malachite alleviates menstrual problems and eases labour. For this reason it is still called the midwife stone in folklore.

Healing

Spiritually Malachite encourages an appreciation of aesthetics, sensuality and beauty, friendship and justice. It helps us imagine ourselves in the position of others and to empathize with them (sense their thoughts and feelings). Malachite gets rid of shyness and awakens the desire for knowledge. Life is experienced more intensely and is more adventurous. Inspired by malachite, we learn to love

Magnesite, Zimbabwe;
malachite, Zaire.

risks and to rely on luck. Malachite helps make us more aware: desires, needs and ideals become visible but the realization of them remains up to us.

Emotionally Malachite stimulates inner imagery. Dreams, imagination and memories become alive and real. Suppressed feelings are suddenly brought out into the open. Malachite takes away inhibitions and encourages the expression of feelings. Moods are experienced more intensely and then rapidly dropped again as fast as they arose. Old pain and traumas may surface and be dissolved if we are in a position to face them. This is one of the weaknesses of malachite: it make many things conscious but does not help much with changing what it has given us an insight into.

Mentally Malachite strengthens the understanding of concepts. We are in a position to absorb information more quickly as the imagination makes us strong and aware of how to handle it. Thoughts flow very fast and decisions are made without having to think a great deal. Malachite fortifies the capacity to observe; even tiny things are perceived much more rapidly and their meaning is recognized. This also increases the ability to criticize and confront and the willingness to do so.

Physically Malachite dissolves cramp. It helps with menstruation problems and facilitates labour. In addition, malachite encourages the development of the female sexual organs and heals their ailments. It also helps with sexual problems, particularly if bad experiences were the cause. Malachite stimulates liver activity, has a detoxifying effect, alleviates rheumatism and helps reduce acidification of the tissues. It stimulates the nerves and brain activity.

Application
To experience the effect of malachite, it will be sufficient to carry it around or lay it directly on the body. Malachite essence has a very pronounced effect and should be taken in very low doses to begin with.

Marble, Switzerland.

Marble

CRYSTAL SYSTEM: trigonal
TYPE BY MANNER OF FORMATION: tertiary
MINERAL CLASS: carbonate
COLOUR: white, yellow, brown, black marbled
CHEMICAL FORMULA, MINERAL-FORMING SUBSTANCES: $CaCO_3$ + Fe,Mn

Mineralogy

Marble is a metamorphic, or so-called 'monomineral' rock that consists entirely of calcite. It is formed through the transformation of limestone under great pressure at high temperatures. This metamorphosis squeezes the tiny calcite crystals of limestone into larger crystals which give the marble its transparency and typical grainy appearance. In the widest sense, limestones are often termed 'marble' even if they have only undergone a partial metamorphic transformation.

Mythology

Marble (Greek *marmaros*, 'white stone') was a collective term in antiquity for 'special stones that appeal through their marking and patterning' (Isidorus). Not much is therefore known that relates specifically to what we now call marble. However, there are traditions about the transforming power of the stones the Greeks and Romans understood by this name, and how they turned sorrow into joy, and their symbolism for wealth, splendour and glory.

Healing

Spiritually Marble transforms unhappy circumstances. It helps change dynamically things we believed we had to put up with.

Emotionally Marble brings the repressed contents of our consciousness to the surface. It helps us rid ourselves of all emotional dissatisfaction.

Mentally Marble opens up new perspectives and stimulates creative solving of problems that we would previously have resigned ourselves to.

Physically Marble improves the processing of calcium in the body. In this, its effect is similar to that of calcite.

Application

Marble quickly shows its effects as a building medium but long periods of wearing it or carrying it make the experience of it more conscious.

Moldavite

CRYSTAL SYSTEM: amorphous
TYPE BY MANNER OF FORMATION: tertiary
MINERAL CLASS: oxide
COLOUR: bottle green
CHEMICAL FORMULA, MINERAL-FORMING SUBSTANCES:
  SiO_2 + Al,Ca,Fe,K,Na

Mineralogy

Moldavite was formed approximately 15 million years after the impact of a giant meteorite in present day Nordlinger Ries (Bavaria). Splatters of rocks that were melted by the impact were propelled over a radius of about 400 kilometres (250 miles). These cooled while they were airborne and many fell to the ground in the general area of the present day Moldavia. Moldavite is now found along the banks of the river Moldau, which is how it got its name.

Mythology

Finds from the Stone Age have proven moldavite's early use as an amulet stone. Its reputation as a magical stone for luck, the fulfilment of wishes and fertility magic has survived to this day.

Healing

Spiritually Moldavite allows the wearer to experience immense spiritual dimensions, enhances clairvoyance and gives us inklings of what actual spiritual greatness humans could be capable of.

Emotionally Moldavite brings memories and dream images that allow an insight into the meaning and duties of our lives. Moldavite also encourages sympathy and compassion.

Mentally Moldavite helps us detach our attention and awareness from strongly materialistic leanings and blocks, as well as from money problems and worries about the future. Moldavite encourages spontaneous, unconventional ideas and solutions to problems.

Physically Moldavite supports healing processes by making us aware of the cause of the illness and the gain that can be had from experiencing the illness.

Application

Moldavite unfolds its fullest effect if it is worn on the forehead ('third eye'). Generally, it will be sufficient, however, to carry it on persons.

Moonstone

CHRYSTAL SYSTEM: monoclinic
TYPE BY MANNER OF FORMATION: primary
MINERAL CLASS: lattice silicate, feldspar family
COLOUR: white, brownish with light or a blueish shimmer
CHEMICAL FORMULA, MINERAL-FORMING SUBSTANCES:
$K[AlSi_3O_8]$ + Na,Fe,Ba

Mineralogy

Moonstone is a potassium feldspar (orthoclase) whose inner laminate structure bends light. In the polished stone, this leads to a white to blueish, almost undulating shimmering light.

Mythology

As the name indicates, the moonstone has been assigned to the moon and, therefore, is traditionally considered to be a stone associated with intuition, feelings, the heart and fertility. In the Far East, the orient and Europe it was thought to be a lucky stone and was used for love magic.

Healing

Spiritually The moonstone increases mediumistic abilities and clairvoyance. It encourages lucid dreaming, particularly at the time of a full moon.

Emotionally The moonstone refines our (subconscious) perception of light, thereby enhancing intuition. It bestows depth of feeling, improves the remembering of dreams and diminishes any tendencies to sleepwalking.

Mentally The moonstone makes us more open to sudden, irrational impulses. This means that it encourages 'happy coincidences', but can just as easily let us trip up on our own illusions.

Physically The moonstone stimulates the functioning of the pineal gland and, via this gland's sensitivity to light, balances the internal hormone cycles with nature's rhythms. In this way, the moonstone also enhances women's fertility and helps with menstrual problems, after childbirth and during the menopause.

Application

The moonstone should be worn on the forehead for spiritual experiences and laid on the heart area for soul (emotional) experiences. For all other purposes, it will be sufficient to carry it about with you.

*Moldavite, Czech Republic
moonstone, India*

Mookaite

CRYSTAL SYSTEM: trigonal
TYPE BY MANNER OF FORMATION: secondary
MINERAL CLASS: oxide, quartz group
COLOUR: red, yellow, beige, marbled
CHEMICAL FORMULA, MINERAL-FORMING SUBSTANCES: SiO_2 + Fe,O,OH

Mineralogy
Mookaite is an Australian jasper that unites the lighter colours of yellow and red jasper. It is formed as a sediment in erosion zones and as a filler in cracks.

Mythology
In Australia, mookaite was and is considered to be a healing stone that bestows strength. It was not one of the taboo stones, on which white people have still not been given any information regarding its cult uses, but was a stone for regeneration and the healing of wounds for 'everyday use'.

Healing
Spiritually Mookaite encourages the desire for variety and new experiences. It helps keep a harmonious balance between the external activities and internal processing of the impressions derived from such experiences.

Emotionally Mookaite simultaneously bestows both a deep inner calm and a desire for adventure simultaneously. It helps us experience the possibility that meditation is actually possible during any activity.

Mentally Mookaite makes us mobile and flexible. It helps us recognize several possibilities at the same time and still choose the most suitable solution without any problems.

Physically Mookaite stabilizes health. It fortifies the immune system and stimulates the purification of the blood in the liver and spleen. Mookaite encourages wounds to heal and alleviates suppuration.

Application
Mookaite should be worn on the body for long periods of time as its effects only accumulate gradually.

Moss agate

CRYSTAL SYSTEM: trigonal
TYPE BY MANNER OF FORMATION: secondary
MINERAL CLASS: oxide, quartz group
COLOUR: clear, pale, light blue with moss green inclusions
CHEMICAL FORMULA, MINERAL-FORMING SUBSTANCES:
   SiO_2 + Al,Ca,F,Fe,K,Mg,Na,OH,Si

Mineralogy
Moss agate belongs to the chalcedony family and is formed in sedimentary processes out of viscous silicic acid into which iron silicate solutions have penetrated, but without becoming mixed or mingled in. The chalcedony formed in this way contains moss green, fibrous and streak-like inclusions.

Mythology
Right through into modern literature, there has been a consistent suggestion that moss agate enhances a love for nature because of its plant-like signature. There are, however, no other indications as to its healing properties.

Healing
Spiritually Moss agate liberates us from spiritual fetters and blocks. It encourages new initiatives after long periods of hesitation or holding back. Moss agate bestows inspiration and makes it possible to begin anew again and again.

Emotionally Moss agate liberates us from pressure and stress. It helps loosen deep fear and encourages trust and hope. Moss agate brings recovery and refreshes the soul.

Mentally Moss agate encourages the ability to communicate. It enhances certainty, helps us understand even the most difficult set of circumstances, and enlivens the intellect.

Physically Moss agate encourages the flow of lymphatic fluid, alleviates swellings of the lymph nodes and, in cases of stubborn infections, has an immune-boosting effect, lowers fevers, is anti-inflammatory, mucous-forming (in cases of a dry cough) and tones down oversensitivity to changes in the weather.

Application
Moss agate should, in all cases, be worn in contact with the skin or be laid on it.

Morganite

CRYSTAL SYSTEM: hexagonal
TYPE BY MANNER OF FORMATION: primary
MINERAL CLASS: ring silicate, beryl family
COLOUR: pink
CHEMICAL FORMULA, MINERAL-FORMING SUBSTANCES:
   $Be_3Al_2(Si_6O_{18})$ + K,Li,Na + (Cu,Mn,Ni)

Mineralogy
Morganite is a type of beryl that has been coloured pink by lithium and manganese. It is formed in pegmatites whenever the magmatic solution is sufficiently enriched with beryllium and lithium.

Mythology
Morganite was not discovered until this century, and was named after the mineral collector, banker and secret society member John Pierpoint Morgan. This is why there are no extant traditions on its effects.

Healing
Spiritually Morganite helps us recognize self-importance, fanaticism, blinkered views and habitual escapism as such, and instead inclines us to devote ourselves to a more contemplative lifestyle. Morganite awakens a love of life itself, and with it a love of all living things.

Emotionally Morganite helps reduce stress and the pressure to succeed. Morganite brings an awareness of the ignored needs of the soul and helps us become aware of feelings and to live them out.

Mentally Morganite helps us let go of ambition and to experience the joy of engaging in spiritual activities that serve neither gain nor success. Morganite creates space for leisure.

Physically Morganite alleviates illnesses caused by stress such as heart problems, nervous complaints, vertigo and impotence.

Application
Morganite can be laid on the heart area as a meditation stone. Spending time in a morganite stone circle will rapidly alleviate stress symptoms, after which the stone should be worn on the body for long periods of time.

Nephrite

CRYSTAL SYSTEM: monoclinic
TYPE BY MANNER OF FORMATION: tertiary
MINERAL CLASS: chain silicate, actinolite family
COLOUR: green
CHEMICAL FORMULA, MINERAL-FORMING SUBSTANCES:
$$Ca_2(Mg,Fe)_5(Si_8O_{22})(OH,F)_4 + OH,F$$

Mineralogy

Nephrite is a cryptocrystalline variety of actinolite with dense, matted crystal fibres. It is formed metamorphically during the formation of actinolite slates

Mythology

The name nephrite is derived from the Greek word *nephron*, 'kidney'. Even in antiquity and in the early cultures of South America and New Zealand, nephrite was known as a healing stone. In addition, it was used as an amulet and for the manufacture of images of the gods.

Healing

Spiritually Nephrite is numbered among the stones that protect against hostile influences. It renders us unable to be influenced by means of applying pressure (blackmail) and helps us preserve our identity.

Emotionally Nephrite bestows certainty. It helps reduce tension and worry and the discharging of violent emotions but, in the long term, it leads to inner peace and dampens aggression.

Mentally Nephrite encourages neutrality and tolerance. It helps with indecisiveness and dissolves doubt and senseless brooding. Nephrite makes us creative and ready for action.

Physically Nephrite improves the functioning of the kidneys, alleviates kidney infections and prevents deposits in the urinary tract and kidney stones. In this way, it also encourages detoxification of the body fluids and of the tissues.

Application

Nephrite should be worn on the body for long periods of time until an inner equilibrium has been attained. In acute cases, it can be laid directly on the kidney area or stuck on with plaster.

Obsidian

CRYSTAL SYSTEM: amorphous
TYPE BY MANNER OF FORMATION: primary
MINERAL CLASS: oxide
COLOUR: black, brown, silvery or colourfully iridescent
CHEMICAL FORMULA, MINERAL-FORMING SUBSTANCES:
$SiO_2 + Fe_2O_3 + H_2O + Al,C,Ca,K,Na,Fe$

Mineralogy

Obsidian is formed volcanically when lava rich in silicic acid cools extremely rapidly. The lava hardens so quickly that no crystalline structures are able to form ('temperature shock'). The result is an amorphous 'solidified molten mass' containing large amounts of minerals, water and gas inclusions. For this reason, obsidian is also called 'rock glass' or 'volcanic glass'. The basic colour of obsidian is black and, as a rule, it is also opaque. Transparent obsidian can only form out of lava that is very poor in foreign substances, so-called smoky obsidian ('Apache's tears'). Obsidian may obtain a silvery shimmer through finely distributed gas bubbles or a colourful iridescence through trapped water bubbles and is then called silver obsidian or rainbow obsidian. Should obsidian occasionally begin to crystallize after all, you will find small inclusions of grey feldspar: this results in the formation of snowflake obsidian. The crystallization process may continue until the obsidian has been transformed completely into feldspar. A high iron content will sometimes result in brown patches – so-called mahagony obsidian.

Mythology

Obsidian was used for some of the oldest cultural artefacts of man. As early as in Palaeolithic times, obsidian blades were used for cult purposes as has been shown by finds from burials. In antiquity, it was regarded as a stone that would drive out demons and in the Middle Ages, as an aid for magical rituals. The Mayan priests of the god Tetzcatlipoca ('Smoking Mirror') employed obsidian mirrors for predicting the future. According to very ancient traditions, obsidian was also used for healing wounds and alleviating pain – an interesting connection since as it also supplied the material for some of the first blades and also weapons made by man. Obsidian is supposed to derive its name from the Roman Obsius who, according to Pliny's reports, found the stone in present day Ethiopia.

Obsidian, Mexico;
mahagony obsidian, Mexico.

Healing

Spiritually Obsidian helps us attain integrity through helping us to see our shadow sides in their true nature, so they can once more become part of the self. This is how to attain the 'unimpeachability of the warrior', a spiritual invulnerability and freedom (liberty). In this manner, forgotten capabilities may be retrieved and our perception refined to the point of clairvoyance.

Emotionally Obsidian dissolves shocks, fear, blocks and traumatization. It has an enlivening effect and brings hidden inner images to light. Obsidian bestows an unimagined depth on our emotional nature and helps with any type of obsession. It purifies the atmosphere of negative, spiritual influences and serves as a protection against psychic attacks.

Mentally Obsidian expands the consciousness and helps change restricting beliefs, communication and behavioural patters. It sharpens the senses and helps the intellect penetrate mysterious phenomena, experiences and accounts.

Physically Obsidian dissolves pain, tensions, energy blocks and vascular contraction. Shock sustained through injury is dissolved on a cellular level and it thus helps staunch bleeding and accelerate the healing of wounds. Obsidian improves the circulation, even in extreme cases such as hardening of the arteries in the legs caused by smoking, and also ensures warming of the extremities, for example, chronically cold hands and feet.

Application

For effects on the emotions/soul, obsidian should be used as a meditation stone in the form of a mirror or a sphere and contemplated quietly. For a final 'clearing', it is recommended to end the meditation every time with rock crystal. Black, rainbow and silver obsidian are best suited to meditation. Smoky obsidian worn next to the skin will rapidly alleviate pain, while the circulation will be best improved with mahagony or snowflake obsidian (worn on the body).

Silver obsidian, Mexico;
rainbow obsidian, Mexico;
snowflake obsidian, USA.

Onyx

CRYSTAL SYSTEM: trigonal
TYPE BY MANNER OF FORMATION: primary
MINERAL CLASS: oxide, quartz group
COLOUR: black
CHEMICAL FORMULA, MINERAL-FORMING SUBSTANCES: SiO_2 + C,Fe

Mineralogy

Onyx is a chalcedony that is coloured black through the presence of iron and carbon. It is formed hydrothermally or out of cooler solutions in hollows in rock.

Mythology

In the Middle Ages onyx was thought to bring bad luck, sadness, fear and images of madness during sleep, as well as inciting discord and dispute. To this day, it has a bad reputation as the 'stone of egotists'.

Healing

Spiritually Onyx encourages self-realization. It helps us to pursue our own goals with determination and is, therefore, particularly suited to people who are easily influenced and led.

Emotionally Onyx fortifies our self-confidence and sense of responsibility. It encourages a healthy egotism and the willingness to get involved in a dispute if necessary.

Mentally Onyx improves the ability to assert ourselves. It stimulates analytical thought and logic, improves concentration and helps us to argue in a conclusive and determined manner. Onyx makes us sobre and realistic and improves our control over our own actions.

Physically Onyx sharpens our sense of hearing and heals diseases of the inner ear. It improves the functioning of the sensory and motor nervous system, helps with weaknesses of the eyes, and fortifies the immune system against susceptibility to infections.

Application

Onyx should be worn for long periods of time as its effect takes some time to unfold.

Opal

CRYSTAL SYSTEM: amorphous
TYPE BY MANNER OF FORMATION: secondary
MINERAL CLASS: oxide
COLOUR: all colours, iridescent
CHEMICAL FORMULA, MINERAL-FORMING SUBSTANCES:
  $SiO_2 + H_2O + C,Ca,Fe,Mg$

Mineralogy

Opal is formed by secondary processes through the solidification of silicic acid gel by loss of water. The drop-shaped silicic acid in the gel forms tiny silicon dioxide globules between which up to 20% water and gas still remain enclosed. It is the bending of light by these globules that gives the opal its wonderful colourful iridescence. Where the basic colour is bluish (Ca + Fe), it is called boulder opal, white (Ca + Mg) is called milk opal and black (C + Fe) is called black opal.

Mythology

Opal is known both as a lucky and unlucky stone. According to Greek mythology it was formed out of the tears of joy of Zeus after his victory over the Titans, while in India it was thought to be the Goddess of Rainbows, turned to stone when fleeing from the unwanted advances of other gods.

Healing

Spiritually Opal bestows joy in our worldly life. It draws our attention to the more colourful sides of life and awakens the desire for variety and distraction.

Emotionally Opal strengthens desire, eroticism and sexuality. It makes us emotional, seductive, unconventional, in love with life and enhances optimism.

Mentally Opal makes us light-hearted, sometimes even a little light-headed. It encourages spontaneity, poetry and an interest in the arts of the Muses.

Physically Opal has a generally health-enhancing effect because it strengthens the will to live.

Application

Opal is effective when it is carried about or worn, laid on (heart area) and during meditative contemplation.

Boulder opal, Australia;
milk opal, Mexico;
black opal, Australia.

Opal, chrysopal

CRYSTAL SYSTEM: amorphous
TYPE BY MANNER OF FORMATION: secondary
MINERAL CLASS: oxide
COLOUR: green, blue-green
CHEMICAL FORMULA, MINERAL-FORMING SUBSTANCES: $SiO_2 + H_2O + Cu$

Mineralogy

Chrysopal is formed by sedimentary processes from silicic acid gel containing copper that has solidified by losing water. When the copper content is high, it will transform in a flowing manner into chrysocolla.

Mythology

Chrysopal is considered to be the stone assigned to oceans, great distances and to the yearning for a (spiritual) home. In South America it is used, to this day, as a magical stone for matters of the heart.

Healing

Spiritually Chrysopal makes us open to new impressions. It makes us open towards other people and encourages community experiences. Chrysopal also imparts enthusiasm.

Emotionally Chrysopal liberates the feelings. It helps allow grief to run its normal course and to get rid of emotional burdens by having a good cry. Chrysopal has a mood-lifting effect and transmits a pleasant exciting–melancholic feeling for life. It helps with lack of courage and stimulates a child-like curiosity that sees the whole world as a huge adventure.

Mentally Chrysopal stimulates us to observe the world with astonished eyes and to appreciate the wonder of life.

Physically Chrysopal encourages the regenerative power of the liver, has an detoxifying effect and lowers temperatures. It liberates the heart and chest of feelings of constriction.

Application

Chrysopal should be worn near the heart or laid on, and can be contemplated during meditation or laid out in a stone circle.

Chrysopal, Peru,
green opal, Mexico

Opal, fire opal

CRYSTAL SYSTEM: amorphous
TYPE BY MANNER OF FORMATION: primary
MINERAL CLASS: oxides
COLOUR: red, orange, yellow
CHEMICAL FORMULA, MINERAL-FORMING SUBSTANCES: $SiO_2 + H_2O + Fe$

Mineralogy
Fire opal is formed by igneous processes from the solidification of magmatic silicic acid gels in volcanically active areas with hot springs and geysers. Its colour is due to iron.

Mythology
Fire opal is a Mars stone. It is considered to be the stone of discoverers and conquerors and will bestow good outcomes, success and the overcoming of all danger on the wearer.

Healing
Spiritually Fire opal bestows dynamism, initiative and new ideas. It awakens the inner fire, helping us to accomplish much more in a short time and to fire others with enthusiasm. Fire opal makes us spontaneous and impulsive.

Emotionally Fire opal makes us lively, open and ready to take risks. It wakens us up, lifts the spirits, and brings cheerfulness, enthusiasm, *joie de vivre* and enjoyment of sexuality. Occasionally, fire opal makes us a little explosive, so that bottled up emotions are suddenly and violently discharged.

Mentally Fire opal helps us to initiate things. It shakes us out of the habit of thinking too long, makes us quick on the uptake, and stimulates action. With fire opal our thought processes are determined by emotions, and outbursts may occur when we are challenged.

Physically Fire opal gets rid of all energy deficiencies. It stimulates the sexual organs and activates the adrenal glands.

Application
Fire opal has a very strong effect when worn in the pubic area or when carried in a trouser pocket. For meditating, it is recommended to contemplate it (as calmly as we can...).

Opal, green

CRYSTAL SYSTEM: amorphous
TYPE BY MANNER OF FORMATION: secondary
MINERAL CLASS: oxide
COLOUR: green
CHEMICAL FORMULA, MINERAL-FORMING SUBSTANCES: SiO_2 + H_2O + Fe,Ni

Mineralogy

Green opal is formed in the sedimentary manner out of silicic acid gel containing iron and nickel which then solidifies by losing water. It is rarely pure but will usually also contain larger amounts of quartz. For this reason green opal is sometimes reckoned to be an opalite (opal-bearing rock).

Mythology

Green opal originates in Mexico and has only been available in Europe for a few years. Unfortunately, no traditions are known about its use as a healing mineral.

Healing

Spiritually Green opal helps us to find new perspectives on life. It makes it possible to see a meaning in everyday life or to give life a meaning.

Emotionally Green opal encourages recovery, relaxation and regeneration following exhaustion brought on by strenuous mental activity. It liberates us from fear and feelings of guilt and helps us sleep peacefully.

Mentally Green opal helps with orientation problems. It encourages the ability to select and to filter out intuitively the most important facts from a confusing profusion of information.

Physically Green opal is a strong detoxifying agent. It stimulates the body fluids, the liver and kidneys and the functioning of the gonads and ovaries.

Application

Green opal should be worn on the body or in the general area of the liver. Its liberating and regenerating effects rapidly become apparent if it is used in meditation. Spending time in a circle of opal stones has a very powerful effect.

Opal, pink

CRYSTAL SYSTEM: amorphous
TYPE BY MANNER OF FORMATION: secondary
MINERAL CLASS: oxide
COLOUR: pink
CHEMICAL FORMULA, MINERAL-FORMING SUBSTANCES: $SiO_2 + H_2O + Mn$

Mineralogy

Pink opal is formed in a sedimentary process out of silicic acid gel containing manganese which then solidifies through loss of water. It is found in the oxidation zone of manganese ore deposits.

Mythology

Pink opal has only been available in Europe for a few years. Unfortunately, no traditional stories about its use as a healing stone are known.

Healing

Spiritually Pink opal encourages generosity towards guests and commitment to idealized communities. It helps us submit to a higher ideal and to act in unselfish ways.

Emotionally Pink opal bestows an unhibited, easy manner and lightness. It dissolves worries and a downcast mood and encourages warmth towards our fellow human beings. Pink opal helps us express ourselves openly as our true nature and liberates from shyness, shame and inhibitions. Pink opal helps with the enjoyment of sexuality.

Mentally Pink opal stimulates dreamy introspection in which a mixture of memories and desirable images are spun into new ideas and concepts.

Physically Pink opal alleviates heart problems. It is particularly helpful with heart neuroses, that is, symptoms that only arise due to worry about the heart without there being a physical diagnosis.

Application

Pink opal should be worn near the heart or laid on and can be used for contemplative meditation or laid out in a stone circle.

Fire opal, Mexico;
pink opal, Peru.

Peridot, olivine, chrysolite

CRYSTAL SYSTEM: rhombic
TYPE BY MANNER OF FORMATION: primary
MINERAL CLASS: island silicate
COLOUR: colourless, bottle green, olive green, greeny yellow
CHEMICAL FORMULA, MINERAL-FORMING SUBSTANCES:
  $(Mg,Fe)_2[SiO_4]$ + Al,Ca,Mn,Ni,Co,Cr,Ti

Mineralogy

Peridot is formed igneously in deep rock out of ultra-alkaline magma. It is often torn away and brought to the surface by rising magma during volcanic eruptions. It is then found as an 'olivine bomb' embedded in volcanic rock.

Mythology

Peridot was being used in ancient Egypt as a stone for jewellery and for healing two thousand years before the birth of Christ. In ancient writings it is often referred to as topaz, so it is thought that the 'topaz' in the breast plate of the high priest mentioned in the Old Testament might actually be a peridot. In the Middle Ages, it was employed for warding off evil spirits and to bestow wisdom and friendship.

Healing

Spiritually Peridot helps us detach ourselves from outside influences. It helps us live our own lives and to cull some wisdom from the abundance of experience.

Emotionally Peridot dissolves oppressive feelings that arise from self-blame and a bad conscience. It helps with stored up anger and fury.

Mentally Peridot helps us to admit our mistakes and to forgive ourselves. It makes us aware of things we have neglected to do and stimulates us to make up for damage caused.

Physically Peridot has a strong detoxifying effect and stimulates the liver. It enhances the liver and gallbladder, stimulates the metabolism and helps with skin problems, even warts.

Application

Peridot should be worn with skin contact or laid over the liver.

Peridot (chrysolite), USA;
peridot (olivine), Lanzarote.

Pietersite

CRYSTAL SYSTEM: trigonal
TYPE BY MANNER OF FORMATION: secondary
MINERAL CLASS: oxide, quartz group
COLOUR: blue-black/brown flecks
CHEMICAL FORMULA, MINERAL-FORMING SUBSTANCES:
$$SiO_2 + Na_2(Mg,Fe,Al)_5(OH/Si_4O_{11})_2$$

Mineralogy

Pietersite is a breccia cemented together with quartz out of falcon's eye and tiger's eye, thus displaying a patched pattern of crocidolite fibres.

Mythology

Pietersite has only been found recently in the desert of Namibia and was given the name of its discoverer, Sid Pieters. The gemstone therapy school run by Jane Ann Dow in New Mexico calls it the 'stormstone', a stone that offers help during chaotic periods.

Healing

Spiritually Pietersite helps us to master periods of fast and stormy (personal or collective) changes and to build a new order out of chaos. It loosens stubborn blocks and clears up confusion.

Emotionally Pietersite helps us cope with unprocessed images and inner conflict and, connected with this, all kinds of unpleasant feelings. Pietersite helps us remain distanced, if necessary, without lacking feelings.

Mentally Pietersite helps us process impressions faster and to remain open to absorb spiritual content. It enables us to remain concentrated and collected, even when there are a multitude of distractions and diversions.

Physically Pietersite supports the healing of illnesses that arise through confusion or unfulfilled desire for rest. It is particularly effective with all respiratory problems.

Application

Pietersite can be worn or laid on the solar plexus. Spending time in a stone circle has a strongly centring effect.

Prase

CRYSTAL SYSTEM: trigonal
TYPE BY MANNER OF FORMATION: primary or tertiary
MINERAL CLASS: oxide, quartz group
COLOUR: leek green
CHEMICAL FORMULA, MINERAL-FORMING SUBSTANCES:
$$SiO_2 + Ca_2(Mg,Fe)_5[OH,F]/Si_4O_{11}]_2$$

Mineralogy

Prase is a quartz that owes its green colour to masses of actinolite needles embedded in it. It can be formed hydrothermally, when it makes crystals whose sides flow straight into its tips, but this is rare. More frequently, however, it is formed in chunky masses during the metamorphosis of rocks containing iron silicate and quartz.

Mythology

Prase has been known since antiquity. Even Pliny (first century AD) knew it as 'prasius'. During the Middle Ages, it was used for healing the eyes, for high temperatures and for the healing of bruises and contusions.

Healing

Spiritually Prase encourages control, particularly the control of our own lives. It bestows a calm, simply pragmatic quality to life.

Emotionally Prase calms hot temper, anger and eruptions of violent fury. It has a calming effect and is particularly good for people who hold grudges as it helps them make it up again.

Mentally Prase helps us not to lose control of our own actions, even when we experience violent emotional reactions.

Physically Prase has a pain-alleviating, temperature-lowering effect. It allows swellings and bruises to reduce rapidly and helps with problems caused by the sun's rays, such as sunburn, sun stroke or heat stroke.

Application

Prase should be worn for longer periods of time as its effect unfolds quite slowly. The stone should be warmed up first, before using it to heal pain and swelling.

Prase, Serifos, Greece.

Prehnite

CRYSTAL SYSTEM: rhombic
TYPE BY MANNER OF FORMATION: primary
MINERAL CLASS: group silicate
COLOUR: colourless, greenish
CHEMICAL FORMULA, MINERAL-FORMING SUBSTANCES:
  $Ca_2Al[(OH)_2/AlSi_3O_{10}]$

Mineralogy

Prehnite was not discovered until the end of the eighteenth century and was named after a Major Prehn, who brought back the mineral from the Cape of Good Hope (South Africa). There are no traditions about its healing effects.

Healing

Spiritually Prehnite helps dissolve avoidance and substitution mechanisms. It also helps us to accept unpleasant truths, helping us to understand our own identities.

Emotionally Prehnite helps us face up to avoided images and memories and to dissolve unpleasant feelings connected with them. Prehnite does not itself throw up many memories, but it helps at moments when they are activated and become acute as a result of new experiences.

Mentally Prehnite encourages analytical thinking and accelerates the processing of sensory perceptions. Prehnite imperceptibly but continuously increases our perception levels.

Physically Prehnite stimulates the metabolism of fat and accelerates the removal of toxins stored in it. Prehnite stimulates all regeneration processes of the body.

Application

Prehnite should be worn directly on the body, definitely with skin contact. It is most effective for dissolving fat if several prehnite stones at once are placed over the liver and pancreas and in the general area of the small intestine.

Pyrite

CRYSTAL SYSTEM: cubic
TYPE BY MANNER OF FORMATION: primary, secondary or tertiary
MINERAL CLASS: sulphide
COLOUR: golden metallic
CHEMICAL FORMULA, MINERAL-FORMING SUBSTANCES:
FeS_2 + Co,Ni,Sb + (Cu,Au,Ag,Zn)

Mineralogy

Small clusters of pyrites with characteristically shaped crystals are formed, for the most part, hydrothermally, as chunky and spherical pyrites; the precisely shaped cubes are formed in sediments in clay and coal. The well-known pyrite 'sunbursts' are formed in the tertiary manner during the metamorphosis of these sediments.

Mythology

The name pyrite means 'fire stone' as it forms sparks when struck and was used, even in the Stone Age, to start fires. As 'fire lives in it' it was worked into amulets as a magic stone, and was used in healing as a 'warming stone'.

Healing

Spiritually Pyrite encourages self-realization. It confronts us with our own character and shows up its light and dark sides.

Emotionally Pyrite uncovers secrets and memories that were held back and thus provides an opportunity for openness and honesty.

Mentally Pyrite clarifies the causes of certain life circumstances and illnesses and thus enables us to intitiate necessary changes.

Physically Pyrite clarifies confusing presentations of diseases and unclear symptoms. It shows up the causal symptoms of an illness. Special pyrite 'suns' have a pain-alleviating effect.

Application

Pyrite should only be worn for a short period of time with skin contact, as longer contact (sweat) makes it secrete black iron sulphide that irritates the skin and stains clothing. It is better to use it for meditation or place it in a position where it can be seen regularly.

Pyrite, Peru,
pyrite cubes, Spain.

Smoky quartz

CRYSTAL SYSTEM: trigonal
TYPE BY MANNER OF FORMATION: primary
MINERAL CLASS: oxide, quartz group
COLOUR: light to dark brown
CHEMICAL FORMULA, MINERAL-FORMING SUBSTANCES: SiO_2 + (Al,Li,Na)

Mineralogy

Smoky quartz is formed mainly in pegmatites or hydrothermally in druses and clefts. It obtains its brown colour from aluminium and lithium as well as from the influence of radioactivity.

Mythology

Smoky quartz is considered to be a protective stone against bad luck in Alpine countries and, to this day, polished crucifixes are still made of it. It was often worn by soldiers in the past.

Healing

Spiritually Smoky quartz increases our tolerance of stress. It helps us bear sorrow and produce great effort, cope more easily with hard times, and do the work that has to be done.

Emotionally Smoky quartz has a relaxing effect. It is the classic 'antistress stone' that, in the long term, also takes away the tendency to allow ourselves to be 'stressed' and makes us more resistant to stress factors.

Mentally Smoky quartz encourages sober, realistic and pragmatic considerations. It encourages concentration and helps dissolve contradictions, as well as separate feelings and thoughts.

Physically Smoky quartz has a pain-alleviating effect and dissolves cramps. It is especially helpful with back problems. Smoky quartz fortifies the nerves, protects us against the effects of radiation and helps alleviate the damage caused by radiation.

Application

Smoky quartz should be worn as a chain or pendant for longer periods of time to give strength. In situations of stress, two polished crystals or rough crystals held in each hand will help. In order to dissolve pain, smoky quartz can be laid directly on the afflicted part of the body.

Smoky quartz, Switzerland;
smoky quartz [Gwindel], Switzerland.

Rhodochrosite

CRYSTAL SYSTEM: trigonal
TYPE BY MANNER OF FORMATION: secondary
MINERAL CLASS: carbonate
COLOUR: raspberry pink to pink
CHEMICAL FORMULA, MINERAL-FORMING SUBSTANCES: $MnCO_3$ + Ca,Fe,Zn

Mineralogy

Rhodochrosite is formed in the sedimentary manner in the oxidation zone of manganese ore deposits. Water containing manganese and carbonic acid collects in hollows and cysts in the rock in the form of rose coloured rhodochrosite stalagmites or fills cracks.

Mythology

Rhodochrosite (Greek for 'rose coloured') has been known for a long time as manganese spar or raspberry spar. However, there are no indications as to a traditional use of it as a healing stone.

Healing

Spiritually Rhodochrosite bestows a positive, enthusiastic attitude towards life. It stimulates an impersonal, all-encompassing love.

Emotionally Rhodochrosite encourages activity, liveliness, eroticism and spontaneous expressions of feeling. It has a mood-lifting effect, bestows energy and makes us light and cheerful.

Mentally Rhodochrosite imparts wakefulness and dynamism: it causes us to be busy, fills us with ideas and helps make work appear easy, so that we can succeed.

Physically Rhodochrosite stimulates the circulation, blood pressure, kidneys and sexual organs of reproduction. It makes the blood vessels more elastic, thus helping with migraines.

Application

During an attack of migraine, the rhodochrosite should be laid on the medulla oblongata ,which is a pressure-sensitive point right behind the back of the head where the spinal cord passes through the opening in the skull into the central (oldest) part of the brain. Otherwise, it will be sufficient to wear the stone directly on the body.

Rhodochrosite, Argentina;
rhodonite, USA.

Rhodonite

CRYSTAL SYSTEM: triclinic
TYPE BY MANNER OF FORMATION: tertiary
MINERAL CLASS: chain silicate
COLOUR: pink
CHEMICAL FORMULA, MINERAL-FORMING SUBSTANCES:
  $CaMn_4[Si_5O_{15}]$ + Al,Ca,Fe,Li,K,Na

Mineralogy

Rhodonite is only rarely formed in the primary manner from hydrothermal solutions at relatively low temperatures. Considerably larger proportions are formed through the regional metamorphosis of sedimentary manganese ore deposits. The result is chunky rose coloured masses that may then be partially oxidized through weathering. This creates the typical black patches and veins of manganese dioxide. Tertiary rhodonite deposits often produce such large quantities that monolithic blocks of rhodonite are also used for stonemasonry and architectural work.

Mythology

Rhodonite (Greek *rhodon*, 'rose') has been known under this name for about 200 years. Unfortunately, no traditions on its healing effects have been found.

Healing

Spiritually Rhodonite helps us to forgive and thereby brings about reconciliation between people who have been hurting each other for some time. It helps us realize that strife is very often caused by a lack of self-love and that the triggering 'misdeeds' of the other person are not the real cause. This facilitates mutual understanding, strengthens friendships and helps solve conflicts in a constructive manner. Rhodonite stimulates learning from life and bestows spiritual maturity.

Emotionally Rhodonite helps heal old 'wounds' and 'scars'. It enables us to forgive harm and injustice received and liberates us from deep mental pain as well as festering anger and persistent annoyance. Rhodonite also helps with renewed injury: it dissolves shock and helps with fear, confusion and panic. Rhodonite can be looked upon as a 'rescue' or 'first aid' stone that can prevent traumatization if used immediately.

Mentally Rhodonite makes it possible to remain clear and conscious even in extreme situations, when in danger, when threatened or under great pressure. It helps us understand that revenge has a mainly self-destructive effect and makes it easier to deal calmly with provocation and insults and to remain prudent and level-headed in all our actions. Rhodonite elucidates the meaning or gain in any experience, even if it is unpleasant, thus showing the way out of seemingly hopeless situations.

Physically Rhodonite is the best wound-healing stone of all. Minor injuries like small cuts, for example, will heal in a matter of minutes. It heals suppurating wounds, helps eliminate toxins out of the tissues (also insect stings) and makes sure that healthy tissue without scar tissue is formed during the healing of a wound. To a lesser degree it will even enable later transformation of scars in the case of wounds that have already healed. Rhodonite will also heal internal injuries and stimulates regeneration during illnesses that involve processes of self-dissolution, for example autoimmune diseases, stomach ulcers, even multiple sclerosis. Rhodonite strengthens the heart and circulation and encourages fertility in both sexes.

Application

Rhodonite should be worn near the heart for healing emotional injuries. Daily meditation in a rhodonite stone circle will also have a strongly spiritual, soul and mental effect. In cases of minor injuries, immediately press a moistened piece of rhodonite on the wound and apply pressure on it for five or ten minutes. Alternatively, or in cases of more serious injuries, a diluted rhodonite essence may be applied to the injury (approximately ten drops to 0.2 litres (7 fluid ounces) of water). The essence, in particular, will help with accidents or similar, dissolve shock and prevent trauma. It is also helpful if the injured person is able to tell a calm listener what happened. This helps the mind deal with it.

Rhyolite (orbicular jasper and leopard skin jasper)

CRYSTAL SYSTEM: trigonal (mainly)
TYPE BY MANNER OF FORMATION: primary
MINERAL CLASS: silicate/oxide
COLOUR: white, grey, greenish, reddish with clearly visible speckled inclusions
CHEMICAL FORMULA, MINERAL-FORMING SUBSTANCES:

$SiO_2 + (Ca,K,Na)[AlSi_3O_8] + Ca_2NaK(Mg,Fe)_3(Fe,Al)_2[O,OH,F]_2/Al_2Si_6O_{22}]$

Mineralogy
Rhyolite is a volcanic rock. It consists mainly of quartz, feldspar and hornblende. Green rhyolite with chalcedony inclusions ('orbicular jasper') or sandy coloured rhyolite with glassy inclusions ('leopard skin jasper') are mainly used as healing stones. The term jasper is derived from the definition 'jasper = grainy quartz with a high content of foreign substances', but is a little misleading here.

Mythology
The name rhyolite originates from the Greek *rhyx*, 'stream of lava'. No traditions for its healing properties are known.

Healing
Spiritually Rhyolite has the interesting effect of strengthening the existing spiritual state and clarifying it without, however, effecting any changes.

Emotionally Rhyolite fortifies our self-respect and feeling of self-value. It helps us accept ourselves as we are and has an emotionally balancing effect.

Mentally Rhyolite helps us deal with strenuous life situations in a calm, concentrated manner and with awareness of our own strength.

Physically Rhyolite fortifies our natural resistance. 'Leopard skin jasper', due to its signature, helps with skin diseases, hardened tissues and the formation of stones, 'orbicular jasper' helps with influenza, colds and infections.

Application
Spending time on rhyolite rock naturally has the strongest effect; otherwise, rhyolite should be worn on the body.

Rhyolite ('orbicular jasper'), Australia; rhyolite ('leopard skin jasper'), Mexico.

Rose quartz

CRYSTAL SYSTEM: trigonal
TYPE BY MANNER OF FORMATION: primary
MINERAL CLASS: oxide, quartz group
COLOUR: pink
CHEMICAL FORMULA, MINERAL-FORMING SUBSTANCES: SiO_2 + Na,Al,Fe,Ti + (Ca,Mg,Mn)

Mineralogy

Rose quartz is formed magmatically in young pegmatites and forms chunky masses. Very rarely, crystal groups may arise through hydrothermal formation. Asterism (formation of stars) may occur due to oriented rutile (TiO_2) crystals embedded in the quartz which become visible when the rose quartz is polished into spherical shapes (beads).

Mythology

For centuries, rose quartz has been considered to be a fertility crystal. It has been used for healing heart problems and female disorders, but also for love magic, therefore, in 'matters of the heart'.

Healing

Spiritually Rose quartz makes us gentle yet firm. There is no question of pliability or giving in, rather there is an awareness of the 'gentle, soft nature overcoming the hard, strong one'. Rose quartz encourages helpfulness, openness and the desire for a pleasant ambience.

Emotionally Rose quartz imparts empathy, sensitivity and sometimes over-sensitiveness. It encourages proper self-love, a strong heart, romance and the ability to love.

Mentally Rose quartz liberates us from worry and helps us discriminate (sympathy/antipathy). Rose quartz draws attention to the fulfilment of elementary needs.

Physically Rose quartz stimulates the blood circulation in the tissues. It fortifies the heart and sexual organs, helps with sexual problems and encourages fertility.

Application

Rose quartz is effective even as a rough stone situated nearby. It can be used in any manner.

Rose quartz, Brazil;
rutilated quartz, Brazil.

Rutilated quartz

CRYSTAL SYSTEM: trigonal/tetragonal
TYPE BY MANNER OF FORMATION: primary
MINERAL CLASS: oxide, quartz group
COLOUR: clear, brown with copper red or golden fibres
CHEMICAL FORMULA, MINERAL-FORMING SUBSTANCES: SiO_2 + TiO_2

Mineralogy

Rutilated quartz consists of needle-shaped rutile crystals that are enclosed by rock crystal and smoky quartz. It is formed magmatically in pegmatites or hydrothermally in clefts.

Mythology

Rutilated quartz was termed 'Venus hair' in ancient times; later it was called sagenite. It was thought to be captured sunlight and to be helpful for dark moods and coughs.

Healing

Spiritually Rutilated quartz gives us new hope and transmits uprightness, independence and spiritual greatness. It helps us to defend ourselves without losing sight of our goals.

Emotionally Rutilated quartz has a mood-lifting and antidepressive effect. It dissolves hidden, unacknowledged fear and liberates us from feelings of anxiety and constriction. Rutilated quartz also helps with sexual problems caused by severe tension, such as potency problems and premature ejaculation.

Mentally Rutilated quartz helps develop vision. It helps us to think big and not to limit our visionary power because of supposed pressure of circumstances.

Physically Rutilated quartz helps with diseases of the respiratory tract, particularly with chronic bronchitis. It stimulates the regenerating power of all cells and the flow of energy and body growth. Rutilated quartz encourages an upright posture.

Application

Rutilated quartz can be used for meditation, for stone circles, or for wearing or laying on the chest or solar plexus.

Ruby

CRYSTAL SYSTEM: trigonal
TYPE BY MANNER OF FORMATION: primary or tertiary
MINERAL CLASS: oxide, corundum family
COLOUR: red
CHEMICAL FORMULA, MINERAL-FORMING SUBSTANCES: Al_2O_3 + Cr,Ti

Mineralogy

Ruby is formed either magmatically as a liquid in aluminium-rich rock like granite, syenite or pegmatites, or during the metamorphosis of similar rocks into gneiss, crystalline slate or marble. It belongs to the corundum family and obtains its red colour through the presence of chromium. Oriented rutile needles embedded in the ruby give rise to asterism (star formation).

Mythology

Ruby (Latin *rubeus*, 'red') was unanimously considered to be the stone of the Sun in all the old cultures of Europe and India. It represents the life force, inner fire, love and passion

Healing

Spiritually Ruby lends style and vigour to life. It bestows passion as a driving force, but still prevents any tendencies towards self-destruction in its role as a life-loving stone.

Emotionally Ruby brings healthy tension and dynamism. It is enlivening, rejuvenates, fires us with enthusiasm, and lifts us out of lethargy and exhaustion; it has a balancing effect on hyperactivity. Ruby stimulates sexual activity.

Mentally Ruby leads to joyful commitment to all social tasks. It makes us awake and aware in thought and action, able to perform well, active, courageous, impulsive and spontaneous.

Physically Ruby stimulates the spleen, adrenal glands and the circulation. It helps with infectious diseases, for example intestinal infections, and encourages fever in its function as resistance:

Application

Ruby can be worn as a chain, pendant or hand 'comforter' on the body or laid on the pubic bone. The latter course will activate a great deal of 'power' ...

Sapphire

CRYSTAL SYSTEM: trigonal
TYPE BY MANNER OF FORMATION: primary or tertiary
MINERAL CLASS: oxide, corundum family
COLOUR: colourless, yellow, blue, black
CHEMICAL FORMULA, MINERAL-FORMING SUBSTANCES: Al_2O_3 + Fe,Ti

Mineralogy

Sapphire is formed either magmatically as a liquid in aluminium-rich rock like granite, syenite or pegmatite or during the metamorphosis of similar rock into gneiss, crystalline slate or marble. It belongs to the corundum family and obtains its colour from iron and titanium. Oriented rutile needles embedded in the sapphire give rise to asterism (star formation).

Mythology

Sapphire (from Sanskrit *Sani*, 'Saturn') was always considered to be the stone of Saturn in all the old cultures of Europe and India. It represents the heavens, the sphere of the angels, magic, fidelity and friendship.

Healing

Spiritually Sapphire bestows straightforwardness and the ability to direct scattered spiritual energies towards a single goal. By using sapphire, we are made to look at our own lives in a critical way and throw away everything that does not stand up to scrutiny. Sapphire encourages the desire for knowledge and wisdom.

Emotionally Sapphire has a calming effect. It helps with depression, psychic illnesses and delusions. Sapphire strengthens the power of belief and the love of truth.

Mentally Sapphire encourages sobriety, the ability to criticize and the organization of thoughts. Our intentions and will become so clear that both ideas and thoughts are realized very rapidly.

Physically Sapphire encourages all healing processes through a mental decision to get well. It alleviates pain, lowers fevers and is particularly helpful with intestinal, brain and nervous diseases.

Application

Sapphire can be worn, laid on the stomach or forehead, or taken internally in the form of an essence.

Sardonyx

CRYSTAL SYSTEM: trigonal
TYPE BY MANNER OF FORMATION: primary
MINERAL CLASS: oxide, quartz group
COLOUR: black-white-red brown banded
CHEMICAL FORMULA, MINERAL-FORMING SUBSTANCES:
SiO_2 + C + (Fe,O,OH)

Mineralogy

Sardonyx is a chalcedony that is coloured black and white, sometimes also red-brown due to iron and carbon inclusions. It is formed hydrothermally in hollows and cysts in rock.

Mythology

Sardonyx has been known since antiquity and right into the Middle Ages was considered to be a stone of abundance, virtue, fearlessness and eloquence. It was thought to bestow a good intellect and common sense. Its name is a composite of the reddish brown sard it contains (carnelian) and onyx.

Healing

Spiritually Sardonyx stimulates the striving for a meaningful existence. It increases willpower and strengthens a virtuous character, making us friendly and helpful.

Emotionally Sardonyx bestows stability, self-confidence and a hopeful attitude. It helps overcome sadness and brings joy that is easily transferred to others.

Mentally Sardonyx strengthens the perceptions and the absorption of information and intensifies perceptions. It helps us understand more easily all the things that happen on a daily basis.

Physically Sardonyx invigorates all the sensory organs and improves all perceptions of the senses. It regulates all body fluids, the immune system, cell metabolism and the activity of the intestines and encourages absorption of nutrients and elimination of wastes.

Application

Sardonyx can be worn as a pendant or carried about as a hand 'comforter'. Physically it is most effective if it is laid on the stomach.

Sardonyx, Brazil.

Schalenblende

CRYSTAL SYSTEM: cubic (+ hexagonal)
TYPE BY MANNER OF FORMATION: primary
MINERAL CLASS: sulphide
COLOUR: yellow-brown/silver-grey banded
CHEMICAL FORMULA, MINERAL-FORMING SUBSTANCES:
  $ZnS + Mn + (Cu,Sb,Sn,Pb)$

Mineralogy

Schalenblende consists of cubic (sphalerite) and hexagonal zinc sulphide (wurtzite); the wurtzite that is contained gradually transforms into sphalerite. Schalenblende is formed hydrothermally from a zinc and sulphur gel which gives it its undulating, banded appearance.

Mythology

Schalenblende has been known as 'blende' in mines since the Middle Ages. There are, however, no traditions about its healing effects.

Healing

Spiritually Schalenblende breaks up outworn structures and bestows idealism. It helps one survive dramatic changes in life and uses them for the meaningful creation of better cicumstances.

Emotionally Schalenblende helps combat exhaustion, weakness, lack of courage and fear. It balances inner unrest and helps us get to sleep whenever thoughts are keeping us awake.

Mentally Schalenblende encourages concentration, abstract thinking, spontaneity and intuition as well as the ability to communicate. It helps end fruitless brooding.

Physically Schalenblende encourages the development of the brain as well as of the senses of smell and taste. It stimulates the retina (enhancing vision in half-light), assists regeneration and wound-healing, supports the immune system and alleviates diabetes. It helps with prostate trouble and stimulates the gonads and ovaries. Schalenblende protects the organism from harmful substances and radiation.

Application

Schalenblende works best when it is worn on the body.

Schalenblende, Poland

Serpentine

CRYSTAL SYSTEM: monoclinic
TYPE BY MANNER OF FORMATION: tertiary
MINERAL CLASS: phyllo or sheet silicate
COLOUR: olive green, yellow-green, light green, silvery fibrous
CHEMICAL FORMULA, MINERAL-FORMING SUBSTANCES:

$Mg_6[(OH_8/Si_4O_{10}] + Al,Cr,Fe,Mn,Ni$

Mineralogy

Serpentine is formed during the metamorphosis of alkaline igneous rocks, for example peridot to crystalline slate. It occurs in rock-forming processes as green 'leaf' serpentine (antigorite) or as silvery fibrous serpentine (chrysotile). Whenever both varieties are united in alternating bands, the trade call it 'silver eye'.

Mythology

Serpentine ('serpent stone') probably received its name from its scaly, patchy appearance, which is reminiscent of snake skin. From pre-Roman times until well into the Middle Ages, serpentine was considered to protect against disease and sorcery. 'Fright stones' were carved out of this mineral in the shape of ugly-faced amulets that were supposed to drive away 'frightening things'

Healing

Spiritually Serpentine helps us to establish boundaries and find inner peace. It is an outstanding meditation stone.

Emotionally Serpentine balances mood swings, is calming in cases of nervousness and stress and protects from negative energy effects. It helps women who are unable to reach orgasm because of tension.

Mentally Serpentine stimulates the urge to solve conflicts in a peaceful way; however, it can sometimes make us too eager to compromise for the sake of peace.

Physically Serpentine helps with disturbances to the heart rhythm, kidney and stomach complaints, and also when diarrhoea and constipation keep alternating. It balances over-acidification and stimulates the magnesium metabolism, relaxes cramps and alleviates menstrual pain.

Application

Serpentine should be worn directly on the skin or laid on it.

Silver eye, Australia;
serpentine, Austria.

Emerald

CRYSTAL SYSTEM: hexagonal
TYPE BY MANNER OF FORMATION: primary or tertiary
MINERAL CLASS: ring silicate, beryl family
COLOUR: emerald green
CHEMICAL FORMULA, MINERAL-FORMING SUBSTANCES:
$Be_3Al_2(Si_6O_{18})$ + K,Li,Na + (Cr)

Mineralogy
Emerald is formed magmatically in pegmatites or through metamorphosis in the contact zone between rocks containing beryllium and chromium.

Mythology
In the old cultures of Europe and India, emerald was assigned to Mercury, the messenger of the gods and god of the pathways and roads, of sleep and dreams, and was, therefore, always considered to be the stone of divine inspiration. In antiquity, it was in use as a medium for healing the eyes; in the Middle Ages, it was used for all 'weaknesses and illnesses in mankind' (Hildegard von Bingen).

Healing

Spiritually Emerald encourages spiritual growth, clairvoyance and a sense of beauty, harmony and justice. It makes us upright, goal-orientated and life-affirming. Emerald enhances friendship, love and unity between partners. It keeps us mentally young.

Emotionally Emerald helps overcome misfortunes and blows dealt by fate. It bestows a balanced nature, openness, recovery and regeneration. Emerald also stimulates us to live intensely and enjoy life.

Mentally Emerald bestows clarity, wakefulness and a broad vision. It improves cooperation in groups, as it enhances mutual understanding.

Physically Emerald improves the ability to see and heals inflammations of the sinuses and upper respiratory tract. It fortifies the heart, stimulates the liver, has a detoxifying effect and alleviates rheumatic complaints. Emerald strengthens the immune system and encourages recovery after infectious illnesses.

Application
Emerald can be worn, laid on or used for meditation. The gem essence has a very pronounced effect.

Emerald, Brazil.

Sodalite

CRYSTAL SYSTEM: cubic
TYPE BY MANNER OF FORMATION: primary
MINERAL CLASS: lattice silicate
COLOUR: dark blue
CHEMICAL FORMULA, MINERAL-FORMING SUBSTANCES:

$$Na_8[Cl_2/(AlSiO_4)_6] + Be,K,Mg$$

Mineralogy
Sodalite is formed in the primary manner in pegmatites that are poor in silicic acid, or in vulcanites such as trachyte.

Mythology
The meaning of sodalite is 'sodium stone'. It has been known for about 200 years but there are no known traditions about its healing effects.

Healing

Spiritually Sodalite encourages idealism and the drive for truth. It makes it possible to observe suppressed parts of our nature without judging and once again to accept them. Sodalite makes space for living the life we have chosen freely and consciously. It helps us remain true to ourselves.

Emotionally Sodalite transmits a clear feeling of who we are and creates a strong antipathy against everything that does not correspond to this identity. It helps us avoid unconscious mechanisms and behavioural patterns, once we have recognized them as being a hindrance to our development. Sodalite dissolves feelings of guilt and makes it possible to stand up for our own feelings and to live them out.

Mentally Sodalite increases awareness and helps us to create order and lend expression to our own convictions, either verbally or through actions. It stimulates a departure from restrictive ideas, dogmas, rules and laws. Sodalite increases a yearning for freedom.

Physically Sodalite heals complaints that afflict the throat, larynx and vocal chords, in particular, long-lasting hoarseness. It has a cooling effect, lowers the blood pressure and stimulates absorption of fluids in the body.

Application
Sodalite should be worn as a chain, pendant or hand 'comforter' for long periods of time.

*Sunstone, Norway;
sodalite, Brazil.*

Sunstone

CRYSTAL SYSTEM: triclinic
TYPE BY MANNER OF FORMATION: primary
MINERAL CLASS: lattice silicate, feldspar family
COLOUR: orange brown iridescent
CHEMICAL FORMULA, MINERAL-FORMING SUBSTANCES:
$Na[AlSi_3O_8]Ca[Al_2Si_2O_8] + Fe$

Mineralogy

Sunstone is an orange-brown iridescent feldspar that owes its appearance to the presence of microscopically thin hematite platelets. It is formed primarily in acid plutonites, more rarely meta-morphically in gneiss. The mineralogical term for sunstone is aventurine feldspar; this, unfortunately, often leads to confusion with the green aventurine quartz (see aventurine).

Mythology

Sunstone, as the name indicates, is assigned to the Sun. There are no traditions about its use for healing purposes, however.

Healing

Spiritually Sunstone helps us discover and live out our own inner nature. It helps us to affirm our lives and to allow our strong points and 'sunny sides' to shine. Sunstone brings back the belief in luck and happiness and the 'benevolent gods'.

Emotionally Sunstone bestows *joie de vivre*. It has a mood-lifting, antidepressive effect and helps us detach ourselves from feelings of disadvantage, discrimination and failure, as well as images of a 'bad world'. Sunstone increases a sense of self-worth and self-confidence.

Mentally Sunstone encourages optimism and a desire for action. It helps switch our perception filters to the positive events and gives new perspectives even to stubborn pessimists.

Physically Sunstone stimulates self-healing powers. It stimulates the autonomous nervous system and ensures harmonious functioning between all the organs.

Application

Sunstone can be worn as a chain, pendant or hand 'comforter', or even used for meditation.

Sugilite

CRYSTAL SYSTEM: hexagonal
TYPE BY MANNER OF FORMATION: primary
MINERAL CLASS: ring silicate
COLOUR: violet
CHEMICAL FORMULA, MINERAL-FORMING SUBSTANCES:
  $(K,Na)_2/(Fe,Ti)_2(Li,Al)_3[Si_{12}O_{30}]$

Mineralogy

Sugilite is formed primarily in pegmatites of alkaline magmas. It is very rare and, to date, only two sources in the world have been found, one in Japan and one in South Africa.

Mythology

Sugilite was not discovered until 1944 in Japan, and was named after its discoverer, Dr Kenichi Sugi. It did not become known as a healing mineral until the 1980s, but soon became a fully-fledged 'New Age' stone that is supposed to represent the Age of Aquarius. It is also known under the names luvulite and Royal Azel.

Healing

Spiritually Sugilite helps us maintain our own point of view. It encourages us to live in accordance with our inner truth and not to allow ourselves to be deflected from it, either through pressure or persuasion.

Emotionally Sugilite improves the ability to face up to unpleasant things. It dissolves tension in the soul, alleviates sorrow and grief and helps with fears, paranoia and schizophrenia.

Mentally Sugilite allows us to deal with and overcome conflicts without entering into compromise. It helps find solutions that are based on agreement and do not put any party at a disadvantage.

Physically Sugilite has a harmonizing effect on the nerves and brain and alleviates severe pain. It helps with epilepsy, dyslexia and motor disturbances.

Application

Sugilite should be worn on the body and in cases of pain it should be laid on or held in the hand. Its spiritual effect can be experienced through regular meditation with it.

Thulite

CRYSTAL SYSTEM: rhombic
TYPE BY MANNER OF FORMATION: tertiary
MINERAL CLASS: group silicate, zoisite family
COLOUR: reddish, pink
CHEMICAL FORMULA, MINERAL-FORMING SUBSTANCES:
$(Ca,Mn)_2Al_3[O/OH/SiO_4/Si_2O_7] + Mg,Cr$

Mineralogy

Thulite is formed during the metamorphosis of alkaline igneous rocks containing manganese, and forms chunky, massy lumps. Thulite is a zoisite containing manganese.

Mythology

Thulite received its name after the legendary island 'Thule' of Germanic lore that is supposed to form the northernmost rim of the world, probably because the mineral was first found in Norway. Unfortunately, there are no traditions about its healing properties or use.

Healing

Spiritually Thulite stimulates the life force. It bestows strength and courage for all undertakings and encourages creativity of a kind that is inspired whenever there is resistance and challenge.

Emotionally Thulite encourages lust, sensuality and sexuality. It helps us to live life to the full and to immerse ourselves in our feelings. Beauty, adventure, melancholy, romance and eerie atmospheres are all equally loved.

Mentally Thulite fortifies curiosity and the gift for inventions. It stimulates us to search for new ways to solve personal and collective problems.

Physically Thulite enhances fertility. It helps with diseases of the ovaries, testicles and sexual organs. Thulite stimulates regeneration, fortifies the entire nervous system and prevents fainting fits when the body is severely weakened.

Application

Thulite should be worn on the body or laid on the pubic bone. Spending time in a thulite stone circle has a very interesting effect ... (more I will not say here!).

Thulite, Norway;
sugilite, South Africa.

Tiger's eye

CRYSTAL SYSTEM: trigonal
TYPE BY MANNER OF FORMATION: tertiary
MINERAL CLASS: oxide, quartz group
COLOUR: golden brown
CHEMICAL FORMULA, MINERAL-FORMING SUBSTANCES: SiO_2 + FeOOH

Mineralogy
Tiger's eye is formed out of falcon's eye through oxidation of the original crocidolite fibres so that they are transformed into limonite. This means tiger's eye consists of limonite fibres embedded in quartz.

Mythology
The silken sheen produced by limonite fibres causes an interesting light effect when the mineral is polished into a round shape, and looks like an eye. This is how the stone gets its name and this is also the origin of the ancient belief that tiger's eye heals eye problems and is a protective stone. In the Middle Ages, it was used to make amulets that protected the wearer against spells, demons and the evil eye.

Healing

Spiritually Tiger's eye helps us get through difficult phases in life without losing courage. It helps preserve that spark of trust in God that leads us on in dark moments.

Emotionally Tiger's eye helps us to distance ourselves from external influences that may come storming in on us; it also mitigates the influence of moods and stressful situations.

Mentally Tiger's eye helps us retain an overall view in complicated, difficult situations and also helps with doubts and difficulties in making decisions.

Physically Tiger's eye has a pain-alleviating effect. It slows down the flow of energy in the body and dampens overexcitation of the nerves and overstimulation of the adrenal glands.

Application
As tiger's eye slows down the flow of energy in the body, it should never be worn for more than a week. Meditation is preferable for effects on the soul and spirit.

Tiger's eye, South Africa,
tiger iron, Namibia.

Tiger iron

CRYSTAL SYSTEM: trigonal
TYPE BY MANNER OF FORMATION: tertiary
MINERAL CLASS: oxide
COLOUR: grey-red-yellow banded
CHEMICAL FORMULA, MINERAL-FORMING SUBSTANCES:

$Fe_2O_3 + SiO_2 + Al,Na,Fe,Mg$

Mineralogy

Tiger iron is formed by a metamorphic process from rock containing iron and quartz. It has a layered structure made of jasper, hematite and tiger's eye formed under the influence of tectonic displacements.

Mythology

Tiger iron has only been known as such for a few years (it is a trade name) and there are no traditions about its healing effects.

Healing

Spiritually Tiger iron inspires new impulses when our own lives have been crying out for change for a very long time. It clarifies the areas where spiritually we have moved on long ago and actively helps these cycles to be closed, if necessary, and a new start to be made.

Emotionally Tiger iron imparts the kind of endurance that is necessary in order to overcome typical difficulties at the beginning of an undertaking or phase. It lends strength and dynamism to tackle all obstacles (a 'tiger in your tank'). Tiger iron helps with tiredness and exhaustion.

Mentally Tiger iron helps us to find very simple, pragmatic solutions. It clarifies thought according to the notion that 'truth lies in simplicity' and thus helps us act quickly and with determination.

Physically Tiger iron heightens vitality by accelerating the formation of red blood corpuscles and the transportation of oxygen by the blood. Tiger iron eliminates any kind of energy deficiency.

Application

Tiger iron works very quickly if it is worn in contact with the skin. It is a good idea to carry it in your pocket and to hold it in your hand whenever you need extra energy.

Topaz

CRYSTAL SYSTEM: rhombic
TYPE BY MANNER OF FORMATION: primary
MINERAL CLASS: island silicate
COLOUR: clear, light blue, brownish
CHEMICAL FORMULA, MINERAL-FORMING SUBSTANCES:
$Al_2[F_2/SiO_4] + OH + (Cr,Fe,Mn)$

Mineralogy

Topaz is formed magmatically through pneumatolytic processes during the formation of acid plutonites, more rarely also during the formation of vulcanites. Chromium gives topaz a yellow colour, iron a blue colour and manganese a brownish colour.

Mythology

In all the old cultures of Europe and India, topaz was unanimously considered to be the stone of Jupiter. It represented rule over one's own life, self-realization and wisdom. In Mexico, it was used for finding out the truth in cases of disagreement.

Healing

Spiritually Topaz encourages self-realization and the shaping of our lives according to our own wishes. It can enable a breakthrough in spiritual development whenever things have been very laborious and difficult for a long time. Topaz helps us to gain wisdom from of the vagaries of fate.

Emotionally Topaz helps us discover our own inner riches of soul images, abilities and knowledge. It encourages openness, honesty and a fulfilled emotional life.

Mentally Topaz helps us become fully aware of the influence we exert based on ability and real knowledge gained through hard work, and then to use this meaningfully.

Physically Topaz fortifies the nerves and stimulates the energy flow in the meridians. It improves the digestion and even helps with anorexia. Topaz stimulates the metabolism and the combustion processes of the organism.

Application

Topaz should be worn or chosen for contemplative meditation or laid on the head.

Topaz, Imperial

CRYSTAL SYSTEM: rhombic
TYPE BY MANNER OF FORMATION: primary
MINERAL CLASS: island silicate
COLOUR: golden yellow to pink
CHEMICAL FORMULA, MINERAL-FORMING SUBSTANCES: $Al_2[F_2/SiO_4] + P$

Mineralogy

Imperial topaz is formed magmatically through pneumatolytic processes during the formation of acid plutonites, more rarely also during the formation of vulcanites. Its golden yellow colour is due to phosphorus.

Mythology

Imperial topaz was considered to be a stone of the Sun, as was underlined by the phosphorus, a light-giving, fiery element, contained in it (Greek *phosphoros*, 'light carrier'). Imperial topaz was always a royal stone.

Healing

Spiritually Imperial topaz encourages self-realization. It helps us view our own abilities in a realistic light and encourages the self-confidence necessary to show them in public. Imperial topaz encourages striving for fame and recognition.

Emotionally Imperial topaz strengthens self-confidence and the awareness of our own importance. It makes us proud and self-confident but also big-hearted and generous. It bestows charisma.

Mentally Imperial topaz encourages the development of great plans and ideas.It helps us overcome apparent limitations without losing sight of reality.

Physically Imperial topaz helps with states of nervous exhaustion. It fortifies the nerves and increases their activity, which makes the entire organism more willing to react. Imperial topaz stimulates the appetite and even helps with anorexia. It activates the life force, processes of combustion in the body and the entire metabolism.

Application

Imperial topaz should be worn in the area of the solar plexus or laid on the body.

*Topaz, Pakistan.
Imperial topaz, Brazil.*

Turquoise

CRYSTAL SYSTEM: triclinic
TYPE BY MANNER OF FORMATION: secondary
MINERAL CLASS: phosphate
COLOUR: green to turquoise
CHEMICAL FORMULA, MINERAL-FORMING SUBSTANCES:
$$CuAl_6[(OH)_2/PO_4]_4 \cdot 4\,H_2O + Fe$$

Mineralogy

Turquoise is formed in the sedimentary manner as coatings and fillings in clefts, when solutions containing copper react with rock rich in aluminium phosphates.

Mythology

Turquoise received its name from Turkey, where European crusaders first came into contact with the stone. In many cultures, turquoise was looked upon as a protection against harmful spells and was worn as an amulet for strength, good health and *joie de vivre*. According to tradition, turquoise was also thought able to warn the wearer about the threat of danger.

Healing

Spiritually Turquoise helps us recognize the causes of fate that we have created for ourselves and the results of which we feel later. This means turquoise makes us aware that we really are the creators of our own luck.

Emotionally Turquoise balances extreme fluctuations of mood and dissolves an apathetic self-martyring attitude. It also refreshes us when tired, downcast or exhausted, and protects us from sensitivity to outside influences.

Mentally Turquoise bestows inner calm but still enables us to be wide awake, lively and ready to act. It encourages good intuition and foresight.

Physically Turquoise neutralizes overacidity and alleviates rheumatism, gout, stomach problems and viral infections. It increases growth, muscular strength, creation of warmth, the ability to regenerate, brain activity and sensory perception and also alleviates pain, relaxes cramps, and has anti-inflammatory and detoxifying effects.

Application

Turquoise should be worn on the solar plexus.

Turquoise, USA.

Tourmaline and tourmaline quartz

CRYSTAL SYSTEM: trigonal
TYPE BY MANNER OF FORMATION: primary
MINERAL CLASS: ring silicate (+ oxide)
COLOUR: all colours in various different combinations
CHEMICAL FORMULA, MINERAL-FORMING SUBSTANCES:

$Me^+Me^{2+}{}_3Me^{3+}{}_6[(OH,F)_4(BO_3)_2Si_6O_{18}]$

Mineralogy

Tourmaline is formed magmatically in acid plutonites, particularly in pegmatites, where it forms freely grown, large and many-coloured crystals. When neighbouring rock is influenced by gases in the magma that contain boron, tourmaline can also come into being as a pneumatolytic displacement. The crystals are then found firmly embedded in the rock. Tourmaline consists of very different mineral-forming substances, but it always displays the same structure: the cations consist of one-, two- or three-valent metal ions in a ratio of 1 : 3 : 6, the anions are of alkaline groups (hydroxide or fluoride), borate groups and silicate rings in a ratio of 4 : 2 : 1, so the simplified summary formula of tourmaline can be demonstrated as follows: $Me^+Me^{2+}{}_3Me^{3+}{}_6[(OH,F)_4(BO_3)_2Si_6O_{18}]$. Within this stable and un-changeable structure, it is the metals in particular that provide the colourful combinations, thus ensuring a similarly colourful display for tourmaline.

Classifying the tourmalines according to their different com-position of mineral-forming substances, there are seven varieties. However, this subdivision is only appropriate for single colour tourmalines. In the case of so-called 'polychrome tourmalines', the whole thing becomes mixed up again.

Variety	Formula, mineral-forming substances	Colour
Dravite:	$NaMg_3(Al,Fe,Cr)_6[(OH,F)_4(BO_3)_2Si_6O_{18}]$	brown, yellow, green, grey
Elbaite:	$Na(Li,Al)_3Al_6[(OH,F)_4(BO_3)_2Si_6O_{18}]$	all colours incl. colourless
Indicolite:	$Na(Fe,Li,Al)_3(Fe,Al)_6[(OH,F)_4(BO_3)_2Si_6O_{18}]$	blue
Rubellite:	$Na(Li,Mn,Al)_3Al_6[(OH,F)_4(BO_3)_2Si_6O_{18}]$	red, pink

Tourmaline, Brazil (left); indicolite, Brazil.

Verdelite:	$Na(Li,Al)_3(Al,Cr,V)_6[(OH,F)_4(BO_3)_2Si_6O_{18}]$	green
Schorl:	$NaFe_3(Al,Fe)_6[(OH,F)_4(BO_3)_2Si_6O_{18}]$	black
Uvite:	$CaMg_3(Al_5Mg) [(OH,F)_4(BO_3)_2Si_6O_{18}]$	light to dark brown

Tourmaline needles consisting of schorl enclosed in rock crystal are called tourmaline quartz. The healing effects of tourmaline quartz can, therefore, be equated with those of schorl.

Mythology

Tourmaline was probably already known in antiquity, but was always equated with other precious stones depending on its colour. It was not until the eighteenth century that it appeared as the 'stone of wisdom, that is clear and resistant to all vagaries of fate...' (Bernardus Caesius). According to Arabic traditions, tourmaline is a stone of the Sun that strengthens the heart and protects from nightmares.

Healing

All tourmalines possess a wide spectrum of healing effects that are based on their unimaginable variety. In the following, the individual effects are assigned to particular varieties that are most suited. However, at a pinch, other varieties can be used. Multi-coloured tourmalines combine several of the different qualities.

Spiritually Multi-coloured *elbaite* helps combine the spirit, soul, intellect and body into one harmonious whole. This experience of 'wholeness' gives rise to wisdom and creativity. *Indicolite* strengthens an urge for spiritual freedom. It encourages fidelity, ethics and a love of truth. *Dravite* encourages a sense of community spirit, helpfulness and social commitment. *Verdelite* bestows *joie de vivre*. It makes us grateful for the wonders of life. *Rubellite* makes us targeted but still flexible enough to check our goals and correct them, if necessary. *Schorl* gives neutrality and a relaxed attitude. *Watermelon tourmaline* encourages understanding, love and friendship.

Emotionally Multi-coloured *elbaite* stimulates imagery as well as creative daydreams and dreams at night. *Indicolite* dissolves sadness and blocked feelings and lends relief. *Dravite* strengthens the facility for empathy and identifying. It helps with family problems and feelings of apprehension in larger groups. *Verdelite* makes us patient and open. It encourages an interest in our fellow human beings. *Rubellite* makes us sociable and outgoing, ready for action and charming. *Schorl* discharges tensions and protects us from negative

Dravite, Namibia; watermelon tourmaline, Afghanistan.

thoughts and also helps with stress. *Watermelon tourmaline* makes us patient, loving and tender. It alleviates depression and fears and helps us to protect ourselves and to develop our own inner sense of security.

Mentally Multi-coloured *elbaite* encourages thinking in images and a heightened degree of perception, and enhances the imagination. *Indicolite* broadens the horizons and promotes tolerance and a sense of responsibility. *Dravite* stimulates a pragmatic, simple creativity and gives us skill at crafts. *Verdelite* helps us to see a number of possible solutions in any situation from which the best one (according to knowledge and conscience) can be chosen. *Rubellite* helps us devote ourselves actively and with devotion to a task. *Schorl* stimulates clear, logical and rational thought processes. It helps us recognize mistakes and analyse them. *Watermelon tourmaline* helps us express our intentions clearly and in a focused way

Physically Multi-coloured *elbaite* stimulates the activity of the glands (hormones), the metabolism and the immune system. *Indicolite* stimulates the water metabolism as well as the kidneys and the bladder. It allows burns to heal without scar tissue. *Dravite* stimulates the powers of regeneration in the cells, tissues and organs. It helps with chronic tensions and skin diseases. *Verdelite* strengthens the heart and has a detoxifying effect. It encourages elimination and helps with constipation and diarrhoea. *Rubellite* improves the flow of energy and the conductivity of the nerves. It strengthens the functioning of the sexual organs and stimulates blood circulation and blood purification in the spleen and liver. *Schorl* has a pain-alleviating effect and conducts body energy. It can be used to stimulate the formation of scars and will neutralize the influence of radiation. *Watermelon tourmaline* encourages regneration of the nerves. It also helps with paralysis and multiple sclerosis.

Application

Tourmaline can be worn on the body or, when required, placed on certain parts of it. For stimulating the energy flow in the meridians, crystals should be placed on the body with their tips pointing in the same direction as the flow. Essences also work very strongly and rapidly.

Schorl, Brazil;
tourmaline quartz, Brazil.

Variscite

CRYSTAL SYSTEM: rhombic
TYPE BY MANNER OF FORMATION: secondary
MINERAL CLASS: phosphate
COLOUR: colourless, grey, green
CHEMICAL FORMULA, MINERAL-FORMING SUBSTANCES:
$$AlPO_4 \cdot 2 H_2O + Cu,Fe,Mg$$

Mineralogy

Variscite is formed in the sedimentary manner on the Earth's surface through the weathering of aluminium-rich rock under the influence of rainwater containing phosphoric acid. Variscite is deposited during this process as a filling in cracks.

Mythology

Variscite obtained its name after the place where it was found, 'Variscia', the Latin name for Vogtland. No traditions about its healing properties are known.

Healing

Spiritually Variscite encourages authenticity and truthfulness. As long as we carry variscite, it will be difficult for us to indulge in pretence; we just show ourselves as we are. Variscite also helps us develop interests and remain spiritually aware.

Emotionally Variscite has an enlivening effect and lifts the spirit. It helps with chronic tiredness, for example in the spring, but also has a calming effect on nervousness and inner unrest.

Mentally Variscite bestows a wakeful attitude, sobriety and clear, rational thinking. It helps us to express ourselves clearly and in a fashion that can be easily understood. It also increases our level of perception.

Physically Variscite stimulates energy reserves. It neutralizes over-acidification and helps with acid indigestion, gastritis, stomach ulcers, rheumatism and gout. Variscite helps loosen cramp and calms the nerves.

Application

Variscite should be worn as a pendant or hand 'comforter' for a long period of time and, when needed, held in the left hand.

Variscite, USA;
fossilized wood, Australia.

Fossilized wood

CRYSTAL SYSTEM: triclinic or amorphous
TYPE BY MANNER OF FORMATION: secondary
MINERAL CLASS: oxide
COLOUR: brown, reddish, yellow
CHEMICAL FORMULA, MINERAL-FORMING SUBSTANCES: SiO_2 + C,Fe,O,OH

Mineralogy

Fossilized wood is formed when dead wood is saturated with silicic acid in the absence of air and then solidifies through loss of water. Depending on the exact circumstances of formation, the substance of the wood is replaced either by quartz or, more rarely, by opal.

Mythology

Fossilized wood in the form of cult objects has been found in a 4300 year old Etruscan temple. In some cases, fossilized wood was looked upon in bygone times as giants' bones or tools of the gods and was, therefore, used in magic as an object of power. Nowadays, in esoteric circles, fossilized wood is thought to be an aid in remembering past lives.

Healing

Spiritually Fossilized wood bestows the feeling of a bond with the Earth, and feelings of being at home on this planet. It also bestows the feeling of being in the right place at the right time.

Emotionally Fossilized wood stimulates inner imagery. It stimulates recovery, is calming, helps us collect ourselves and helps us keep our feet firmly planted in reality.

Mentally Fossilized wood stimulates us to create a pleasant atmosphere, live a simple life and grant ourselves enough time for leisure and reflection.

Physically Fossilized wood stabilizes our health. It stimulates the metabolism, calms the nerves, creates a feeling of well-being and helps with obesity, which is often caused by 'inadequate earthing'.

Application

Fossilized wood should be worn or used in a stone circle. A slice of fossil wood is ideal for meditating, if it is large enough to sit on.

Zircon

CRYSTAL SYSTEM: tetragonal
TYPE BY MANNER OF FORMATION: primary
MINERAL CLASS: island silicate
COLOUR: red, orange, brown, yellow
CHEMICAL FORMULA, MINERAL-FORMING SUBSTANCES:
$ZrSiO_4$ + Al,Ca,Fe,P,Y,Ce,Hf,Th,U

Mineralogy

Zircon is formed as a liquid out of acid magmas and is, therefore, found as a component of granites and seyenites. It forms larger, usually double-ended crystals in pegamatites. Some types of zircon may be slightly radioactive due to deposits of up to 10% hafnium, thorium and uranium.

Mythology

Zircon was known in antiquity as hyacinth and was used for healing. It was reputed to heal madness, make us resistant to temptations and strengthen the intellect. Nowadays, only the red-brown variety of zircon is called hyacinth.

Healing

Spiritually Zircon helps us become detached from materialism and experience spiritual reality. Zircon stimulates dealing with the meaning of existence.

Emotionally Zircon helps us overcome loss. It also helps us to let go of pain, sadness and fear, as well as all kinds of 'hanging on to' things. Zircon encourages lucid dreaming.

Mentally Zircon makes us aware of the ephemeral nature of all things. It stimulates us to re-evaluate the 'important things in life' from this viewpoint and to shed our adherence to material things.

Physically Zircon has a liver-stimulating, pain-alleviating and cramp-dissolving effect. It helps with menstrual pains that are caused by delayed menstruation.

Application

Zircon should be worn or laid on only for a maximum of one hour daily (except in cases of pain or menstrual complaints).

Zoisite

CRYSTAL SYSTEM: rhombic
TYPE BY MANNER OF FORMATION: tertiary
MINERAL CLASS: group silicate
COLOUR: green
CHEMICAL FORMULA, MINERAL-FORMING SUBSTANCES:
$Ca_2Al_3[O/OH/SiO_4/Si_2O_7] + Mg,Cr,Sr,V$

Mineralogy

Zoisite is formed during the metamorphosis of alkaline igneous rocks. It forms rough masses and obtains its green colour from the presence of chromium and vanadium. Zoisite may also contain ruby.

Mythology

Zoisite was first found in Carinthia (Karnten, Austria) towards the end of the eighteenth century and named after the mineral collector Freiherr von Zois. There are no traditions about its healing powers.

Healing

Spiritually Zoisite helps us to avoid conforming to others and being affected by outside influences, and helps us to realize our own ideas and desires. It makes it possible to transform destructive attitudes into a constructive way of life.

Emotionally Zoisite encourages recovery after illnesses or heavy stress. It helps us rediscover suppressed feelings and gradually live through them and express them.

Mentally Zoisite makes us creative. After a short or longer interruption, it will always help us to find our way back to the point of departure, to what we had really intended to do.

Physically Zoisite helps with diseases of the testicles and ovaries. It stimulates fertility and, in combination with ruby, will increase potency. Zoisite detoxifies the tissues, neutralizes overacidification and stimulates regeneration of the cells. It hinders inflammation and strengthens the immune system.

Application

Zoisite should be worn on the body for long periods of time or regularly laid on the afflicted part of the body in contact with the skin. Zoisite takes a while to unfold its full effect, so only continued use will ensure success.

Zircon (Hyacinth), Brazil; zoisite with ruby, Tanzania.

Index of synonyms

The minerals described in this volume are currently available in the trade under many different names. Together with these and the proper mineralogical terms, you will also find a wide profusion of ancient names and mythological terms. The modern trade names are generally imaginary and freely adapted on the principle of 'Give it a good name and it will sell!'.

This index of synonyms is intended to shed some light on the confusion: it gives an alphabetical list of the synonyms currently used for all the healing crystals described in this volume. Where appropriate, as well as indicating the proper name, a short description is given so as to explain what is behind the term

African jade prase
Amazon stone amazonite
Andes opal chrysopal or pink opal
Apache's tear smoky obsidian
apricot agate carnelian
Atlantis stone larimar
aventurine feldspar sunstone
birthing stones biotite lenses
bitter-spar dolomite or magnesite
bixbite red beryl
blood agate red agate or red chalcedony
blood jasper heliotrope
bloodstone hematite
breccia jasper red jasper
bubble stone aragonite
buddstone prase
callacite turquoise
carneol carnelian
cat's eye a shape made by undulating light in chrysoberyl, moonstone or tourmaline; burnt red tiger's eye
chalk calcite
chevron amethyst amethyst banded with quartz
chrysolite peridot

chyta serpentine from Mexico
citrinocalcite brown calcite
copper emerald dioptase
copper silicate chrysocolla
cross stone chiastolite or staurolite
dendritic quartz dendritic chalcedony
double spar calcite rhombohedron
dravite brown tourmaline
eagle stone agate with water inclusions
elbaite tourmaline (all colours)
emerald quartz prase
enhydros agate with water inclusions
fish eye stone apophyllite
flesh agate red agate or red chalcedony
flower jasper epidote (unakite)
fluorspar fluorite
girasol clear opal-containing quartz
golden beryl beryl, golden colour
golden obsidian silver obsidian

golden topaz Imperial topaz
goldstone artificial (imitation) sunstone
goshenite beryl, clear
grey antimony antimonite
heliodor beryl, yellow to blue-green
howlite calcium silicate, often confused with magnesite
hyacinth zircon
Iceland spar calcite rhombohedron
indicolite blue tourmaline
iron gleam hematite
iron rose a shape of hematite
ivorite magnesite (until recently 'ivory magnesite')
Kalahari picture stone yellow jasper
kyanite disthene
landscape jasper yellow (sandy) jasper
lavender quartz light amethyst or chalcedony (pink)
layer stone agate
lazurite lapis lazuli
leek quartz prase

leopard skin jasper rhyolite
ligurius amber
lithium mica lepidolite
lucky geodes agate geodes
luvulite sugilite
manganese calcite pink calcite,or pink aragonite
manganese silicate rhodonite
manganese spar rhodochrosite
mica mineral group containing biotite and lepidolite
midge stone dendritic chalcedony
midwife stone malachite
milk stone white, light blue or pink chalcedony
morion dark smoky quartz
New Age stone sugilite
new jade serpentine (usually)
olivine peridot

opalite opal-containing rock, for example, green opal
orbicular jasper rhyolite
paparadscha salmon coloured sapphire
peace agate grey agate or white quartz
picture jasper landscape jasper
pistacite epidote
pop rocks boji stones
poppy jasper red/green/yellow jasper
praseolite burnt green quartz, not aventurine!
prasius prase
rainforest jasper rhyolite
raspberry spar rhodochrosite
ray stone actinolite
red iron ore hematite
Royal Azel sugilite
rubellite red tourmaline
sard brown carnelian
schorl black tourmaline
serpent stone serpentine
silex red jasper
silver eye serpentine

silver topaz clear topaz
spectrolite Finnish labradorite
spodumene mineral family of kunzite
storm stone pietersite
succinite amber
tree quartz fossilized wood
tree stone fossilized wood
turitella jasper yellow (brown) jasper with fossils
unakite epidote
uvite brown tourmaline
Venus hair rutilated quartz
verdelite green tourmaline
verdite serpentine
water agate agate with water inclusions
wood stone fossilized wood
zebra jasper serpentine (silver eye)

Therapeutic Index

The following index is intended to give an overview, in alphabetical order, of the beneficial qualities and healing properties attributed to crystals. Please, only use this index for reference and not to choose your crystal! Selecting a stone for particular symptoms according to a list of key words may seem nice and simple, but will too often result in error. You would be ignoring your general situation, your lifestyle, the mineral-forming substance and its colour, all described in Part 1 of this book, with the result that you would not be making an informed decision. The entries here should be checked against the detailed descriptions of the minerals (Part 3), and you should also consult the information on the mineralogical and therapeutic background (Part 1). Only by proceeding this way will you be able to get the information necessary for a sound, reliable choice.

A

abilities,realizing actinolite, dioptase, Imperial topaz, obsidian, rock crystal, topaz,

ability to take things in pietersite, prehnite, sardonyx, tourmaline, variscite

abundance dioptase, sardonyx

acceptance aventurine, chalcedony (blue), kunzite, lapis lazuli, rutilated quartz

accomplishment, ease of (*see* success)

achieve, ability to epidote, fire opal, hematite, ruby, tiger iron

acid indigestion antimonite, turquoise, variscite

acid/alkaline metabolism/balance jade, nephrite

action, readiness for/joy of amethyst, ametrine, chrysoberyl, disthene, fire opal, nephrite, onyx, prase, rhodonite, tiger iron, turquoise

action, urge for /energy for ametrine, charoite, garnet (almandine), jade, jasper, sodalite, sunstone

activity (*see also* over-activity) Imperial topaz, jade, mookaite, rhodochrosite, ruby, tourmaline (rubellite)

adapting biotite lenses, zoisite

addiction amethyst, dumortierite

admiration chrysopal, tourmaline (verdelite)

adrenal glands jade, fire opal, ruby, tiger's eye

adrenalin (*see* adrenal glands) fire opal

adventure, urge for chrysopal, malachite, mookaite, thulite

aesthetics antimonite, chrysoprase, copper chalcedony, malachite

aggression apatite, heliotrope, jasper, nephrite

allergies apophyllite, aquamarine, aventurine, fluorite

ambition chrysoberyl, morganite

ambitions dioptase

anger chrysoprase, peridot, prase

annoyance apatite, aventurine, lapis lazuli, peridot, rhodonite

anorexia Imperial topaz, topaz

anxiety chalcedony (pink), opal

apathy apatite, turquoise

appetite apatite, Imperial topaz

argumentativeness (*see also* communication) onyx

arteriosclerosis (*see also* blood vessels/fat metabolism) aventurine, magnesite

arthritis fluorite, garnet (grossular)

arthrosis (*see also* cartilage) apatite

assertiveness onyx

asthma apophyllite

atmosphere fossilized wood, obsidian (black), thulite

attentiveness boji stones, chrysoprase, copper chalcedony, dendritic chalcedony, variscite

authority chrysoberyl, topaz

autoimmune diseases (*see also* immune system) aquamarine, rhodonite

avoidance mechanisms prehnite

B

back problems smoky obsidian, smoky quartz

bad luck azurite-malachite, aventurine, marble, opal
bad conscience (*see* conscience)
balance chalcedony (blue), copper chalcedony, dendritic chalcedony, dolomite, jade, mookaite, morganite, rhyolite
balance, consistency actinolite, chrysocolla, emerald, jasper (green)
beauty copper chalcedony, chrysoprase, dioptase, emerald, malachite, thulite
beginnings, new garnet, rutilated quartz, tiger iron
behavioural patterns boji stones, chiastolite, chrysoberyl, chrysoprase, dumortierite, fluorite, garnet, obsidian (black), rainbow obsidian, silver obsidian, sodalite
belief/faith amber, larimar, black obsidian, rainbow obsidian, silver obsidian, sapphire, sunstone
birth amazonite, biotite lenses, malachite, moonstone
bladder agate, chalcedony, citrine, tourmaline (indicolite)
blinkered attitudes aquamarine, beryl, morganite
blocks, energy boji stones, garnet, larimar, obsidian, tourmaline (indicolite)
blood clotting calcite, chalcedony (red), marble, magnesite
blood pressure (*see also* circulation) – raising: jasper, rhodochrosite, ruby; lowering: chalcedony (blue), chrysocolla, labradorite, lapis lazuli, sodalite; stabilizing: chalcedony (red)
blood purification mookaite, tourmaline (rubellite)
blood sugar (*see* diabetes)
blood vessels agate, aventurine, hematite, carnelian, magnesite, mahogany obsidian, obsidian, snowflake obsidian, rhodochrosite
blood, formation of garnet (andradite), hematite, tiger iron

blood, quality of carnelian, dolomite, garnet (pyrope)
body fluids chalcedony (blue), dendritic chalcedony, garnet, jade, nephrite, onyx, opal, (green), sardonyx
bones apatite, calcite, fluorite, garnet (melanite), marble
boundlessness moldavite
brain amazonite, azurite, diamond, disthene, fluorite, larimar, malachite, rock crystal, sapphire, schalenblende, sugilite, turquoise
breastfeeding chalcedony (blue and pink)
bronchitis, chronic rutilated quartz
brooding nephrite, schalenblende
bruises amethyst, prase
building up actinolite, dendritic agate, epidote
burns chrysocolla, tourmaline (indicolite)

C

calcium metabolism apatite, aragonite, calcite, dolomite, marble
calming amazonite, charoite, chiastolite, chrysopal, disthene, fossilized wood, labradorite, magnesite, prase, sapphire, serpentine, variscite
carefree attitude chalcedony (blue), pink opal
cartilage apatite, amber
cells, growth of apatite, azurite-malachite, calcite, tourmaline (dravite), zoisite
cellular metabolism ametrine, sardonyx
centring chiastolite
certainty rose quartz
challenge dendritic agate, garnet, fire opal, thulite
changes charoite, chrysocolla, diamond, epidote, larimar, marble, pietersite, pyrite, schalenblende, tiger iron
chaos pietersite
character chalcedony (blue), diamond, pyrite, sardonyx
charisma garnet (pyrope), Imperial topaz

charm tourmaline (rubellite)
cheerfulness amber, fire opal
cholesterol (*see also* fat metabolism) aventurine, magnesite
chronic feeling of coldness chrysopal, emerald, obsidian, mahogany obsidian, snowflake obsidian, opal (green), rhodonite, rutilated quartz, schalenblende, thulite, tourmaline (dravite), turquoise, watermelon tourmaline, zoisite
circulation (blood supply) carnelian, obsidian, mahagony obsidian, snowflake obsidian, rose quartz, tourmaline (rubellite)
circulation (*see also* blood pressure) – stimulating: chalcedony (red), garnet (pyrope), hematite, jasper (red), rhodochrosite, ruby, tiger iron; calming: chalcedony (blue), lapis lazuli, sodalite; stabilizing: dolomite, garnet, rhodonite
clairvoyance aquamarine, alexandrite, emerald, moldavite, moonstone, obsidian, zircon
clarity chrysocolla, diamond, emerald, rhodonite, rock crystal, watermelon tourmaline
clearness amethyst, dendritic chalcedony, fluorite, obsidian, pietersite, pyrite, rock crystal
coldness, feelings of labradorite, mahogany obsidian, obsidian, rock crystal, snowflake obsidian
colds chalcedony (blue), dendritic chalcedony, labradorite, rhyolite (orbicular jasper)
colic dumortierite
commitment ruby, tourmaline (rubellite)
communication chalcedony (blue and pink,) copper chalcedony, lapis lazuli, moss agate, obsidian (black), onyx, rainbow obsidian, sardonyx, schalenblende, silver obsidian, variscite

community, sense of carnelian, chalcedony (blue), chrysopal, dendritic chalcedony, dolomite, garnet, pink opal, tourmaline (dravite)
competence calcite
composure, inner agate, fossilized wood, pietersite
compromise, readiness for serpentine
compromise, unwillingness to diamond, fluorite, lapis lazuli, sugilite
compulsions charoite, chrysoprase, dumortierite
concentration agate, amethyst, aragonite, lepidolite, onyx, pietersite, smoky quartz, rhyolite, sapphire, schalenblende
confidence (faith, trust) chalcedony (red), dumortierite, garnet, moss agate, sardonyx
conflicts chalcedony (pink), jasper, lapis lazuli, pietersite, rhodonite, serpentine, sugilite
confrontation, readiness for amethyst, carnelian, citrine, copper chalcedony, diamond, malachite, onyx, prehnite, pyrite, sugilite
confusion aquamarine, carnelian, dendritic chalcedony, fluorite, pietersite, pyrite, rhodonite
conjunctiva agate
conscience apophyllite, peridot, tourmaline (verdelite)
consciousness amethyst, ametrine, azurite, chalcedony (blue), copper chalcedony, chiastolite, disthene, fluorite, larimar, malachite, moldavite, moss agate, obsidian (black), rainbow obsidian, silver obsidian, rhodonite, rhyolite, sodalite, topaz, turquoise, zircon
consistency actinolite, aquamarine, beryl, chiastolite, chrysocolla, emerald, onyx, sugilite, zoisite
constipation (see also elimination, intestines, large intestine) biotite lenses, serpentine, tourmaline (verdelite)
constitution epidote

contemplation labradorite
contentment chrysoprase, dolomite
control ametrine, apophyllite, chrysoprase, dumortierite, heliotrope, onyx, prase, tourmaline
contusions prase
conversion calcite, carnelian, chalcedony (blue), chalcedony (red), chiastolite, diamond, dioptase, dolomite, epidote, garnet, jade, jasper, lepidolite, zoisite
coolness chalcedony (blue), chrysocolla, sodalite
cooperation emerald
copper metabolism azurite, azurite-malachite, dioptase, chrysocolla, copper chalcedony, malachite, turquoise
coronary blood vessels magnesite
coughs moss agate, rutilated quartz
courage carnelian, dendritic agate, diamond, dumortierite, garnet (general), garnet (pyrope), jasper, ruby, thulite, tiger's eye
courage, lack of chrysopal, marble, schalenblende
cramps amazonite, azurite-malachite, charoite, chrysocolla, dioptase, dolomite, dumortierite, magnesite, malachite, smoky quartz, serpentine, turquoise, varscite, zircon
creativity ametrine, antimonite, amber, biotite lenses, chalcedony (blue), dioptase, garnet (andradite), labradorite, larimar, marble, nephrite, thulite, tourmaline, zoisite
crises diamond, garnet
criticism, ability to criticize (see also self-criticism) azurite, malachite, sapphire, tourmaline (rubellite)
cuts rhodonite
cycles, unfinished business aquamarine, carnelian, tiger iron

D

danger fire opal, rhodonite
daydreams tourmaline, labradorite

decisions, power to make biotite lenses, charoite, diamond, falcon's eye, jade, lepidolite, nephrite, tiger's eye, tourmaline (verdelite)
delimiting/boundaries dendritic chalcedony, heliotrope, lavender jade, lepidolite, serpentine
depression citrine, diamond, garnet (spessartite), kunzite, rutilated quartz, sapphire, sunstone, watermelon tourmaline
depth obsidian (black), rainbow obsidian, silver obsidian
desires/wishes, fulfilment of alexandrite, amber, chalcedony (blue), hematite, malachite, moldavite (pink), opal, zoisite
determination biotite lenses, charoite, disthene, jade, malachite, sapphire, tiger iron
detoxification actinolite, azurite, azurite-malachite, beryl, biotite lenses, chrysocolla, chrysopal, chrysoprase, emerald, heliotrope, jasper (green), magnesite, malachite, opal (green), peridot, prehnite, rhodonite, tourmaline (verdelite), turquoise, zoisite
devaluation/debasement epidote
development, physical aragonite, calcite, tourmaline
development, spiritual aragonite, rock crystal, beryl, calcite, epidote, hematite, lepidolite, schalenblende, sodalite, topaz
devotion kunzite, tourmaline (rubellite)
dexterity disthene
diabetes chalcedony (blue), citrine, schalenblende
dialogue, inner amethyst
diarrhoea amethyst, dumortierite, rock crystal, serpentine, tourmaline (verdelite)
difficulties, solving carnelian, chalcedony (red), dumortierite, garnet, moss agate, smoky quartz, tiger's eye, tree agate

digestion agate, antimonite, aragonite, chrysocolla, citrine, epidote, jasper, topaz

dignity lapis lazuli

dimensions, spiritual moldavite

diplomacy chalcedony (blue)

discipline chrysoberyl

discrimination sunstone

discs, intervertebral aragonite

displacement/repression/ suppression, mechanisms prehnite

distance disthene, falcon's eye, malachite, pietersite, tiger's eye

distinction/discrimination aquamarine, calcite, lepidolite, opal (green), rose quartz, tourmaline (verdelite), garnet, sardonyx

distraction agate, lepidolite, pietersite

disunity, inner conflict azurite-malachite

doubts falcon's eye, nephrite, tiger's eye

downheartedness pink opal, turquoise

dreams alexandrite, amethyst, aventurine, charoite, dioptase, emerald, heliotrope, jade, malachite, moldavite, moonstone (pink), opal, tourmaline

drive/lack of drive apatite, beryl (bixbite), chrysocolla, ruby

dynamism aquamarine, beryl (bixbite), citrine, fire opal, fluorite, garnet in general, garnet (andradite), hematite, jasper (red), marble, rhodochrosite, ruby, tiger iron

dyslexia chalcedony (blue), sugilite

E

ears chalcedony (blue), dendritic chalcedony, onyx

Earth, connection with fossilized wood

eczema (see also skin) antimonite

effect, increasing diamond, rock crystal, topaz (clear)

effectivity amethyst, beryl, rhodochrosite

egotism chrysoprase, onyx

ejaculation, premature rutilated quartz

elation/exhilaration chalcedony (blue), dumortierite, rhodochrosite

elimination (see also kidneys, intestines, large intestine) agate, actinolite, sardonyx, tourmaline (indicolite), tourmaline (verdelite)

eloquence sardonyx

embryo (see pregnancy)

emotions (see also moods) azurite-malachite, beryl, boji stones, carnelian, epidote, fire opal, larimar, nephrite, opal, prase, rhyolite

empathy kunzite, malachite, moldavite, rose quartz, tourmaline (dravite)

energy apatite, fire opal, rhodochrosite, rock crystal, tiger iron, variscite

energy flow – stimulating: boji stones, jasper (red), rutilated quartz, tiger eye, topaz, tourmaline; slowing: falcon's eye, tiger eye

enlivening turquoise, variscite

enterprise, spirit of thulite, tourmaline (rubellite)

enthusiasm aventurine, chrysopal, fire opal, garnet (uvarovite), labradorite, rhodochrosite

environment azurite-malachite, copper chalcedony, turitella jasper

epilepsy dumortierite, kunzite, sugilite

eratic behaviour aragonite

eroticism fire opal, opal, rhodochrosite, ruby, thulite

eruptions, skin (see also skin) antimonite, aventurine

escape, habits morganite

ethics diamond, tourmaline (indicolite)

evaluation copper chalcedony, sodalite

excessive demanding aragonite

excitement (see calming)

exertion opal (green), smoky quartz, rhyolite, rose quartz

exhaustion apatite, epidote, heliotrope, Imperial topaz, opal (green), ruby,

schalenblende, tiger iron, turquoise

existence, meaning of (see life, meaning of)

expansion, feeling of moldavite

experiences, new azurite, citrine, malachite, mookaite, peridot

extreme situations, ability to handle garnet, rhodonite

extrovertedness apatite, citrine, dioptase, Imperial topaz

eyes (see also seeing, sight) agate, aquamarine, beryl, chalcedony (blue), emerald, prase, schalenblende

F

failure sunstone

fainting emerald, thulite

faith in God amazonite, chrysoprase, tiger's eye

fame dioptase, Imperial topaz

family tourmaline (dravite)

fanaticism beryl, morganite

farsightedness (see also eyes, seeing, sharp sight) aquamarine, beryl (heliodor)

fat metabolism aventurine, magnesite, prehnite

fate/belief in fate amazonite, disthene, emerald, topaz, turquoise

fear/fears/anxiety/ apprehension apophyllite, chiastolite, chrysoberyl, diamond, dumortierite, larimar, magnesite, moss agate, obsidian, onyx, opal (green), rhodonite, rutilated quartz, schalenblende, sugilite, watermelon tourmaline, zircon

feelings alexandrite, apophyllite, azurite-malachite, chrysocolla, chrysopal, citrine, dolomiote, labradorite, malachite, moonstone, morganite, chrysopal, pietersite, rhodochrosite, sodalite, thulite, tourmaline (indicolite), zoisite

feelings of being oppressed, apprehension or trepidation amazonite, apophyllite, chrysoberyl, chrysopal, rutilated quartz, tourmaline (dravite)

feelings, depth of
chrysopal, dioptase,
labradorite, malachite,
moonstone, emerald
feelings, expression of
azurite-malachite, lapis
lazuli, malachite,
rhodochrosite, zoisite
feelings, lack of pietersite,
rock crystal, tourmaline,
tourmaline quartz
fertility chrysoprase,
Imperial topaz, moldavite,
moonstone, rhodonite, rose
quartz, thulite, zoisite
fever – lowering:
chalcedony (blue),
chrysocolla, chrysopal, moss
agate, prase, rock crystal,
sapphire; bringing on:
garnet (uvarovite),
rhodochrosite, ruby
fiery temper fire opal,
prase, ruby
fire, inner chalcedony
(pink), fire opal, garnet,
ruby
first aid stone rhodonite
flawlessness obsidian
flexibility aragonite, amber,
biotite lenses, chalcedony
(red), garnet (andradite),
heliotrope, mookaite,
tourmaline (verdelite,
rubellite)
**fluid intake and
absorption** sodalite,
tourmaline (indicolite)
**foolishness/thoughtless-
ness** opal
foresight, view of future
aquamarine, turquoise
**formation of stones (in
organs)** nephrite, rhyolite
(leopard skin jasper)
free will/free spirit fluorite,
sodalite
freedom diamond, fluorite,
garnet, lapis lazuli, obsidian,
sodalite, tourmaline
(indicolite)
friendship emerald, lapis
lazuli, malachite, peridot,
rhodonite, sapphire,
sardonyx, watermelon
tourmaline
frugality fossilized wood
frustration disthene,
epidote
fufilment sardonyx, topaz
fun fire opal
fungal infections
chalcedony (blue),
combination of chrysoprase

and smoky quartz, copper
chalcedony
fury aventurine, peridot,
prase, rhodonite

G

gallbladder amber,
epidote, magnesite, peridot
gastritis (*see also* stomach)
agate, variscite
**generosity/generousness
of spirit** Imperial topaz
generosity towards guests
pink opal
gentleness amethyst,
amber, rose quartz
glands (*see also* hormones)
chalcedony (blue), dendritic
chalcedony, diamond, rock
crystal, tourmaline
glaucoma chalcedony
(blue)
goal orientedness
aquamarine, beryl, emerald,
rutilated quartz, tourmaline
(rubellite)
goals, setting of actinolite,
diamond, labradorite,
lepidolite, sapphire,
tourmaline, watermelon
gonads opal (green),
rhodochrosite,
schalenblende, thulite,
zoisite
gout biotite lenses,
chiastolite, chrysoprase,
labradorite, turquoise,
variscite
gratification, substitute
antimonite
greatness, spiritual
alexandrite, moldavite,
rutilated quartz
gregariousness apatite,
azurite-malachite,
chalcedony (blue), copper
chalcedony, lapis lazuli, pink
opal, tourmaline (rubellite,
verdelite)
grief epidote, sugilite
groups, shyness in
tourmaline (dravite)
goodness chalcedon, (pink)
growth, physical agate,
actinolite, aquamarine,
azurite, calcite, rutilated
quartz, turquoise
growth, spiritual agate,
aquamarine, emerald,
garnet (hessonite)
grudges prase

guilt, feelings of
chiastolite, opal (green),
peridot, sodalite

H

habits antimonite, dendritic
chalcedony, fluorite, garnet
**hardening of skin (also
lumps, knots)** rhyolite
(leopard skin jasper)
harmony agate, ametrine,
azurite-malachite, beryl
(golden beryl, heliodor),
copper chalcedony,
chrysocolla, dumortierite,
emerald, mookaite,
sunstone, sugilite,
tourmaline
hayfever (*see also* allergies)
aquamarine
head/headache amethyst,
dioptase, dumortierite,
emerald, larimar,
magnesite, smoky obsidian
healing epidote, garnet,
rhodonite, sapphire
**health,
preventive/stabilizing**
agate, dendritic agate,
dolomite, fossilized wood,
hematite, mookaite, opal,
sapphire
hearing, sense onyx,
sardonyx
heart amazonite,
aventurine, calcite,
chalcedony (pink), charoite,
chrysopal, dolomite,
emerald, garnet
(spessartite), heliotrope,
kunzite, magnesite, marble,
moonstone, morganite,
pink opal, rhodonite, rose
quartz, tourmaline
(verdelite)
heart attack, prophylactic
aventurine, magnesite
heart rhythm calcite, rose
quartz, serpentine
heartiness copper
chalcedony, chalcedony,
chalcedony (pink), garnet
(rhodolite), pink opal, rose
quartz
heat stroke prase
heavy metal poisoning
chrysoprase, emerald,
peridot
helper, spiritual
chrysoprase
helpfulness azurite-
malachite, carnelian,
chalcedony (pink), garnet,
garnet (spessartite), rose

quartz, sardonyx,
tourmaline (dravite)
hesitation charoite, moss
agate
hiding/covering up
apophyllite, rutilated quartz
hoarseness lapis lazuli,
sodalite
holding back/suppressing
amethyst, apophyllite,
fluorite, malachite,
moldavite, moss agate,
pietersite, tourmaline
(indicolite), zircon
holding on apophyllite,
chiastolite, zircon
home chrysopal, fossilized
wood
honesty amethyst,
apophyllite, jasper, lapis
lazuli, pyrite, sodalite,
topaz, variscite
honesty/sincerity
amethyst, aquamarine,
emerald, garnet (melanite),
jasper, lapis lazuli, rutilated
quartz
hope dioptase, garnet,
moss agate, rutilated quartz
horizons, broadening of
fluorite, garnet, lapis lazuli,
tourmaline (indicolite)
hormones (see also glands)
aquamarine, diamond,
falcon's eye, garnet
(hessonite), moonstone,
tourmaline
hostility/attacks, spiritual
copper chalcedony, garnet,
obsidian (black), rhodonite
humility kunzite
hunger pangs chalcedony
(red)

I

ideals/idealism antimonite,
carnelian, chrysoprase,
malachite, pink opal,
schalenblende, sodalite
ideas/abundance of ideas
aventurine, fire opal, garnet,
Imperial topaz, jade,
labradorite, moldavite, pink
opal, rhodochrosite,
sapphire, zoisite
ideés fixes fluorite
identity, finding/keeping
chiastolite, dolomite, lapis
lazuli, nephrite, prehnite,
sodalite, variscite
illness, gain from/causes
boj stones, moldavite, pyrite
illnesses, prophylaxis boji
stones

illusions chiastolite,
labradorite, moonstone
images, inner alexandrite,
amethyst, azurite,
chrysoprase, copper
chalcedony, dendritic
chalcedony, fossilized wood,
jade, malachite, obsidian
(black), rainbow obsidian,
silver obsidian, sunstone,
topaz, tourmaline
**imagination/power of
imagination** alexandrite,
antimonite, azurite,
dioptase, garnet
(almandine), jasper,
labradorite, malachite,
sodalite, tourmaline
immune system
aquamarine, aragonite,
azurite malachite, calcite,
chalcedony (blue), dendritic
chalcedony, copper
chalcedony, chalcedony
(pink), emerald, epidote,
garnet, heliotrope, jasper
(yellow), marble, mookaite,
moss agate, onyx,
sardonyx, schalenblende,
tourmaline, tree agate,
zoisite
**impartiality/
uninhibitedness** pink opal
importance zircon
impotence (see also
potency) morganite,
rutilated quartz
impressions (see
processing, spiritual)
impulsiveness fire opal,
moonstone, rhodochrosite,
ruby
independence chrysoberyl,
chrysoprase, lepidolite,
rutilated quartz
individuality aventurine,
biotite lenses, citrine, garnet
(uvarovite), tourmaline
indulgence copper
chalcedony, emerald, pink
opal, thulite
industriousness
rhodochrosite
infections dendritic agate,
chalcedony (blue),
chrysocolla, chrysoprase,
emerald, heliotrope, moss
agate, onyx, rhyolite
(orbicular jasper), ruby,
turquoise
infertility (see fertility)
inflammation of joints (see
arthritis)

inflammations aventurine,
alexandrite, chalcedony
(blue), copper chalcedony,
chrysoberyl, dendritic
chalcedony, emerald,
garnet (uvarovite),
heliotrope, jasper (green),
moss agate, turquoise,
zoisite
influences, external biotite
lenses, charoite, fluorite,
peridot, topaz, zoisite
**influencing people/ability
to be influenced** lepidolite,
nephrite, obsidian, onyx,
serpentine
influenza chalcedony
(blue), heliotrope, jasper
(green), moss agate,
rhyolite (orbicular jasper)
inhibitions garnet,
malachite, pink opal
initial difficulties tiger iron
initiative fire opal, moss
agate
injuries amethyst, obsidian,
rhodonite
injustice fluorite, rhodonite
inner ear onyx
inner voice alexandrite,
anitmonite
inquisitiveness/curiosity
chalcedony (pink),
chrysopal, thulite
insect bites rhodonite
insight tiger's eye
inspiration amethyst,
chalcedony (blue),
chalcedony (red), emerald,
kunzite, moss agate, thulite
insult rhodonite
integrity biotite lenses,
obsidian, sodalite
intelligence/mental grasp
fire opal, fluorite
intentions chalcedony
(red), labradorite, lepidolite,
sapphire, watermelon
tourmaline, zoisite
interest antimonite,
aragonite, azurite-
malachite, tourmaline
(verdelite), variscite
intestine, large (see also
elimination, diarrhoea,
constipation) agate,
amethyst, hematite (kidney)
intestine, small (see also
iron absorption, nutrient
absorption, etc.) carnelian,
chalcedony (red), epidote,
hematite, prehnite
intestines agate, amethyst,
calcite, garnet, jasper,

magnesite, marble, ruby, sapphire, sardonyx
intoxication amethyst
intuition alexandrite, amazonite, amethyst, ametrine, biotite lenses, fossilized wood, kunzite, labradorite, moonstone, schalenblende, turquoise
inventiveness fluorite, thulite
invincibility diamond
iron, absorption of garnet (almandine), hematite, tiger iron
irritability heliotrope, jade, magnesite
itching antimonite, emerald, rhodonite

J

jealousy chrysoprase
joie de vivre/life force ametrine, beryl, citrine, emerald, fire opal, garnet, opal, ruby, sunstone, thulite, tourmaline (verdelite)
joints apatite, amber, fluorite, kunzite, lepidolite
joy morganite, opal, rhodochrosite, sardonyx
judge, ability to amethyst, copper chalcedony
justice amethyst, azurite, chrysoprase, diamond, emerald, malachite, sugilite

K

kidneys actinolite, amber, biotite lenses, garnet (grossular), hematite (kidney), jade, nephrite, opal (green), rhodochrosite, serpentine, tourmaline (indicolite)
knowledge jade, lapis lazuli, malachite, sapphire, topaz

L

labour pains (*see also* birth) biotite lenses
laissez faire larimar
language chalcedony (blue)
larynx chalcedony (blue), lapis lazuli, sodalite
laws diamond, sodalite
laziness calcite, chrysocolla, jade
leadership qualities chrysoberyl

learning/ability to learn amethyst, chalcedony (blue), diamond, fluorite, rhodonite, rock crystal, sapphire
lethargy fire opal, rhodochrosite, ruby, tiger iron
letting go (*see* blocks)
level-headedness/calm charoite, rhodonite
liberation diamond, moss agate, opal (green)
life, affirming azurite-malachite, chrysoprase, dumortierite, Imperial topaz, magnesite, rhodochrosite, sunstone, zoisite
life, liveliness apatite, chalcedony (pink), fire opal, morganite, rhodochrosite
life, meaning of antimonite, copper chalcedony, chiastolite, moldavite, opal (green), sardonyx, topaz, zircon
life, perspectives on marble, opal (green), sunstone, zircon
life, quality of garnet (pyrope)
life, trials and tests azurite, chalcedony (blue), diamond, garnet, sapphire
life, will for jasper, opal
life's work (*see* meaning of life)
light, insight apophyllite, garnet
light, sensitivity to/perception of light moonstone
lightheartedness aquamarine, chalcedony (blue), dumortierite, opal, rhodochrosite
limitations, boundaries (overcoming) Imperial topaz, larimar, rock crystal (phantom quartz)
listening chalcedony (blue and pink), dendritic chalcedony, magnesite
liver actinolite, amazonite, azurite, azurite-malachite, copper chalcedony, chrysoberyl, alexandrite, chrysocolla, chrysoprase, emerald, epidote, garnet, malachite, opal (green), peridot, tourmaline (rubellite), zircon
logic (*see* thinking, logical)

loss amethyst, zircon
love copper chalcedony, chalcedony (pink), chrysopal, chrysoprase, emerald, moonstone, morganite, pink, opal, rhodochrosite, rose quartz, ruby, watermelon tourmaline
love of life garnet (rhodolite), opal
love, sorrows of chrysoprase
loyalty/fidelity diamond, kunzite, sapphire, sodalite, tourmaline (indicolite)
lucid dreams (*see also* dreams) emerald, moonstone, zircon
luck agate, ametrine, aventurine, amber, chrysoprase, garnet, malachite, moldavite, moonstone, opal, sunstone, turquoise
lungs amethyst, chalcedony (blue), dendritic chalcedony, fluorite, moss agate, rutilated quartz
lymph/lymph nodes chalcedony (blue and pink), dendritic chalcedony, heliotrope, moss agate

M

madness sapphire, zircon
magic alexandrite, sapphire
magnesium metabolism dolomite, magnesite, serpentine
making up/atonement peridot
manipulation larimar
many-sidedness/variety beryl, tourmaline (verdelite)
materialism moldavite, zircon
maturity agate, rhodonite
meaning/meaninglessness (*see also* meaning of life) copper chalcedony, diamond, rhodonite, schalenblende, topaz
meditation amethyst, citrine, fossilized wood, mookaite, obsidian (black), rainbow obsidian, rock crystal, rose quartz, serpentine, silver obsidian
mediumistic abilities aquamarine, alexandrite, labradorite, moonstone
melancholy chrysopal, thulite

memory agate, aquamarine, calcite, chalcedony (blue), copper chalcedony, kunzite, labradorite, malachite, moldavite, pink opal, pyrite, rock crystal

menopause moonstone

menstruation chrysocolla, lapis lazuli, malachite, moonstone, serpentine, zircon

mental illnesses diamond, sapphire

meridians boji stones, topaz, tourmaline

metabolism amazonite, amber, calcite, carnelian, copper chalcedony, charoite, fossilized wood, garnet in general, garnet (rhodolite), heliotrope, Imperial topaz, peridot, sardonyx, topaz, turquoise, tourmaline

migraine magnesite, rhodochrosite

milk, production of chalcedony (blue and pink)

minerals, absorption of carnelian

mistakes/failures diamond, epidote, tourmaline (schorl), tourmaline quartz

mobility/motion chiastolite, disthene, fluorite, mookaite, ruby, sugilite

modesty magnesite

money worries moldavite, zircon

mood-lifting ametrine, citrine, rhodochrosite, rutilated quartz, sunstone, variscite

moods (see also emotions) boji stones, chrysopal, dendritic chalcedony, diamond, kunzite, malachite, rhodochrosite, tiger's eye

moods shifts amazonite, chrysocolla, falcon's eye, serpentine, turquoise

mortality zircon

motivation, increase of apatite, amber, chalcedony (blue), chrysoprase

motor nervous system disthene, onyx, sugilite, tourmaline (dravite)

mucous membranes apophyllite, amber, chalcedony (blue), dendritic chalcedony, fluorite, garnet (grossular), moss agate

multiple sclerosis rhodochrosite, rhodonite, watermelon tourmaline

muscle power hematite, tiger iron, turquoise

muscles aragonite, magnesite

N

narrow-mindedness fluorite

nature, spiritual amber, amethyst, jade, moldavite, rock crystal, sunstone

nausea antimonite, dumortierite, rock crystal

neck/throat chrysocolla, lapis lazuli, larimar, sodalite

needs chalcedony (blue), hematite, malachite, morganite, rose quartz

negativity chrysoprase, sunstone, tourmaline (schorl), tourmaline quartz, zoisite

neglect peridot

nerves, motor disthene, onyx, sugilite, tourmaline (indicolite, rubellite, verdelite), watermelon tourmaline

nerves, sensory amethyst, jade, onyx, tourmaline (indicolite, rubellite, verdelite), watermelon tourmaline

nerves/nervous system amethyst, charoite, chiastolite, diamond, dumortierite, fluorite, Imperial topaz, jade, kunzite, lepidolite, malachite, morganite, smoky quartz, sapphire, sugilite, topaz, tourmaline (indicolite, rubellite, verdelite), watermelon tourmaline, variscite

nervous system, autonomous amazonite, ametrine, beryl, charoite, citrine, Imperial topaz, sunstone, tourmaline (rubellite)

nervousness aragonite, beryl (golden beryl), chiastolite, chrysocolla, falcon's eye, magnesite, serpentine, variscite

neuralgia kunzite, lepidolite, sugilite

neurodermatitis chrysoprase, fluorite

neutrality azurite-malachite, rock crystal, copper chalcedony, chrysocolla, nephrite, tourmaline (schorl), tourmaline quartz

nightmares amethyst, chrysoberyl, chrysoprase, garnet (spessartite), tourmaline

non-influenceability dendritic agate, nephrite, serpentine, sugilite, tiger's eye, turquoise

normalization after birth agate

nose/sinuses emerald

nutrients, proper absorption of (see also small intestine) carnelian, chalcedony (red), epidote, garnet, sardonyx

O

obesity fossilized wood

observation, talent for charoite, malachite

obsession/possession obsidian

oedema (see also water retention) chalcedony (blue), dendritic chalcedony

openmindedness/ receptiveness azurite malachite, amber, chrysopal, fire opal, rose quartz, tourmaline (verdelite)

openness apatite, apophyllite, chalcedony (blue), copper chalcedony, chalcedony (red), emerald, Imperial topaz, pink opal, pyrite, topaz

opinion chalcedony (blue), dendritic chalcedony, lapis lazuli, sodalite

optimism ametrine, chalcedony (blue), opal, sunstone

order aquamarine, diamond, fluorite, pietersite, sodalite

organs, inner ametrine, amazonite, carnelian, sunstone, tourmaline (dravite)

orgasm ruby, serpentine, thulite

orientation, new actinolite

orientation, alignment sapphire, watermelon tourmaline

orientation, spiritual opal (green), zoisite

ovaries (*see also* gonads) opal (green), thulite, zoisite

overacidification biotite lenses, chiastolite, heliotrope, malachite, serpentine, turquoise, variscite, zoisite

overcoming calcite, carnelian, emerald, fire opal, garnet, jasper, sardonyx, sodalite

overview diamond, falcon's eye

overwork epidote

oxygen, supply hematite, tiger iron

P

pain amethyst, apatite, aventurine, charoite, dioptase, falcon's eye, malachite, obsidian, , prase, pyrite sunburst, obsidian, smoky quartz, rhodonite, rock crystal, sapphire, sugilite, tiger's eye, tourmaline (schorl), tourmaline quartz, turquoise, zircon

pain, mental azurite-malachite, rhodonite, turquoise

pancreas citrine, prehnite

panic dumortierite, rhodonite

paralysis rock crystal, chiastolite, rhodochrosite, rhodonite, watermelon tourmaline

paranoia sugilite

parasites amethyst, peridot

pardoning peridot, rhodonite

partnership emerald

passion ruby

past life memories agate

patience actinolite, aventurine, chrysoprase, epidote, heliotrope, magnesite, tourmaline (verdelite), watermelon tourmaline

peace, inner agate, amber, amethyst, apophyllite, chalcedony (pink), dendritic jade, disthene, jasper (yellow), larimar, lavender jade, lepidolite, marble, mookaite, nephrite, prase,

rhyolite, serpentine, turquoise

peace, need for pietersite

perception alexandrite, amethyst, ametrine, chalcedony (blue), chiastolite, chrysoprase, dumortierite, malachite, obsidian, rock crystal, sardonyx, sunstone

persistence chalcedony (red), tree agate

perspectives, new (*see* life's perspectives)

pessimism sunstone

pineal gland amazonite, aquamarine, moonstone

planning alexandrite, chrysoberyl, diamond, Imperial topaz

pleasure antimonite, apatite, fire opal, garnet, malachite, opal, pink opal, ruby, thulite

pliability/compliance amber, biotite lenses, kunzite, rose quartz

poetry opal

poisoning (*see also* detoxification) chrysoprase, dumortierite, heliotrope, turitella jasper

positive attitude towards life (*see* life affirming)

posture, upright apatite, fluorite, garnet (melanite), rutilated quartz

potency garnet, rutilated quartz, zoisite with ruby

pragmatism (*see also* thinking, pragmatic) agate, carnelian, dolomite, prase, smoky quartz, tiger iron, tourmaline (dravite)

prediction rock crystal, obsidian

pregnancy agate

prenatal memories agate

presence of mind chrysoprase

pressure, inner apophyllite, moss agate

pride Imperial topaz

problem solving agate, amazonite, carnelian, chalcedony (pink), diamond, garnet, marble, pietersite, sugilite, thulite, tourmaline (verdelite), tiger iron

processing/dealing with/digesting spiritually agate, amethyst, copper chalcedony, fluorite,

mookaite, pietersite, prehnite

prostate schalenblende

protection agate, dendritic agate, biotite lenses, heliotrope, jasper (green), lepidolite, nephrite, smoky quartz, serpentine, tiger's eye, turquoise, tourmaline (schorl), tourmaline quartz, watermelon tourmaline

psychiatric illnesses diamond, sapphire

psychosomatic illnesses chalcedony (pink), diamond

purification, physical ametrine, chrysoprase, diamond, lepidolite, peridot

pus calcite, fluorite, heliotrope, mookaite, rhodonite

R

radiation dumortierite, turitella jasper, prase, smoky quartz, rose quartz, schalenblende, tourmaline (schorl)

realism fossilized wood, Imperial topaz, labradorite, onyx, smoky quartz

reality, sense of agate, carnelian, chiastolite

reality, spiritual chrysoprase, falcon's eye, jade, larimar, moldavite, tiger's eye, zircon

realization/insight (*see also* self-realization) azurite, boji stones, chrysoberyl, diamond

reason amethyst, sardonyx

reasoning/intellect amazonite, azurite-malachite, chiastolite, citrine, dolomite, moss agate, obsidian, prehnite, sardonyx, zircon

recognition/acceptance Imperial topaz

reconciliation prase, rhodonite

recovery aventurine, charoite, emerald, epidote, fossilized wood, moss agate, opal (green), zoisite

reactions, speed of Imperial topaz, jade

red blood corpuscles hematite, tiger iron

reflection azurite, fossilized wood, kunzite, larimar, pink opal

regeneration agate, aventurine, alexandrite, dioptase, epidote, garnet, mookaite,
rejuvenation emerald, ruby
relativity zircon
relaxation (see also stress, tension) amazonite, aventurine, chrysocolla, dolomite, garnet (grossular), magnesite, smoky quartz
relief tourmaline (indicolite)
rescue stone rhodonite
resignation (see courage, lack of)
resistance, power of dendritic agate, chrysocolla, garnet (melanite), turitella jasper, smoky quartz, rhyolite
resistances amber, chalcedony (blue), charoite, garnet, kunzite, thulite
respiratory tract amethyst, apophyllite, chalcedony (blue), dendritic chalcedony, emerald, fluorite, pietersite, rutilated quartz
responsibility for self disthene, larimar, turquoise
responsibility, sense of onyx, tourmaline (indicolite)
restraint, reserve, caution apophyllite, chiastolite, lapis lazuli, moss agate, rutilated quartz
restriction moss agate
retreat agate
revenge rhodonite
reverence/awe chalcedony (pink), chrysopal
revival/stimulation obsidian, ruby
rhetoric chalcedony (blue)
rheumatism biotite lenses, carnelian, chiastolite, emerald, garnet (grossular), labradorite, malachite, turquoise, variscite
rhythms of nature moonstone
risks, readiness to take alexandrite, fire opal, malachite
romance pink opal, rose quartz, thulite

S

sacrificial attitudes amazonite, larimar, turquoise
sadness amazonite, amethyst, chrysopal, epidote, onyx, sardonyx, tourmaline (indicolite), zircon
safety/security agate, beryl, nephrite, tree agate
salt metabolism jade, nephrite
scars rhodonite, tourmaline (schorl)
scattering of attention/diffusion of feelings/distraction opal, pietersite
schizophrenia sugilite
sciatica biotite lenses, kunzite, lepidolite
scurvy apatite, aragonite, calcite
secrecy pyrite
security, feeling of agate, chrysoprase, watermelon tourmaline
seduction/enticement/temptation opal, malachite
seeing/sharpness of vision (see also eyes, senses, sensory organs) aquamarine, beryl, emerald, onyx, schalenblende
self-acceptance magnesite, peridot, rhyolite, sodalite
self-awareness amber, dioptase, Imperial topaz, lapis lazuli, onyx
self-confidence calcite, citrine, fluorite, garnet, Imperial topaz, sardonyx, sunstone
self-control chrysoberyl
self-criticism tourmaline (rubellite)
self-destruction rhodonite, ruby
self-determination amazonite, aventurine, fluorite, larimar, peridot, sodalite, topaz, turquoise
self-discipline chrysoberyl
self-expression citrine, dioptase, Imperial topaz, variscite
self-healing power alexandrite, chrysoberyl, larimar, sunstone
self-importance Imperial topaz, morganite

self-knowlege (see also, knowledge, insight) azurite, rock crystal, epidote, jade, kunzite, peridot, pyrite
self-love magnesite, rhodonite, rose quartz
self-observation chrysocolla
self-pity epidote
self-realization biotite lenses, citrine, dioptase, dolomite, garnet, Imperial topaz, jade, onyx, topaz
self-recrimination chrysoprase, peridot
self-respect garnet (hessonite), rhyolite
self-worth, feeling of actinolite, rhyolite, sunstone
senses alexandrite, obsidian (black), prehnite, rainbow obsidian, rock crystal, silver obsidian, turquoise
sensitivity to weather chalcedony (blue), moss agate
sensitivity/oversensitivity aragonite, falcon's eye, rainbow obsidian, rose quartz, silver obsidian, turquoise
sensory organs (see also eyes, balance, ears, nose) agate, aquamarine, beryl, chalcedony (blue), dendritic chalcedony, diamond, kunzite, sardonyx
sensory perception sardonyx, turquoise
sensuality copper chalcedony, emerald, malachite, thulite
serving kunzite
severity chrysoberyl
sexual organs antimonite, chalcedony (blue), copper chalcedony, fire opal, jasper, malachite, rose quartz, thulite, tourmaline (rubellite)
sexuality antimonite, chrysoprase, fire opal, garnet (general), garnet (rhodolite, spessartite), malachite, opal, pink opal, rose quartz, rutilated quartz, ruby, serpentine, thulite, zoisite with ruby
shadow sides boji stones, obsidian, pyrite
shame pink opal
short-sightedness (see also eyes, seeing, sharpness of

vision) aquamarine, beryl (heliodor)

shyness malachite, pink opal

simplicity chrysoprase, fossilized wood, prase, tiger iron

sinus, frontal emerald

skill tourmaline (dravite)

skin agate, amethyst, antimonite, apophyllite, aventurine, amber, calcite, chrysoprase, dumortierite, fluorite, garnet, (grossular), lepidolite, marble, peridot, rhyolite (leopard skin jasper), tourmaline (dravite)

sleep amethyst, aventurine, chalcedony (blue), charoite, chrysoprase, emerald, lepidolite, opal, green, schalenblende

sleepwalking moonstone

slowing down chiastolite

smell, sense of sardonyx, schalenblende

smoking, consequences of chalcedony (blue), dendritic chalcedony, moss agate

smoking, problems with legs due to obsidian, mahogany obsidian, snowflake obsidian

sober, becoming amethyst

sobriety amethyst, chiastolite, onyx, smoky quartz, sapphire, variscite

sociability (*see* community, sense of)

social commitment tourmaline (dravite)

sorrow amazonite, apatite, epidote, nephrite, sugilite

speed fire opal, Imperial topaz

spine garnet (melanite)

spirit of discovery apophyllite, dendritic chalcedony, tree agate

spirituality amethyst

spleen amber, citrine, mookaite, ruby, tourmaline (rubellite)

spontaneity amber, charoite, fire opal, moldavite, opal, rhodochrosite, ruby, schalenblende

stability agate, aragonite, dendritic agate, calcite, chiastolite, dolomite, fluorite, fossilized wood,

hematite, mookaite, sardonyx

stamina (*see also* perserverance) aquamarine, chalcedony (red), dendritic agate, epidote, garnet, jasper (red and yellow), tiger iron

state, intensification of rhyolite

steadfastness calcite, carnelian, rhyolite, rock crystal, sugilite

stomach agate, antimonite, amber, citrine, magnesite, rhodonite, serpentine, turquoise, variscite

storytelling, art of chalcedony (pink)

straightforwardness actinolite, aquamarine, beryl, sapphire

strength chalcedony (red), hematite, rhyolite, rock crystal, tiger iron, tree agate

strength/strengthening chalcedony (red), diamond, epidote, sunstone, thulite, tree agate

stress ametrine, antimonite, apophyllite, beryl, chalcedony (blue), charoite, chrysocolla, disthene, epidote, magnesite, morganite, moss agate, peridote, smoky quartz, rhodonite, serpentine, tiger's eye, topaz, tourmaline (schorl), tourmaline quartz, zoisite

strife onyx, rhodonite, topaz

structure fluorite, schalenblende

success ametrine, aquamarine, amber, calcite, epidot, fire opal, Imperial topaz, rhodochrosite

suffering larimar, smoky quartz, rhodonite

sunburn prase

sunny sides sunstone

sunstroke prase

suppression azurite-malachite, citrine, fluorite, marble, nephrite, sodalite, sugilite

suppuration (*see* pus)

survival hematite, schalenblende, tiger iron

swellings amethyst, prase, rock crystal

T

taboos garnet, malchite

take-it-easy stone dumortierite

taste, sense of sardonyx, schalenblende

team spirit emerald

teeth/teething apatite, amber, fluorite

tenderness chalcedony (pink), pink opal, rhodochrosite, rose quartz, watermelon tourmaline

tenseness (*see also* relaxation) amethyst, chrysocolla, obsidian, smoky quartz, serpentine, tourmaline (dravite)

tension agate, kunzite, nephrite, ruby, rutilated quartz, sugilite, tourmaline (schorl), tourmaline quartz

testicles opal (green), thulite, zoisite

thankfulness tourmaline (verdelite)

thinking (*see* reflection)

thinking patterns chrysoprase, fluorite

thinking, abstract schalenblende

thinking, analytical agate, chiastolite, dendritic chalcedony, onyx, prehnite, tourmaline (schorl), tourmaline quartz

thinking, clear/wakeful amethyst, antimonite, smoky quartz, ruby, rutilated quartz, sapphire, tourmaline quartz, variscite

thinking, fast fire opal, fluorite

thinking, logical/rational agate, chrysoprase, citrine, diamond, disthene, kunzite, lepidolite, onyx, tourmaline (schorl), tourmaline quartz, variscite

thinking, simple pragmatic dolomite, hematite, tiger iron

thinking, strategic alexandrite, chalcedony (red), chrysoberyl

thinking, visual tourmaline

thoughts apophyllite, azurite, boji stones, chrysoberyl, smoky quartz, sapphire, schalenblende

threats (*see* hostility)

thyroid gland aquamarine, azurite, chrysocolla, lapis lazuli
timing actinolite, fossilized wood
tiredness heliotrope, tiger iron, turquoise, variscite
tissue, connective (see tissue)
tissues rose quartz, agate, aventurine, ametrine, calcite, carnelian, lepidolite, magnesite, malachite, marble, nephrite, rhodonite, rhyolite (leopard skin jasper), tourmaline (dravite), zoisite
tolerance aragonite, aventurine, copper chalcedony, kunzite, nephrite, tourmaline (indicolite)
tonsils chalcedony (blue), chrysocolla, heliotrope
toxins peridot, schalenblende
tradition, sense of amber, dolomite
tranquillity, quietness agate, morganite
tranquillity, relaxedness apophyllite, aquamarine, copper chalcedony, charoite, larimar, tourmaline (schorl), tourmaline quartz
transformation marble, zoisite
trauma malachite, obsidian, rhodonite
trembling, shaking aragonite, falcon's eye
trust amber, chalcedony (pink), chrysoprase, dumortierite, garnet (rhodolite)
truth/truthfulness chrysoprase, lapis lazuli, prehnite, sapphire, sodalite, sugilite, tiger iron, topaz, tourmaline (indicolite), variscite
tumours azurite-malachite, calcite, fluorite

U
ulcers (see tumours)
uncertainty apophyllite
unconventionality moldavite, opal
understanding chalcedony (blue and pink), citrine, emerald, falcon's eye, fluorite, malachite, rhodonite, rock crystal, sardonyx, variscite, watermelon tourmaline
unrest, inner aragonite, schalenblende, variscite
unselfishness, altruism pink opal
upheavals in life charoite, pietersite
urinary tract nephrite, tourmaline (indicolite)
uterus agate

V
vagina chalcedony (blue), copper chalcedony
vaginal flora chalcedony (blue), copper chalcedony
variety apatite, citrine, heliotrope, mookaite, opal, ruby
verruca (see also skin) amethyst
virtue diamond, sardonyx
virus infections turquoise
vision, far-sightedness aquamarine, beryl, emerald
vision, sense of rutilated quartz
vitality hematite, heliotrope, rock crystal, tiger iron, tree agate
vitamins, absorption carnelian
vocal chords lapis lazuli, sodalite
vomiting antimonite, dumortierite

W
wakefulness amethyst, ametrine, chiastolite, emerald, fire opal, rhodochrosite, ruby, turquoise, variscite

warmth chalcedony (pink), citrine, turquoise
warrior nature jasper, tree agate
warts peridot
water metabolism jade, tourmaline (indicolite)
water retention chalcedony (blue), dendritic chalcedony, jade, nephrite
water, reabsorption of in intestines amethyst
weakness chiastolite, epidote, schalenblende, thulite
wealth, inner dioptase, garnet, topaz
well-being, sense of ametrine, aquamarine, aragonite, azurite-malachite, chrysopal, fossilized wood, hematite, rose quartz
wholeness chrysoprase, obsidian, sodalite, tourmaline
will alexandrite, garnet, hematite, jasper (red), sapphire
wisdom amethyst, lapis lazuli, peridot, sapphire, topaz, tourmaline
worries/carefree apophyllite, amber, chalcedony (pink), charoite, pink opal, rose quartz
work, energy for garnet (almandine), smoky quartz, rhodochrosite
work, pressure of beryl, emerald, morganite
worries about the future moldavite
wound healing amber, calcite, garnet (general), garnet (almandine), mookaite, obsidian, rhodonite, schalenblende

Y
yearning, longing chrysopal
youth, spiritual emerald

The author

Michael Gienger has been an enthusiastic mineral collector since childhood and an amateur mineralogist since his teens. After an unfinished university chemistry course, he became a student at the School of Natural Healing and also studied different traditional healing methods from Europe, Asia and the Americas. He has been researching the art of healing with crystals since 1985, founded a research group on the subject in Stuttgart in 1989, and formed a company called Karfunkel in 1990. This is a large retail firm trading and specializing in healing minerals. He is the founder of 'analytical healing with crystals', a scientifically based therapy that is presented for the first time in this volume. Michael Gienger is also a founder member of Steinheilkunde e.V., a society dedicated to promoting the art of healing with crystals as a recognized natural method of healing. Today he lives in his favourite part of the world, the Schwabian Forest, working as an author and lecturer on geomancy and the art of healing with crystals. Recently he has launched an academic-length course of studies in the art.